WESTMAR COLLEGE LIBRARY

D1212938

ABOUT THE AUTHORS

THOMAS A. RATCLIFFE is an Associate Professor of Accounting at Texas Tech University. He is a CPA in the state of Texas and a member of the American Institute of CPAs, the National Association of Accountants, American Accounting Association, and the Academy of Accounting Historians. Dr. Ratcliffe earned his Ph.D. in accounting in 1977 from The University of Alabama. He has authored several articles published in numerous professional journals.

PAUL H. MUNTER is an Assistant Professor of Accounting at Texas Tech University. He is a CPA in the state of Colorado and a member of the American Institute of CPAs, the National Association of Accountants, American Accounting Association, and the Academy of Accounting Historians. Dr. Munter received his D.B.A. degree in accounting in 1978 from The University of Colorado. He has authored several articles published in numerous professional journals.

Complete Handbook
of Inflation Accounting

Complete Handbook
of Inflation Accounting

Thomas A. Ratcliffe, Ph.D., CPA
and
Paul Munter, D.B.A., CPA

PRENTICE-HALL, INC., ENGLEWOOD CLIFFS, NEW JERSEY

HF
5658.5
.R 37

Prentice-Hall International, Inc., *London*
Prentice-Hall of Australia, Pty. Ltd., *Sydney*
Prentice-Hall of Canada, Ltd., *Toronto*
Prentice-Hall of India, Private Ltd., *New Delhi*
Prentice-Hall of Japan, Inc., *Tokyo*
Prentice-Hall of Southeast Asia, Pte. Ltd., *Singapore*
Whitehall Books, Ltd., *Wellington, New Zealand*

©1981 by
Prentice-Hall, Inc.
Englewood Cliffs, N.J.

*All rights reserved. No part of this book
may be reproduced in any form or by
any means, without permission in writing
from the publisher.*

Library of Congress Cataloging in Publication Data

Ratcliffe, T   A
    Complete handbook of inflation accounting.

    Includes bibliographical references and index.
    1. Accounting—United States—Effect of in-
flation on—Handbooks, manuals, etc. I. Munter,
Paul, joint-author. II. Title.
HF5658.5.R37   657'.48   80-29378
ISBN O-13-160952-1

Printed in the United States of America

102408

A Word from the Authors

As the inflationary pressures in the United States continue, so do pressures to present financial and managerial accounting data which reflect the impact of inflation upon the reporting entity. Business executives —whether in production, distribution or financing—and financial analysts and investment bankers are all faced with increasingly complex and difficult problems in making the economic decisions they are entrusted with. The complexities of the business environment of today are only compounded further by inflation. Business decision-makers—whether internal or external—need to be informed of the impact of inflation on the reporting entity. *The Complete Handbook of Inflation Accounting* is intended to provide practical guidance to the users of managerial accounting data as well as the users of financial accounting data when inflation accounting information is incorporated into business reports.

The impact of inflation upon businesses has risen in severity in the past decade. It has now reached the point where users of accounting information are demanding information on the impact of inflation upon the reporting entity. Factors causing this demand include:

1. An increased awareness of inflation by expanded government reporting.
2. A squeeze placed upon borrowing ability by rising interest rates. This leads to a more careful scrutiny of alternative investment decisions.
3. The expanding complexities of business placing a greater reliance on accounting information.
4. The increased sophistication of the users of accounting information.
5. The growing demand for more and better information by public agencies, most notably the Securities and Exchange Commission.

5

The expanding scope of accounting reporting, along with the intensifying need for more information, has placed a tremendous demand upon business and the accounting profession.

Purposes and Organization of This Book

The first purpose of this handbook is to provide practitioners with some operational guidance in implementing the new inflation accounting rules in practice. A second purpose is to provide managerial accountants with approaches to incorporating inflationary trends into widely utilized analytical methods. A third purpose is to discuss some particular accounting and reporting problems unique to certain accounting entities, e.g., the oil and gas industry. And a final objective of this book is to aid financial analysts in incorporating inflation-adjusted accounting numbers into some typical analytical techniques. These four objectives serve as a basis for segregating this book into its component parts.

Part One of this book should serve as a perspective builder. While most of the discussion in this section is of an historical slant, sometimes this perspective can keep readers from attempting "to reinvent the wheel."

Part Two contains three chapters that should provide significant operational guidance to those attempting to implement and/or understand SFAS No. 33. Discussions center on both constant dollar and current cost accounting problems, with the emphasis on pragmatic implementation rather than on theoretical justification.

Part Three is an attempt to indicate problems that could result when inflationary impacts are not considered, or are only incidentally considered, in managerial decision-making predicated on accounting numbers. Four chapters are included in this section, and discussions center around cost behavior analysis and budgeting process in general.

Part Four represents a discussion of some special industry accounting problems resulting from inflation-related accounting standards. Special consideration is devoted to the oil and gas industry because of the complex requirements necessary to implement under the Reserve Recognition Accounting requirements of the SEC. Then other industries, e.g., real estate, banking, insurance, and utilities, are accorded slightly less analysis, based solely on relative implementation complexities.

Part Five is an attempt to insert inflation-adjusted accounting numbers into financial statement analysis. Both short-term and long-term analytical tools are assessed, compared, and contrasted, using various valuation bases for the accounting-related numbers.

And, finally, Part Six is comprised of one chapter that attempts to bring all this information into focus and to provide some indications of what may be expected in the process of generating and using inflation-impacted accounting numbers.

Summary

With the issuance of SFAS No. 33, the FASB has now required the implementation of a financial reporting process not based on historical costs. The constant dollar and current cost disclosures currently required by the FASB represent the latest step in the continuing evolvement of financial reporting in periods of changing prices. The organization of this book enables readers to identify quickly the sections most pertinent to their needs. Inflation accounting is now pragmatic in nature; the purpose of this book is to aid in the implementation and understanding of inflation-impacted accounting numbers.

Thomas A. Ratcliffe
Paul Munter
Lubbock, Texas

ACKNOWLEDGMENTS

For their contributions to the completion of this work, we would like to acknowledge two men:

—Professor Robert J. Koester of Texas Tech University, who provided valuable assistance in ensuring the technical accuracy of discussions relating to inflation problems in the oil and gas industry.

—Professor Gary D. Kelley of Texas Tech University, who aided in the statistical analysis of cost-behavior patterns in an inflationary environment.

The ultimate test of any book of this nature is its continued value to its users. To help in assessing this value, comments from users are always welcome.

Table of Contents

9

Complete Handbook
of Inflation Accounting

CHAPTER **1**

How Inflation Accounting Developed

□□□□□□□□□□□□

As inflationary pressures in the United States continue, so do pressures to present financial statements which, in some way, reflect the impact of inflation upon the reporting entity. Furthermore, managerial analysis of financial data needs to incorporate inflationary trends. The idea of accounting for the effects of inflation in financial statements is not new. During the early years of this century, the notion of current cost accounting was being deliberated. For example, Hatfield's works included a discussion on current cost accounting as early as 1909.[1] Canning, in discussing the differences between accounting income and economic income, indicated a preference for current costs as a valuation mechanism.[2] And, in 1939, MacNeal went so far as to say that "truth in accounting" can be attained only when financial statements display the current value of assets and the profits and losses resulting from changes in these asset values. MacNeal also advocated that realized and unrealized profits and losses should be segregated.[3]

---

[1] Henry R. Hatfield, *Modern Accounting* (New York: D. Appleton & Co., 1909).

[2] John B. Canning, *The Economics of Accountancy* (New York: Ronald Press, Co., 1929).

[3] Kenneth MacNeal, *Truth in Accounting* (Philadelphia: University of Pennsylvania Press, 1939).

Seemingly without regard to these and other discussions in the accounting literature, the authoritative rule-making bodies in the accounting field had not, by the 1930s, made any attempts to effectively operationalize the positions of current value advocates. In fact, the trend was to adhere more strictly to historical cost as an approximation of value. However, over the past few decades, several influential accounting bodies have moved toward advocating some form of inflation accounting, although many of these approaches adhere to the principles of historical costing. The purposes of this chapter are to trace the development of inflation accounting from its early stages to its current status and to provide an overview and organization for the remainder of this book.

It may be argued successfully that the development of accounting has been precipitated by a reaction to needs. Exhibit 1.1 summarizes the relationship of changing price levels to the issuance of inflation accounting studies. Exhibit 1.2 then summarizes the valuation approaches advocated in several of these studies.

The Influence of the American Accounting Association

The American Accounting Association (AAA) began issuing a series of publications in 1936 expressing positions concerning the principles of accounting. The series essentially concluded with the publication of *A Statement of Basic Accounting Theory* (ASOBAT) in 1966.

The pre-depression years in this country evidenced rapid growth of business and a rapid growth in the need for accounting data. During the pre-depression period, assets were being valued upward with little or no objective support for the increased values being recorded. This practice resulted in increasing skepticism about accounting data after the depression began.

As a reflection of this skepticism, the AAA's 1936 study, "A Tentative Statement of Accounting Principles Underlying Corporate Financial Statements," strongly advocated the use of historical cost in valuing assets.[4] Not coincidental is the fact that the inflation rate at that time was practically negligible, running less than 2% per year.[5] Under such circumstances, the assumption of a stable monetary unit is not without theoretical merit. In light of existing economic conditions and attitudes, the

---

[4] Executive Committee of the American Accounting Association, "A Tentative Statement of Accounting Principles Underlying Corporate Financial Statements," *Accounting Review* (June, 1936).

[5] Economic Report of the President (Washington: U.S. Government Printing Office, 1979).

EXHIBIT 1.1*
A Developmental Summary of Inflation Accounting Studies

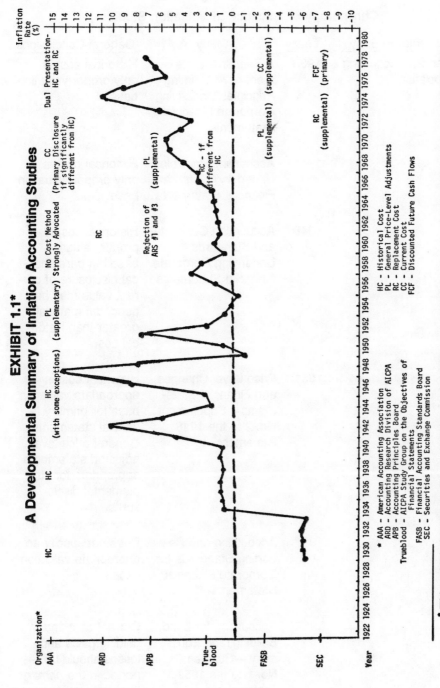

*   AAA – American Accounting Association
     ARD – Accounting Research Division of AICPA
     APB – Accounting Principles Board
Trueblood – AICPA Study Group on the Objectives of
             Financial Statements
    FASB – Financial Accounting Standards Board
     SEC – Securities and Exchange Commission

HC – Historical Cost
PL – General Price-Level Adjustments
RC – Replacement Cost
CC – Current Cost
FCF – Discounted Future Cash Flows

* This exhibit is adapted from Thomas A. Ratcliffe and Paul Munter, "Asset Valuation: An Historical Perspective," *The Accounting Historians Journal* (spring 1980), pp. 73–78.

EXHIBIT 1.2

Chronology of Issuance of Valuation Studies

Authoritative Body	Year	Study	General Conclusions
American Accounting Association	1936	A Tentative Statement of Accounting Principles Underlying Corporate Financial Statements	Historical cost is only proper valuation base.
	1941	Accounting Principles Underlying Corporate Financial Statements	Historical cost is only proper valuation base.
	1948	Accounting Concepts and Standards Underlying Corporate Financial Statements	Historical cost is proper valuation base but parenthetical disclosure of current value may be needed if materially greater than historical cost.
	1951	Price Level Changes and Financial Statements—Supplement No. 2 to the 1948 Statement	Historical cost is appropriate valuation base for primary financial statements. General price-level adjusted statements appropriate for supplemental disclosures.
	1957	Accounting and Reporting Standards for Corporate Financial Statements	Does not specify an appropriate valuation base.
	1964	Accounting for Land, Building, and Equipment—Supplement No. 1 to the 1957 Statement	Current cost and holding gains and losses should be reported in the *primary* financial statements.

EXHIBIT 1.2 (continued)

	1966	A Statement of Basic Accounting Theory	Dual presentation of historical cost and replacement cost in the *primary* financial statements.
Accounting Research Division of the American Institute of Certified Public Accountants (AICPA)	1961	ARS No. 1—The Basic Postulates of Accounting ARS No. 3—A Tentative Set of Broad Accounting Principles for Business Enterprises	Current costs should be incorporated into *primary* financial statements.
Accounting Principles Board	1962	Statement No. 1	Rejects ARS No. 1 and No. 3.
	1969	Statement No. 3—Financial Statements Restated for General Price-Level Changes	Optional use of supplemental disclosure of general price-level statements.
AICPA Study Group on the Objectives of Financial Statements (Trueblood Committee)	1973	Objectives of Financial Statements	Use current values if they differ significantly from historical cost.
Financial Accounting Standards Board	1974	Financial Reporting in Units of General Purchasing Power—Exposure Draft	Mandatory use of supplementary general price-level adjusted statements.
	1978	Financial Reporting and Changing Prices—Exposure Draft	Preference for supplementary current cost information.
Securities and Exchange Commission	1976	ASR No. 190	Supplemental disclosure of replacement

EXHIBIT 1.2 (continued)

			cost of plant assets and inventories with related expenses.
	1978	Reserve Recognition Accounting	Present value of future cash flows used as valuation base in *primary* financial statements.
Financial Accounting Standards Board	1979	SFAS No. 33— Financial Reporting and Changing Prices	Mandates supplemental disclosures on both a constant dollar and a current cost basis.

conclusions in this AAA study appear to have been responsive to the *existing* needs of external users.

Also, in keeping with the prevalent thought of that era, Paton and Littleton's AAA monograph, "An Introduction to Corporate Accounting Standards," also was heavily dependent upon the notion of historical cost. The authors were extremely critical of any proposed efforts to value assets above cost unless there was evidence supporting the upward revaluation that could not be ignored.[6]

In 1941, the AAA updated its statement on accounting principles with the issuance of "Accounting Principles Underlying Corporate Financial Statements." This report contained few noticeable differences from the 1936 report other than the fact that this report no longer was considered "tentative." Historical costing still was strongly advocated as *the* acceptable method of valuing assets.

The 1948 AAA revision entitled "Accounting Concepts and Standards Underlying Corporate Financial Statements" adhered, in general, to the principle of historical costing. The immediate post-war period witnessed some rather significant price increases as the U.S. economy attempted to readjust to a civilian-oriented rather than a war-oriented economy. The annual inflation rate from 1946–1948 exceeded 10 percent. Perhaps more than just coincidentally, the 1948 revision did provide an

---

[6] W.A. Paton and A.C. Littleton, *An Introduction to Corporate Accounting Standards,* American Accounting Association Monograph No. 3 (Sarasota, Florida: American Accounting Association, 1940).

exception to the principle that only historical cost is appropriate for valuing assets:

> When values of assets other than costs applicable to future periods are supported by substantial objective evidence, and are materially higher than the cost applicable to future periods, such data may be essential in interpreting the economic position of the enterprise. Such information, adequately described as to nature and source, may be shown parenthetically, by footnote, or in a supplementary schedule.[7]

The AAA issued eight supplementary statements to clarify or expand upon the 1948 report. The second supplement, entitled "Price Level Changes and Financial Statements," discussed the use of current replacement costs to value assets. While the merits of current replacement cost accounting were believed to be sound, the committee expressed the belief that a reasonably objective measure of current replacement cost did not exist. In light of this operational deficiency, the AAA committee was still of the opinion that some method of disclosing the effects of inflation on an enterprise was needed. This reasoning led the AAA to opt for general purchasing power adjustments as a surrogate measure of the impact of inflation on the firm. The second supplement to the 1948 report was, in effect, a statement by the AAA committee that price level adjusted statements were acceptable, and in some cases necessary, disclosures. The AAA committee believed that the disclosures should nonetheless be of a supplemental type, as evidenced by this statement:

> It is the judgment of the Committee, therefore, that the time has come to give adjusted dollar statements a thorough test. Such statements should now be, and may continue to be, supplementary to the financial statements based on historical dollar cost.[8]

During the Eisenhower administration, the rate of inflation was relatively under control when viewed from an annual perspective. However, it had become clear that a small but persistent rate of inflation can, in the aggregate, result in a material impact upon an enterprise just as surely as can a short-lived, large annual inflation rate. The AAA report "Accounting and Reporting Standards for Corporate Financial Statements" was issued in 1957, a time when external users were becoming increasingly

---

[7] American Accounting Association, *Accounting Concepts and Standards Underlying Corporate Financial Statements* (Columbus, Ohio: American Accounting Association, 1948), p. 5.

[8] American Accounting Association, *Price-Level Changes and Financial Statements*, Supplementary Statement No. 2 (Columbus, Ohio: American Accounting Association, 1951), p. 6.

aware of the impact of inflation on the economy. In the 1957 revision, there was a subtle, yet distinct, shift in position regarding the issue of asset valuation. In discussing the value of an asset, neither historical costing nor a current costing method was favored. The value of an asset was defined as "the money equivalent of its service potentials." In amplifying this point, the report reads:

> Conceptually, this (the money equivalent of its service potentials) is the sum of the future market prices of all streams of service to be derived, discounted by the probability and interest factors to their present worths. However, this conception of value is an abstraction which yields but limited practical basis for quantification. Consequently, the measurement of assets is commonly made by other more feasible methods.[9]

The fact that the report does not specifically indicate a preference for any of the "more feasible methods" of measurement represents a significant shift in the positions espoused by AAA committees. Although current cost accounting is not directly advocated, neither is historical costing promoted as the primary valuation basis.

In 1964, the AAA issued a supplement statement to the 1957 report. The supplement called for current cost disclosures as well as disclosures of holding gains and losses. Perhaps even more significantly, the supplement advocated current costs of existing services to be used as the *primary* valuation tool for financial reporting purposes and advocated immediate adoption of the recommendations.[10]

Shortly after the 1964 supplement was issued, the Committee to Prepare a Statement of Basic Accounting Theory was formed by the AAA. The charge of that committee was:

> . . . to develop an integrated statement of basic accounting theory which will serve as a guide to educators, practitioners, and others interested in accounting. The statement should include adequate support for any position taken and sufficient explanation to provide clarity, yet be as concise as feasible.
>
> The committee should not feel bound in any way by the format or content of previous statements issued by this or other organizations.
>
> Among the subjects the committee may want to consider are the role, nature, and limitations of accounting, both now and in the future; the

---

[9] American Accounting Association, *Accounting and Reporting Standards for Corporate Financial Statements* (Iowa City, Iowa: American Accounting Association, 1957), p. 4.

[10] Committee on Concepts and Standards, "Accounting for Land, Buildings and Equipment—Supplementary Statement No. 1," *Accounting Review* (July, 1964), pp. 693–699.

appropriate conceptual framework for a coordinated statement of accounting theory; and the possibility of implementing its conclusions.

This charge is given with a reminder of the unique opportunity available to the American Accounting Association to contribute to the advancement of accountancy through the conduct of fundamental research and the dissemination of the results of such research.[11]

The result of this committee effort was the 1966 publication of *ASOBAT*. While the committee was not totally successful in developing an "integrated statement of basic accounting theory," *ASOBAT* has undeniably had a significant impact on accounting thought in the years since its issuance. Perhaps most significant is the fact that *ASOBAT*, rather than recommending one valuation approach for the basic financial statements and others as supplemental disclosures, suggested a data expansion approach. *ASOBAT* advocated a dual presentation of both historical cost data and replacement cost data in the primary financial statements. This advocation represented a significant departure from the ideas which any of the authoritative bodies were promoting at that time. When *ASOBAT* was released, neither the American Institute of Certified Public Accountants (AICPA) nor the Securities and Exchange Commission (SEC) had advocated a move to either (1) supplement historical cost disclosures with additional disclosures using another basis, or (2) abandon historical costing in favor of another valuation base.

The Impact of the American Institute of Certified Public Accountants

The AICPA has been a leader in developing accounting principles throughout this century. Its direct influence was perhaps most visible from 1939, when the Committee on Accounting Procedure (CAP) began issuing Accounting Research Bulletins (ARB), until 1973, when the Accounting Principles Board (APB) was disbanded.

Throughout its 20-year existence, the CAP advocated the use of historical costing as the primary basis for valuing assets. Following the doctrine of conservatism, only when a decline in the utility of an asset became apparent would a deviation from historical cost be recognized; and then, this valuation decline would result in the recognition of a loss prior to its realization. Unrealized gains would never be recognized.

A comparison of positions of the CAP and the AAA reveals several commonalities. However, at approximately the same time the spirit of the

---

[11] Committee to Prepare a Statement of Basic Accounting Theory, *A Statement of Basic Accounting Theory* (Sarasota, Florida: American Accounting Association, 1966), p. v.

AAA reports began to change from strong adherences to historical costing, the CAP was receiving heavy criticism. In 1959, as the CAP issued
its final ARB, it still was a strong advocate of historical costing.

In conjunction with the formation of the APB, the AICPA also
established the Accounting Research Division to provide research support
as an aid to the APB in an attempt to establish accounting principles
from a global framework. Immediately upon its formation, the Accounting Research Division began a study in an effort to determine the basic
postulates and broad principles of accounting. This effort resulted in the
publication of Accounting Research Study (ARS) No. 1, entitled "The
Basic Postulates of Accounting," and ARS No. 3, entitled "A Tentative
Set of Broad Accounting Principles for Business Enterprises."

Ideally, the broad principles of ARS No. 3 should have been derived
from the basic postulates of ARS No. 1. In reality, it is not clear that the
conclusions in ARS No. 3 are logically consistent in suggesting valuation
methodologies. For example, receivables would have been valued at the
present value of the future cash flows, while inventories would have been
valued at their net realizable value or their replacement cost, and intangible assets would have been valued at their cost. In spite of the apparent
inconsistencies between and within ARS Nos. 1 and 3, the message was
clear—current values should be utilized in valuing assets in the primary
financial statements.

The APB response to these two documents was that:

> . . . while these studies are a valuable contribution to accounting
> thinking, they are too radically different from present generally accept-
> ed accounting principles for acceptance at the time.[12]

With that response, the authoritative thought of accounting for inflation
was tabled. Not until inflationary pressures on the U.S. economy began
to mount in the late 1960s did the APB again address the issue. Then, in
1969, the APB issued Statement (APBS) No. 3, "Financial Statements
Restated for General Price-Level Changes." The Statement advocated
supplemental disclosures of general purchasing power adjusted statements. However, the APB issued this pronouncement in the form of a
Statement rather than an Opinion, thus only recommending the disclosures rather than requiring that they be made. Since the disclosures were
not required, very few reporting entities chose to adhere to the reporting
guidelines in APBS No. 3.

---

[12] Accounting Principles Board of the American Institute of Certified Public Accountants, "Statement by the Accounting Principles Board," *Statement No. 1* (New York:
American Institute of Certified Public Accountants, 1962).

In 1970, the APB issued APBS No. 4, "Basic Concepts and Accounting Principles Underlying Financial Statements of Business Enterprises." APBS No. 4 was supposed to be a descriptive study on current generally accepted accounting principles (GAAP). APBS No. 4 identified cost as the primary valuation tool and realization as the criterion for recognizing gains in asset values. However, the APB did recognize and acknowledge the possibility that current cost accounting could, in the future, become the primary valuation basis for financial accounting.

Following the completion of APBS No. 4, the AICPA appointed the "Trueblood Committee" to use the objectives of this Statement as a point of departure in attempting to refine the objectives of financial accounting. The Trueblood Committee strongly recommended the use of cash flow related information. In providing information to enable the user to predict future cash flows, the Committee felt that current values should be provided if they differ significantly from historical costs. The Trueblood report, "Objectives of Financial Statements," was issued in October, 1973 —just four months after the formation of the Financial Accounting Standards Board (FASB). At that point, the FASB was given the responsibility of promulgating accounting standards, and still there existed no requirements to disclose any inflation adjusted data.

The Joint Efforts of the Financial Accounting Standards Board and the Securities and Exchange Commission

When the FASB first examined the problem of accounting in an inflationary environment, general purchasing power adjustments seem to be favored. A 1974 FASB Exposure Draft, had it been adopted, would have required supplemental disclosure of general purchasing power adjusted statements. This proposal was based heavily on the recommended approach suggested by the APB in APBS No. 3.

However, before the FASB proposal was adopted in final form, the SEC began *requiring* certain replacement cost information from larger publicly held enterprises in the U.S. on a supplemental basis. Although Accounting Series Release (ASR) No. 190 (the SEC release requiring replacement cost data) only required replacement cost data for fixed assets and related depreciation, inventories, and cost of sales, it marked the first time that any current cost information was *required* to be disclosed. Furthermore, the SEC action clearly moved accounting more in the direction of a replacement cost basis and away from a general purchasing power basis (as advocated by the APB and the FASB).

Since ASR No. 190 was released, the FASB has been studying the entire concept of valuation as a part of an overall conceptual framework project. The FASB issued an Exposure Draft which proposed new current disclosures that far exceeded those required by the SEC.[13] The proposed FASB requirement mandated supplemental disclosure of either

(1) income from continuing operations on a current cost basis and holding gains or losses *net of inflation;* or

(2) income from continuing operations on a general purchasing power adjusted basis. (Emphasis added.)

The FASB specified a definite preference for the first disclosure.

Then, in September 1979, the FASB issued Statement of Financial Accounting Standards (SFAS) No. 33, "Financial Reporting and Changing Prices,"[14] that required certain large, publicly traded enterprises to make selected supplementary disclosures in financial reports on *both* a constant dollar and a current cost basis. So the theoretical debates concerning appropriate valuation bases now represent pragmatic realities. SFAS No. 33, coupled with the SEC's Reserve Recognition Accounting applicable to oil and gas producers, constitutes the most significant change in financial reporting in decades. In this book, an in-depth summary of these reporting rules is presented along with an examination of how inflationary trends should be incorporated into managerial decision-making.

---

[13] Financial Accounting Standards Board, "Financial Reporting and Changing Prices," *Proposed Statement of Financial Accounting Standards* (Stamford, Connecticut: Financial Accounting Standards Board, 1978).

[14] Financial Accounting Standards Board, "Financial Reporting and Changing Prices," *Statement of Financial Accounting Standards No. 33* (Stamford, Connecticut: Financial Accounting Standards Board, 1979).

CHAPTER **2**

Implementing Constant Dollar Accounting Methods and Procedures for External Reporting

▣▣▣▣▣▣▣▣▣▣▣▣

Financial statements traditionally have been prepared on an historical cost basis, measuring financial statement elements at the fair market value of consideration surrendered or fair market value of consideration received—whichever is more clearly determinable. These amounts have not been restated from their initial measurement amount (except in certain cases to reflect lower of cost or market or net realizable value) to reflect either changes in the general purchasing power of the dollar or changes in current costs of specific financial statement elements. The Financial Accounting Standards Board (FASB) now is requiring disclosure of both historical cost/constant dollar (general) amounts and current cost (specific) amounts in financial statements for fiscal years ended on or after December 25, 1979.[1] These disclosure requirements are presented in

---

[1] There is, however, a grandfather provision on the current cost disclosures. Enterprises may defer the current cost disclosures until the first annual report for a fiscal year ended on or after December 25, 1980 is issued.

Statement of Financial Accounting Standards (SFAS) No. 33, issued in September 1979, entitled "Financial Reporting and Changing Prices." The purpose of this chapter is to present and analyze the historical cost/constant dollar disclosure requirements of SFAS No. 33.

Enterprises Required to Disclose Historical Cost/Constant Dollar Information

The SFAS No. 33 requirement to disclose historical cost/constant dollar (hereafter constant dollar) information in external financial reports applies only to public enterprises[2] that prepare their primary financial statements in U.S. dollars and in accordance with U.S. generally accepted accounting principles (GAAP) and that have, at the beginning of the fiscal year for which financial statements are prepared, either

1. inventories and property, plant, and equipment (before deducting accumulated depreciation, depletion, and amortization) amounting in the aggregate to more than $125 million, or
2. total assets amounting to more than $1 billion (after deducting accumulated depreciation).

Except where otherwise stated, inventory and property, plant, and equipment should include land and other natural resources and capitalized leasehold interests, but not goodwill or other intangible assets. Both of the amounts listed in the criteria above should be measured in accordance with GAAP used in developing the primary financial statements of the enterprise.

The FASB defines the reporting entity as the consolidated enterprise. Therefore, constant dollar disclosures need not be presented separately for a parent company, an investee company, or any other enterprise(s) in any financial report that includes the results for that enterprise in the consolidated financial statements. Further, these disclosures need not be made during the year of a business combination accounted for as a pooling of interests by an enterprise created by the pooling of two or more enterprises none of which individually satisfies the aforementioned size tests.

The constant dollar disclosures do not apply to interim reports, segment disclosures, publicly held enterprises not meeting the size tests, and

---

[2] A public enterprise is defined by the FASB as an enterprise:
(a)   whose debt or equity securities trade in a public market on a foreign or domestic stock exchange or in the over-the-counter market, or
(b)   that is required to file financial statements with the Securities and Exchange Commission. SFAS No. 21, "Suspension of the Reporting Requirements of Earnings per Share and Segments Information by Nonpublic Enterprises," par. 13.

nonpublicly held enterprises. The FASB does encourage enterprises to make the constant dollar disclosures even if they are not required to implement the provisions of SFAS No. 33. The FASB emphasizes that, while there are minimum disclosures required by certain enterprises, there is room for experimentation both in the information disclosed and in the reporting format.

Required Supplementary Disclosures on a Constant Dollar Basis

Enterprises meeting the applicable size tests are required to disclose these facts at a minimum:

1. Information on income from continuing operations for the current fiscal year on a constant dollar basis.
2. The purchasing power gain or loss on net monetary items for the current fiscal year. The purchasing power gain or loss should not be included in income from continuing operations.

The constant dollar income from continuing operations may be presented in either a statement format (see Figure 2.5) or a reconciliation format (see Figure 2.6). Regardless of the format selected, disclosures should include material amounts of or adjustments to cost of goods sold, depreciation, depletion, and reductions of historical cost amounts of inventory and property, plant, and equipment to their lower recoverable amounts.

The index used to compute information for the constant dollar disclosures should be the Consumer Price Index for All Urban Consumers (CPI) published by the Bureau of Labor Statistics of the U.S. Department of Labor. Use of this index was prescribed by the FASB for two major reasons: (1) it is published on a monthly basis, and (2) it is not subsequently revised after its initial release.

If the minimum constant dollar disclosures required in SFAS No. 33 are to be made, inventory, property, plant, and equipment, cost of goods sold, depreciation, depletion, and amortization expense, along with any reductions of the historical cost amounts of inventory and property, plant, and equipment to their lower recoverable amounts should be restated in constant dollars represented by the average level over the fiscal year of the CPI. Other financial statement elements need not be restated.

An enterprise that selects to disclose the constant dollar information through the preparation of comprehensive financial statements may measure the financial statement elements in terms of either average-for-the-year constant dollars or end-of-the-year constant dollars.

Constant dollar measurements of financial statement elements should be determined by multiplying the historical cost measurement associated with the item times the ratio of the average-for-the-year or end-of-the-year CPI for the current year to the base CPI at the date the historical cost amount was established. Thus, in general, financial statement elements are restated as follows:

$$\text{Historical Cost Amount} \times \frac{\text{Average-for-the-year or End-of-the-Year CPI}}{\text{Base Period CPI}} = \begin{array}{l}\text{Constant Dollar}\\\text{Restated Amount}\end{array}$$

If it is necessary to reduce measurements of inventory and property, plant, and equipment during the current year from constant dollar amounts, such reductions should be included in income from continuing operations. Except as noted in this paragraph (and as discussed later related to selection of depreciation methods), the accounting principles used in preparing constant dollar income should be the same as those used in determining historical cost income; only the unit of measure changes.

Inventory, property, plant, and equipment, and related cost of goods sold and depreciation, depletion, and amortization expense originally determined in units of a foreign currency should first be translated into U.S. dollars in accordance with U.S. GAAP and then restated in terms of constant dollars.

The required disclosure of the purchasing power gain or loss during the period on net monetary items should be equal to the net gain or loss formed by restating in constant dollars the beginning and ending balances of, and transactions affecting, monetary assets and liabilities. A monetary asset is money or claim to receive a sum of money the amount of which is fixed or determinable without reference to future prices of specific goods or services. A monetary liability is an obligation to pay a sum of money the amount of which is fixed or determinable without reference to future prices of specific goods or services. All other assets and liabilities are nonmonetary. The Appendix to this chapter contains an itemization of common balance sheet accounts and their monetary/nonmonetary classification.

An enterprise that prepares a comprehensive set of supplementary financial statements to fulfill the constant dollar disclosure requirements may measure the purchasing power gain or loss in average-for-the-year or end-of-the-year constant dollars. Other enterprises should measure the purchasing power gain or loss in terms of average-for-the-year constant dollars.

Illustration of Constant Dollar
Financial Statements Prepared
on a Comprehensive Basis

MR Corporation was formed on December 31, 19X4, through the combination of partnerships. As such, all assets and liabilities are stated at their fair values as of the combination date. MR Corporation is in the process of making the constant dollar disclosures on a comprehensive basis for the fiscal year ended December 31, 19X9.

Comparative balance sheets and income statements of MR Corporation for years 19X4 through 19X9 prepared on an historical cost basis are presented in Figures 2.1 and 2.2, and a checklist for preparing the restated financial statements is developed in Checklist 2.1.

Figures 2.3 and 2.4 and related schedules represent the restatement process applicable to converting the financial statement elements from their historical cost measurements to constant dollar amounts. In this example, end-of-the-year constant dollars are utilized since average-for-the-year constant dollars are used in developing the minimum required disclosures in the next section of this chapter. Also, end-of-the-year dollars seem to be more meaningful in the comprehensive disclosures so that monetary items on hand at the end of the current year need not be "rolled back" to average-for-the-year dollars. The CPI indices used in developing these statements are shown in Schedule 2.1.

Schedule 2.2 shows how sales are restated from the historical cost statements to the constant dollar statements. Notice that 19X8 sales are first restated to end of 19X8 constant dollars and then this restated amount is rolled forward to the end of 19X9 constant dollars for inclusion in the comparative financial statements. It should become increasingly apparent that after the constant dollar financial statements are first prepared, the roll-forward technique used in developing information for comparative purposes is relatively simple.

FIGURE 2.1
MR Corporation
Comparative Balance Sheets
December 31, 19X4–19X9

		December 31				
ASSETS	19X4	19X5	19X6	19X7	19X8	19X9
Cash	$ 100,000	$ 176,250	$ 282,500	$ 398,750	$ 410,250	$ 514,250
Receivables (net)	300,000	528,750	847,500	1,196,250	1,230,750	1,542,750
Inventories (FIFO)	300,000	260,000	300,000	400,000	420,000	480,000
Land	80,000	80,000	80,000	80,000	80,000	80,000
Buildings	500,000	500,000	500,000	500,000	500,000	500,000
Accumulated Depreciation—Buildings	-0-	(12,500)	(25,000)	(37,500)	(50,000)	(62,500)
Equipment	420,000	420,000	420,000	420,000	530,000	530,000
Accumulated Depreciation—Equipment	-0-	(52,500)	(105,000)	(157,500)	(221,000)	(284,500)
Total Assets	$ 1,700,000	$ 1,900,000	$ 2,300,000	2,800,000	$ 2,900,000	$ 3,300,000
LIABILITIES AND STOCKHOLDER'S EQUITY						
Current Liabilities	$ 160,000	$ 154,943	$ 192,234	$ 242,891	$ 215,793	$ 227,532
Long-term Liabilities	700,000	774,715	961,167	1,214,456	1,078,963	1,137,657
Deferred Taxes	-0-	14,292	24,499	30,623	35,814	36,221
Capital Stock ($10 par value)	280,000	280,000	280,000	280,000	280,000	280,000
Additional Paid-In Capital	560,000	560,000	560,000	560,000	560,000	560,000
Retained Earnings	-0-	116,050	282,100	472,030	729,430	1,058,590
Total Liabilities and Stockholder's Equity	$ 1,700,000	$ 1,900,000	$ 2,300,000	$ 2,800,000	$ 2,900,000	$ 3,300,000

FIGURE 2.2
MR Corporation
Comparative Statements of Income and Retained Earnings
For the Years Ended December 31, 19X5–19X9

For the Year Ended December 31

	19X5	19X6	19X7	19X8	19X9
Sales (net)	$ 1,600,000	$ 2,000,000	$ 2,400,000	$ 3,200,000	$ 4,000,000
Cost of Goods Sold:					
Beginning Inventories	$ 300,000	$ 260,000	$ 300,000	$ 400,000	$ 420,000
Purchases (net)	1,000,000	1,340,000	1,660,000	2,100,000	2,660,000
Goods Available for Sale	$ 1,300,000	$ 1,600,000	$ 1,960,000	$ 2,500,000	$ 3,080,000
Ending Inventories	260,000	300,000	400,000	420,000	480,000
Cost of Goods Sold	$ 1,040,000	$ 1,300,000	$ 1,560,000	$ 2,080,000	$ 2,600,000
Gross Profit	$ 560,000	$ 700,000	$ 840,000	$ 1,120,000	$ 1,400,000
Operating Expenses (Excluding Depreciation)	$ 192,000	$ 240,000	$ 288,000	$ 384,000	$ 480,000
Depreciation Expense	65,000	65,000	65,000	76,000	76,000
Total Operating Expense	$ 257,000	$ 305,000	$ 353,000	$ 460,000	$ 556,000
Income before Income Taxes	$ 303,000	$ 395,000	$ 487,000	$ 660,000	$ 844,000
Provision for Income Taxes	106,050	138,250	170,450	231,000	295,400
Net Income	$ 196,950	$ 256,750	$ 316,550	$ 429,000	$ 548,600
Beginning Retained Earnings	-0-	116,050	282,100	472,030	729,430
	$ 196,950	$ 372,800	$ 598,650	$ 901,030	$ 1,278,030
Less: Dividends	80,900	90,700	126,620	171,600	219,440
Ending Retained Earnings	$ 116,050	$ 282,100	$ 472,030	$ 729,430	$ 1,058,590

CHECKLIST 2.1
Computational Guidance for Comprehensive Constant Dollar Disclosures

(Paragraph numbers refer to SFAS No. 33.)

1. Determine Purchasing Power Gain or Loss.
   a. Segregate financial statement elements into monetary and nonmonetary categorizations. (par. 23, 50)
   b. Restate beginning net monetary items to average-for-the-year constant dollars or end-of-the-year constant dollars as appropriate. (par. 50, 232)
   c. Restate increases and decreases in net monetary items to average-for-the-year constant dollar or end-of-the-year constant dollars as appropriate. (par. 50, 232)
   d. Restate ending net monetary items to average-for-the-year constant dollars or end-of-the-year constant dollars as appropriate. (When end-of-the-year constant dollars are used, the restatement conversion factor is 1.00 since ending net monetary items are stated in terms of end-of-the-year purchasing power.) (par. 50, 232)
   e. Purchasing power gain (loss) equals beginning net monetary items restated (b) plus increases in net monetary items restated minus decreases in net monetary items restated (c) minus ending net monetary items restated (d). (par. 50, 232)
2. Steps to Prepare Historical Cost/Constant Dollar Income Statement. When using end-of-the-year constant dollars—
   a. Restate operating revenues to end-of-the-year constant dollars. (par. 210)
   b. Restate operating expenses to end-of-the-year constant dollars. (par. 210)
   c. Restate the provision for income taxes to end-of-the-year constant dollars. (par. 210)
   d. Income from continuing operations equals restated operating revenues (a) minus restated operating expenses (b) minus restated provision for income taxes (c). (par. 70)
   e. Add (deduct) purchasing power gain (loss) (1, e). (par. 29)
3. Steps to Prepare Historical Cost/Constant Dollar Income Statement. When using average-for-the-year constant dollars—
   a. Operating revenues may be historical cost operating revenues (consideration should be given to seasonal fluctuations in the generation of revenues). (par. 210)
   b. Operating expenses (exclusive of cost of goods sold and depreciation) may be historical cost operating expenses (consideration should be given to seasonal fluctuations in the incurrence of expenses). (par. 210)

CHECKLIST 2.1 (continued)

   c. Restate cost of goods sold and depreciation expense. (When LIFO method of inventory costing is used, restated cost of goods sold may be approximated by historical cost of goods sold unless a LIFO layer has been depleted. In this case, costs associated with a depleted layer should be restated.) (par. 212, 223–227)

   d. The provision for income taxes should be the historical cost provision for income taxes. (par. 210)

   e. Income from continuing operations equals operating revenues (a) minus operating expenses (b,c) minus provision for income taxes (d). (par. 70)

   f. Add (deduct) purchasing power gain (loss) (1,e). (par. 29)

4. Steps to Prepare Historical Cost/Constant Dollar Balance Sheet. When using end-of-the-year constant dollars—

   a. Monetary items are historical cost monetary items since they are stated in end-of-the-year constant dollars.

   b. Restate nonmonetary items to end-of-the-year constant dollars.

5. Steps to Prepare Historical Cost/Constant Dollar Balance Sheet. When using average-for-the-year constant dollars—

   a. Roll back monetary items to average-for-the-year constant dollars.

   b. Restate nonmonetary items to average-for-the-year constant dollars.

6. Step to Prepare Comparative Historical Cost/Constant Dollar Statements. Roll forward all financial statement elements from previous historical cost/constant dollar statements to average-for-the-current-year or end-of-the-current-year constant dollars as appropriate.

FIGURE 2.3
MR Corporation
Comparative Balance Sheets on an Historical Cost/Constant Dollar Basis

December 31, 19X8 and 19X9

	19X8	19X9
ASSETS		
Cash (see Schedule 2.10)	$ 461,818	$ 514,250
Receivables (net) (see Schedule 2.10)	1,385,455	1,542,750
Inventories (FIFO) (see Schedule 2.11)	473,740	482,112
Land (see Schedule 2.12)	117,586	117,598
Building (see Schedule 2.12)	734,913	734,913
Accumulated Depreciation—Building		
(see Schedule 2.12)	(73,491)	(91,853)
Equipment (see Schedule 2.12)	751,543	751,543
Accumulated Depreciation—Equipment		
(see Schedule 2.12)	(322,086)	(412,675)
Total Assets	$3,529,478	$3,638,638
LIABILITIES AND STOCKHOLDER'S EQUITY		
Current Liabilities (see Schedule 2.10)	$ 242,918	$ 227,532
Long-Term Liabilities (see Schedule 2.10)	1,214,589	1,137,657
Deferred Taxes (see Schedule 2.10)	40,316	36,221
Capital Stock ($10 par value)		
(see Schedule 2.13)	411,551	411,551
Additional Paid-In Capital (see Schedule 2.13)	823,102	823,102
Retained Earnings (see Schedule 2.8)	797,002	1,002,575
Total Liabilities and Stockholder's Equity	$3,529,478	$3,638,638

FIGURE 2.4
MR Corporation
Comparative Statements of Income and Retained Earnings
Restated on an Historical Cost/Constant Dollar Basis
For the Years Ended December 31, 19X8 and 19X9

	For the Year Ended December 31	
	19X8	19X9
Sales (net) (see Schedule 2.2)	$3,740,566	$4,208,400
Cost of Goods Sold (see Schedule 2.3)	2,472,758	2,790,192
Gross Profit	$1,267,808	$1,418,208
Operating Expenses (Excluding Depreciation) (see Schedule 2.4)	$ 448,868	$ 505,008
Depreciation Expense (see Schedule 2.5)	108,960	108,960
Total Operating Expenses	$ 557,828	$ 613,968
Income before Income Taxes	$ 709,980	$ 804,240
Provision for Income Taxes (see Schedule 2.6)	270,022	310,790
Income before Purchasing Power Gain	$ 439,958	$ 493,450
Purchasing Power Gain (Loss) (see Schedule 2.7)	(21,456)	(68,437)
Net Income	$ 418,502	$ 425,013
Beginning Retained Earnings (see Schedule 2.8)	571,670	797,002
	$ 990,172	1,222,015
Less: Dividends (see Schedule 2.9)	193,170	219,440
Ending Retained Earnings (see Schedule 2.8)	797,002	1,002,575

SCHEDULE 2.1

The Consumer Price Index for All Urban Consumers is presented below.

Year	Jan.	Feb.	Mar.	Apr.	May	June	July	Aug.	Sept.	Oct.	Nov.	Dec.	Avg.
19X4	139.7	141.5	143.1	143.9	145.5	146.9	148.0	149.9	151.7	153.0	154.3	155.4	147.7
19X5	156.1	157.2	157.8	158.6	159.3	160.6	162.3	162.8	163.6	164.6	165.6	166.3	161.2
19X6	166.7	167.1	167.5	168.2	169.2	170.1	171.1	171.9	172.6	173.3	173.8	174.3	170.5
19X7	175.3	177.1	178.2	179.6	180.6	181.8	182.6	183.3	184.0	184.5	185.4	186.1	181.5
19X8	187.2	188.4	189.8	191.5	193.3	195.3	196.7	197.8	199.3	200.9	202.0	202.9	195.4
19X9	204.7	207.1	209.1	211.5	214.1	216.6	218.9	221.1	223.4	224.1	226.3	228.4	217.1

SCHEDULE 2.2

Sales are restated on an historical cost/constant dollar basis when comprehensive disclosures are made as follows:

For 19X8 Sales—

Step 1. Restate 19X8 sales to end-of-the-year 19X8 constant dollars:
Sales (historical cost) × (19X8 year-end CPI/1978 average CPI)
= Sales Restated to 19X8 Constant Dollars
$3,200,000 × (202.9/195.4) = $3,322,880

Step 2. Roll forward sales as restated for 19X8 to end-of-the-year 19X9 constant dollars:
Restated 19X8 Sales × (19X9 year-end CPI/19X8 year-end CPI) = Sales Restated to 19X9 Constant Dollars
$3,322,880 × (228.4/202.9) = $3,740,566

For 19X9 Sales—

Step 3. Restate 19X9 sales to end-of-the-year 19X9 constant dollars:
Sales (historical cost) × (19X9 year-end CPI/19X9 average CPI)
= Sales Restated to 19X9 Constant Dollars
$4,000,000 × (228.4/217.1) = $4,208,400

In this example, there is an inherent assumption that sales are being generated evenly throughout the year; therefore, any seasonality problems are not considered. In a later section of this chapter the seasonal revenue issue is addressed and analyzed. Since sales for 19X9 are assumed to have been earned evenly throughout the year, the restatement of 19X9 sales is based on the relationship of the end-of-the-year and average-for-the-year 19X9 CPI.

Schedule 2.3 represents an analysis of the cost of goods sold restatement when inventories are accounted for on a first-in, first-out (FIFO) basis. The problems of restating last-in, first-out (LIFO) inventories are addressed and analyzed in a later section of this chapter. As with sales, the components of cost of goods sold for 19X8 (i.e., beginning inventories, purchases, and ending inventories) should be restated to end-of-the-year 19X8 constant dollars and then rolled forward to end-of-the-year 19X9 constant dollars for inclusion in the comparative statements. Similarly, components of the 19X9 cost of goods sold should be restated to end-of-the-year 19X9 constant dollars. Inventories are assumed to turn over about six times per year so that purchases are restated using the average CPI for the period and ending inventories are restated using an average index of the last two months of the period.

SCHEDULE 2.3

Cost of goods sold is restated on an historical cost/constant dollar basis when comprehensive disclosures are made as follows:

For 19X8 Cost of Goods Sold—

Step 1. Restate 19X8 beginning inventories to end-of-the-year 19X8 constant dollars:
Beginning Inventories (historical cost) $\times$ (19X8 year-end CPI/ Nov.–Dec. 19X7 CPI) = Beginning Inventories Restated to 19X8 Constant Dollars
$400,000 $\times$ (202.9/185.8) = $436,840

Step 2. Restate 19X8 purchases to end-of-the-year 19X8 constant dollars:
Purchases (historical cost) $\times$ (19X8 year-end CPI/19X8 average CPI) = Purchases Restated to 19X8 Constant Dollars
$2,100,000 $\times$ (202.9/195.4) = $2,180,640

Step 3. Restate 19X8 ending inventories to end-of-the-year 19X8 constant dollars:
Ending Inventories (historical cost) $\times$ (19X8 year-end CPI/Nov.– Dec. 19X8 CPI) = Ending Inventories Restated to 19X8 Constant Dollars
$420,000 $\times$ (202.9/202.5) = $420,840

Step 4. Compute 19X8 cost of goods sold restated to end-of-the-year 19X8 constant dollars:
Restated Beginning Inventories + Restated Purchases − Restated Ending Inventories = Cost of Goods Sold Restated to 19X8 Constant Dollars
$436,840 + $2,180,640 − $420,840 = $2,196,640

Step 5. Roll forward cost of goods sold as restated for 19X8 to end-of-the-year 19X9 constant dollars:

SCHEDULE 2.3 (continued)

Restated 19X8 Cost of Goods Sold $\times$ (19X9 year-end CPI/19X8 year-end CPI) = Cost of Goods Sold Restated to 19X9 Constant Dollars

$2,196,640 $\times$ (228.4/202.9) = $2,472,758

For 19X9 Cost of Goods Sold—

Step 6. Restate 19X9 beginning inventories to end-of-the-year 19X9 constant dollars:

Beginning Inventories (historical cost) $\times$ (19X9 year-end CPI/ Nov.–Dec. 19X8 CPI) = Beginning Inventories Restated to 19X9 Constant Dollars

$420,000 $\times$ (228.4/202.5) = $473,718

Step 7. Restate 19X9 purchases to end-of-the-year 19X9 constant dollars:

Purchases (historical cost) $\times$ (19X9 year-end CPI/19X9 average CPI) = Purchases Restated to 19X9 Constant Dollars

$2,660,000 $\times$ (228.4/217.1) = $2,798,586

Step 8. Restate ending inventories to end-of-the-year 19X9 constant dollars:

Ending Inventories (historical cost) $\times$ (19X9 year-end CPI/Nov.– Dec. 19X9 CPI) = Ending Inventories Restated to 19X9 Constant Dollars

$480,000 $\times$ (228.4/227.4) = $482,112

Step 9. Compute 19X9 cost of goods sold restated to end-of-the-year 19X9 constant dollars:

Restated Beginning Inventories + Restated Purchases − Restated Ending Inventories = Cost of Goods Sold Restated to 19X9 Constant Dollars

$473,718 + $2,798,586 − $482,112 = $2,790,192

Schedule 2.4 analyzes the restatement of operating expenses (exclusive of depreciation) which are presumed to have been incurred evenly throughout the year in proportion to sales. Therefore, the operating expense restatement involves use of average indices in restating 19X8 expenses to the end-of-the-year 19X8 constant dollars, rolling forward this amount to the end-of-the-year 19X9 constant dollars, and restating the 19X9 expenses in terms of end-of-the-year dollars.

SCHEDULE 2.4

Operating expenses (exclusive of depreciation) are restated on an historical cost/constant dollar basis when comprehensive disclosures are made as follows:

For 19X8 Operating Expenses—

Step 1. Restate 19X8 operating expenses to end-of-the-year 19X8 constant dollars:

Operating Expenses (historical cost) × (19X8 year-end CPI/19X8 average CPI) = Operating Expenses Restated to 19X8 Constant Dollars

$384,000 × (202.9/195.4) = $398,746

Step 2. Roll forward operating expenses as restated for 19X8 to end-of-the-year 19X9 constant dollars:

Restated 19X8 Operating Expenses × (19X9 year-end CPI/19X8 year-end CPI) = Operating Expenses Restated to 19X9 Constant Dollars

$398,746 × (228.4/202.9) = $448,868

For 19X9 Operating Expenses—

Step 3. Restate 19X9 operating expenses to end-of-the-year 19X9 constant dollars:

Operating Expenses (historical cost) × (19X9 year-end CPI/19X9 average CPI) = Operating Expenses Restated to 19X9 Constant Dollars

$480,000 × (228.4/217.1) = $505,008

Schedule 2.5 relates to the restatement of depreciation. Since the depreciation charge each time period will be measured by multiplying the historical cost depreciation by the relationship of the current period CPI to the purchase period CPI, the first step in this restatement process will be the preparation of fixed asset layers; thereafter, the depreciation restatement follows the same line of reasoning used for other operating expenses. There is a presumption that depreciation methods, estimates of useful lives, and residual value estimates should be the same for constant dollar and historical cost calculations. However, if the methods and estimates used in developing the historical cost amounts were chosen partly to allow for expected price changes, different methods and estimates may be used in preparing the constant dollar amounts.

SCHEDULE 2.5

Depreciation expense is restated on an historical cost/constant dollar basis when comprehensive disclosures are made as follows:

For 19X8 Depreciation Expense—

Step 1. Determine fixed asset layers:

Asset	Historical Cost	Acquisition Date	Depreciation Method
a. Building	$500,000	December 31, 19X4	Straight-line (40 years)
b. Equipment	420,000	December 31, 19X4	Straight-line (8 years)
c. Equipment	110,000	January 1, 19X8	Straight-line (10 years)

Step 2. Determine historical cost depreciation expense:

Asset	Depreciation Expense
a. Building	$12,500
b. Equipment	52,500
c. Equipment	11,000

Step 3. Determine CPI associated with acquisition dates:

Asset	Base CPI
a. Building	155.4
b. Equipment	155.4
c. Equipment	187.2

Step 4. Restate 19X8 depreciation expense to end-of-the-year 19X8 constant dollars

Depreciation Expense (Historical Cost) $\times$ (19X8 year-end CPI/base CPI) = Depreciation Expense Restated to 19X8 Constant Dollars

a.	Building	$12,500 $\times$ (202.9/155.4) =	$16,321
b.	Equipment	$52,500 $\times$ (202.9/155.4) =	68,549
c.	Equipment	$11,000 $\times$ (202.9/187.2) =	11,923
	Total		$96,793

Step 5. Roll forward depreciation expense as restated for 19X8 to end-of-the-year constant dollars:

Restated 19X8 Depreciation Expense $\times$ (19X9 year-end CPI/ 19X8 year-end CPI) = Depreciation Expense Restated to 19X9 Constant Dollars

$96,793 $\times$ (228.4/202.9) = $108,960

SCHEDULE 2.5 (continued)

For 19X9 Depreciation Expense—

Step 6. Determine layers and associated CPI for any new acquisitions: No acquisitions or disposals in 19X9.

Step 7. Restate 19X9 depreciation expense to end-of-the-year 19X9 constant dollars:

Depreciation Expense (historical cost) $\times$ (19X9 year-end CPI/ base CPI) = Depreciation Expense Restated to 19X9 Constant Dollars

a.	Building	$12,500 $\times$ (228.4/155.4) =	$18,373
b.	Equipment	$52,500 $\times$ (228.4/155.4) =	77,166
c.	Equipment	$11,000 $\times$ (228.4/187.2) =	13,421
	Total		$108,960

Schedule 2.6 involves the steps necessary to convert the provision for income taxes from historical amounts to end-of-the-year constant dollars. It has been argued that the provision for income taxes in constant dollar disclosures should be the same as the historical cost provision. In fact, the FASB implements this notion in their *minimum* disclosure requirements for both constant dollars and current costs. However, as will be presented later in this chapter, the minimum disclosures in SFAS No. 33 are required to be based on the average-for-the-year CPI and, in that respect, other income statement elements, e.g., sales and operating expenses exclusive of depreciation, are not restated in constant dollars since they were assumed generated and incurred on an average throughout the year. However, since this comprehensive restatement is prepared using end-of-the-year constant dollars, the provision for income taxes is restated along with other expenses.

SCHEDULE 2.6

Provisions for income taxes are restated on an historical cost/constant dollar basis when comprehensive disclosures are made as follows:

For 19X8 Provision for Income Taxes—

Step 1. Restate 19X8 provision for income taxes to end-of-the-year 19X8 constant dollars:

Provision for Income Taxes (historical cost) × (19X8 year-end CPI/19X8 average CPI) = Provision for Income Taxes Restated to 19X8 Constant Dollars

$231,000 × (202.9/195.4) = $239,870

Step 2. Roll forward provision for income taxes as restated for 19X8 to end-of-the-year 19X9 constant dollars:

Restated 19X8 Provision for Income Taxes × (19X9 year-end CPI/19X8 year-end CPI) = Provision for Income Taxes Restated to 19X9 Constant Dollars

$239,870 × (228.4/202.9) = $270,022

For 19X9 Provision for Income Taxes—

Step 3. Restate 19X9 provision for income taxes to end-of-the-year 19X9 constant dollars:

Provision for Income Taxes (historical cost) × (19X9 year-end CPI/19X9 average CPI) = Provision for Income Taxes Restated to 19X9 Constant Dollars

$295,400 × (228.4/217.1) = $310,790

Schedule 2.7 involves the determination of the purchasing power gain or loss. Since in both 19X8 and 19X9 MR Corporation held net monetary assets, a purchasing power loss results because the conversion of the amounts to cash (or other final use) will result in a net receipt of dollars with a lower purchasing power in a period of rising prices. Notice that the 19X8 purchasing power loss must be rolled forward to end-of-the-year 19X9 constant dollars when the 19X8 amounts are included in the 19X9 financial statements for comparative purposes.

SCHEDULE 2.7

Purchasing power gain or loss is determined as follows:

For 19X8 Purchasing Power Gain or Loss—

Step 1. Compute purchasing power gain or loss for 19X8:

Item	Historical Cost Amounts	×	Conversion Factor	=	Restated to 19X8 Constant Dollars
Net Monetary Assets, December 31, 19X7	$107,030		202.9/186.1		$116,695
Add: Sources of Net Monetary Items— Sales	3,200,000		202.9/195.4		3,322,880
Less: Uses of Net Monetary Items— Purchases	(2,100,000)		202.9/195.4		(2,180,640)
Operating Expenses (excluding depreciation)	(384,000)		202.9/195.4		(398,746)
Provision for Income Taxes	(231,000)		202.9/195.4		(239,870)
Dividends Declared	(171,600)		202.9/202.9		(171,600)
Purchase of Equipment	(110,000)		202.9/187.2		(119,229)
Net Monetary Assets, December 31, 19X8, restated					$329,490
Net Monetary Assets, December 31, 19X8	$310,430				310,430
Purchasing Power Gain (Loss)					$(19,060)

SCHEDULE 2.7 (continued)

Step 2. Roll forward 19X8 purchasing power loss to end-of-the-year 19X9 constant dollars:

Purchasing Power Loss × (19X9 year-end CPI/19X8 year-end CPI) = Purchasing Power Loss Restated to 19X9 Constant Dollars

$(19,060) × (228.4/202.9) = $(21,456)

For 19X9 Purchasing Power Gain or Loss—

Step 3. Compute purchasing power gain or loss for 19X9:

Item	Historical Cost Amounts	×	Conversion Factor	=	Restated to 19X9 Constant Dollars
Net Monetary Assets, December 31, 19X8	$310,430		228.4/202.9		$349,451
Add: Sources of Net Monetary Items— Sales	4,000,000		228.4/217.1		4,208,400
Less: Uses of Net Monetary Items— Purchases	(2,660,000)		228.4/217.1		(2,798,586)
Operating Expenses (excluding depreciation)	(480,000)		228.4/217.1		(505,008)
Provision for Income Taxes	(295,400)		228.4/217.1		(310,790)
Dividends Declared	(219,440)		228.4/228.4		(219,440)
Net Monetary Assets, December 31, 19X9 Restated					$724,027
Net Monetary Assets, December 31, 19X9	$655,590				655,590
Purchasing Power Gain (Loss)					$(68,437)

Schedule 2.8 discusses the determination of the retained earnings balance. In the first year of restatement to constant dollars, the retained earnings amount will be "plugged" as the difference between restated assets and restated equities other than retained earnings. Thereafter, the retained earnings balance may be directly determined by adjusting the original (or updated) amount for any increases, e.g., constant dollar income, or decreases, e.g., constant dollar dividends in retained earnings. In this example, the retained earnings balance is determined on a combined statement of income and retained earnings.

Schedule 2.9 presents the restatement of dividends, which, in this case, is simple since dividends are assumed declared at or near year end, and therefore the dividend amounts measured in terms of historical costs are reflective of end-of-the-year constant dollars. In the event dividends are declared at some other time or multiple times during the year, these amounts should be restated to end-of-the-year constant dollars based on the relationship of the end-of-the-year CPI to the CPI in effect when the dividends are declared.

In the restatement of monetary items, Schedule 2.10 indicates that current year monetary items need not be restated. This is true in that the current year monetary items are already measured in terms of their end-of-the-year monetary equivalent. The 19X8 numbers presented for comparative purposes should be rolled forward based on the relationship of the end-of-the-year 19X9 CPI to the end-of-the-year 19X8 CPI.

Schedule 2.11 represents a constant dollar determination of ending amounts of inventory. These balance sheet amounts tie back to Schedule 2.3 where the inventory amounts used in the computation of cost of goods sold were determined.

The restatement of fixed assets in Schedule 2.12 follows the same rationale as the restatement of related depreciation in Schedule 2.5. The first steps in the restatement of fixed assets involve the layering of the assets into acquisition periods and the determination of the associated CPI. The historical cost amounts should then be restated using the relationship of the end-of-the-year CPI for the current reporting period to the CPI in effect at the acquisition date of the asset. The same logic applies in restating any accumulated depreciation, amortization, or depletion associated with these assets.

SCHEDULE 2.8—Restatement of Retained Earnings

For 19X8 Retained Earnings—

Step 1. In the first year of restatement, ending retained earnings is the balancing figure, i.e., the difference between restated assets and restated equities other than retained earnings.

Step 2. Determine beginning retained earnings:
Ending Retained Earnings + Dividends − Net Income = Beginning Retained Earnings
$797,002 + $193,170 − $418,502 = $571,670

For 19X9 Retained Earnings—

Step 3. Retained earnings amounts for 19X9 are computed on the statement of income and retained earnings.

SCHEDULE 2.9

Dividends are restated on an historical cost/constant dollar basis when comprehensive disclosures are made as follows:

For 19X8 Dividends—

Step 1. It is assumed that dividends are declared at or near year-end. Therefore, the dividends declared already are stated at end-of-the-year constant dollars. If dividends are declared during the year, these amounts should be restated to end-of-the-year constant dollars using the CPI in effect at the date of declaration.

Step 2. Roll forward dividends for 19X8 to end-of-the-year 19X9 constant dollars:
Dividends × (19X9 year-end CPI/19X8 year-end CPI) = Dividends Restated to 19X9 Constant Dollars
$171,600 × (228.4/202.9) = $193,170

For 19X9 Dividends—

Step 3. Procedure is the same as step 1.

SCHEDULE 2.10—Restatement of Monetary Items

For 19X8 Monetary Items—

Step 1. Roll forward 19X8 monetary items to end-of-the-year 19X9 constant dollars:
Monetary Item $\times$ (19X9 year-end CPI/19X8 year-end CPI) = Monetary Item Restated to 19X9 Constant Dollars

a.	Cash	$ 410,250 $\times$ (228.4/202.9) =	$ 461,818
b.	Receivables	1,230,750 $\times$ (228.4/202.9) =	1,385,455
c.	Current Liabilities	215,793 $\times$ (228.4/202.9) =	242,918
d.	Long-term Liabilities	1,078,963 $\times$ (228.4/202.9) =	1,214,589
e.	Deferred Taxes	35,814 $\times$ (228.4/202.9) =	40,316

For 19X9 Monetary Items—

Step 2. Monetary items for 19X9 are stated in end-of-the-year 19X9 constant dollars. Therefore no restatement is necessary.

SCHEDULE 2.11—Restatement of Inventories

For 19X8 Inventories—

Step 1. Restate 19X8 ending inventories to end-of-the-year 19X8 constant dollars (see Schedule 2.3):
Restated amount $420,840

Step 2. Roll forward 19X8 restated ending inventories to end-of-the-year 19X9 constant dollars:
Restated Ending Inventories $\times$ (19X9 year-end CPI/19X8 year-end CPI) = Ending Inventories Restated to 19X9 Constant Dollars
$420,840 $\times$ (228.4/202.9) = $473,740

Step 3. Restate 19X9 ending inventories to end-of-the-year 19X9 constant dollars (see Schedule 2.3):
Restated amount $482,112

SCHEDULE 2.12—Restatement of Fixed Assets

For 19X8 Fixed Assets—

Step 1. Determine fixed asset layers:

	Asset	Historical Cost	Acquisition Date
a.	Land	$ 80,000	December 31, 19X4
b.	Building	500,000	December 31, 19X4
c.	Equipment	420,000	December 31, 19X4
d.	Equipment	110,000	January 1, 19X8

Step 2. Determine CPI associated with acquisition dates:

	Asset	Base CPI
a.	Land	155.4
b.	Building	155.4
c.	Equipment	155.4
d.	Equipment	187.2

Step 3. Restate fixed assets to end-of-the-year 19X8 constant dollars:
Fixed Asset (historical cost) × (19X8 year-end CPI/base CPI) =
Fixed Asset Restated to 19X8 Constant Dollars

a.	Land	$ 80,000 × (202.9/155.4) =	$104,456
b.	Building	500,000 × (202.9/155.4) =	652,850
c.	Equipment	420,000 × (202.9/155.4) =	548,394
d.	Equipment	110,000 × (202.9/187.2) =	119,229

Step 4. Roll forward 19X8 fixed assets as restated to end-of-the-year 19X9 constant dollars:
Restated Fixed Assets × (19X9 year-end CPI/19X8 year-end CPI) = Fixed Assets Restated to 19X9 Constant Dollars

a.	Land	$104,456 × (228.4/202.9) =	$117,586
b.	Building	652,850 × (228.4/202.9) =	734,913
c.	Equipment	548,394 × (228.4/202.9) =	617,327
d.	Equipment	119,229 × (228.4/202.9) =	134,216

Step 5. Restate accumulated depreciation to end-of-the-year 19X8 constant dollars:
Accumulated Depreciation (historical cost) × (19X8 year-end CPI/base CPI) = Accumulated Depreciation Restated to 19X8 Constant Dollars

b.	Building	$50,000 × (202.9/155.4) =	$65,285
c.	Equipment	210,000 × (202.9/155.4) =	274,197
d.	Equipment	11,000 × (202.9/187.2) =	11,923

SCHEDULE 2.12 (continued)

Step 6. Roll forward 19X8 accumulated depreciation as restated to end-of-the-year 19X9 constant dollars:
Restated Accumulated Depreciation $\times$ (19X9 year-end CPI/19X8 year-end CPI) = Accumulated Depreciation Restated to 19X9 Constant Dollars

b.	Building	$65,285 $\times$ (228.4/202.9) =	$73,491
c.	Equipment	274,197 $\times$ (228.4/202.9) =	308,664
d.	Equipment	11,923 $\times$ (228.4/202.9) =	13,422

For 19X9 Fixed Assets—

Step 7. Determine layers and associated CPI for any new acquisitions: No acquisitions or disposals in 19X9.

Step 8. Restate fixed assets to end-of-the-year 19X9 constant dollars:
Fixed Asset (historical cost) $\times$ (19X9 year-end CPI/base CPI) = Fixed Asset Restated to 19X9 Constant Dollars

a.	Land	$80,000 $\times$ (228.4/155.4) =	$117,598
b.	Building	500,000 $\times$ (228.4/155.4) =	734,913
c.	Equipment	420,000 $\times$ (228.4/155.4) =	617,326
d.	Equipment	110,000 $\times$ (228.4/187.2) =	134,217

Step 9. Restate accumulated depreciation to end-of-the-year 19X9 constant dollars:
Accumulated Depreciation (historical cost) $\times$ (19X9 year-end CPI/base CPI) = Accumulated Depreciation Restated to 19X9 Constant Dollars

b.	Building	$62,500 $\times$ (228.4/155.4) =	$91,853
c.	Equipment	262,500 $\times$ (228.4/155.4) =	385,830
d.	Equipment	22,000 $\times$ (228.4/187.2) =	26,845

The paid-in capital restatement in Schedule 2.13 is very similar to the restatement of the fixed assets in Schedule 2.12 since these amounts all represent nonmonetary items. After layers and appropriate indices are determined for paid-in capital, these amounts should be restated to end-of-the-year constant dollars, using the relationship of the end-of-the-year CPI to the CPI in effect when the paid-in capital was generated.

While these comprehensive disclosures are not required in SFAS No. 33, they are permitted and should provide a thorough knowledge of how the minimum disclosures should be generated. The next section of this chapter formulates an example of the required minimum disclosures under SFAS No. 33.

SCHEDULE 2.13—Restatement of Paid-In Capital

For 19X8 Paid-In Capital—

Step 1. Determine appropriate layers for paid-in capital:

	Paid-In Capital	Amount	Issue Date
a.	Capital Stock	$280,000	December 31, 19X4
b.	Additional Paid-In Capital	560,000	December 31, 19X4

Step 2. Determine appropriate CPI:

	Paid-In Capital	Base CPI
a.	Capital Stock	155.4
b.	Additional Paid-In Capital	155.4

Step 3. Restate paid-in capital to end-of-the-year 19X8 constant dollars:
Paid-In Capital (historical cost) × (19X8 year-end CPI/base CPI)
= Paid-In Capital Restated to 19X8 Constant Dollars

a. Capital Stock $280,000 × (202.9/155.4) = $365,596
b. Additional Paid-In Capital 560,000 × (202.9/155.4) = 731,192

Step 4. Roll forward 19X8 paid-in capital as restated to end-of-the-year 19X9 constant dollars:
Restated Paid-In Capital × (19X9 year-end CPI/19X8 year-end CPI) = Paid-In Capital Restated to 19X9 Constant Dollars

a. Capital Stock $365,596 × (228.4/202.9) = $411,551
b. Additional Paid-In Capital 731,192 × (228.4/202.9) = 823,102

For 19X9 Paid-In Capital—

Step 5. Determine layers and associated CPI for any additional issuances:
No additional issuances in 19X9

Step 6. Restate paid-in capital to end-of-the-year constant dollars:
Paid-In Capital (historical cost) × (19X9 year-end CPI/base CPI)
= Paid-In Capital Restated to 19X9 Constant Dollars

a. Capital Stock $280,000 × (228.4/155.4) = $411,551
b. Additional Paid-In Capital 560,000 × (228.4/155.4) = 823,102

Illustration of Minimum Constant Dollar Disclosure Requirements

SFAS No. 33 requires that the reporting enterprises report the following information on a constant dollar basis as a minimum:

1. Income from continuing operations.
2. Purchasing power gain or loss on net monetary items.

Checklist 2.2 provides an overview to the computational steps required to make the minimum constant dollar disclosures.

CHECKLIST 2.2
Computational Guidance for
Minimum Constant Dollar Disclosures

1. Determine Purchasing Power Gain or Loss.
   a. Segregate financial statement elements into monetary and nonmonetary categories. (par. 23, 50)
   b. Restate beginning net monetary items to average-for-the-year constant dollars. (par. 50, 232)
   c. Restate increases and decreases in net monetary items to average-for-the-year constant dollars. (par. 50, 232)
   d. Restate ending net monetary items to average-for-the-year constant dollars. (par. 50, 232)
   e. Purchasing power gain (loss) equals beginning net monetary items restated (b) plus increases in net monetary items restated minus decreases in net monetary items restated (c) minus ending net monetary items restated (d). (par. 50, 232)
2. Steps to Prepare Historical Cost/Constant Dollar Income Statement. When using average-for-the-year constant dollars—
   a. Operating revenues may be historical cost operating revenues (consideration should be given to seasonal fluctuations in the generation of revenues). (par. 210)
   b. Operating expenses (exclusive of cost of goods sold and depreciation) may be historical cost operating expenses (consideration should be given to seasonal fluctuations in the incurrence of expenses). (par. 210)
   c. Restate cost of goods sold and depreciation expense. (When LIFO method of inventory costing is used, restated cost of goods sold may be approximated by historical cost of goods sold unless a LIFO layer has been depleted. In this case, costs associated with a depleted LIFO layer should be restated.) (par. 212, 223–227)
   d. The provision for income taxes should be the historical cost provision for income taxes. (par. 210)
   e. Income from continuing operations equals operating revenues (a) minus operating expenses (b,c) minus provision for income taxes (d). (par. 70)
   f. Add (disclose) purchasing power gain (loss) (1,e). (par. 29)

The reporting enterprise may make the required disclosures in either of two formats. The disclosures may be made either by disclosing a constant dollar income statement (see Figure 2.5) or by using a reconciliation format (see Figure 2.6). In either case, the enterprise must adjust, on a constant dollar basis, its inventories and its depreciation expense. It must also compute the purchasing power gain or loss on net monetary items.

When the minimum disclosures are made, the enterprise is *required* to adjust items to average-for-the-year constant dollars. This, of course, differs from the comprehensive disclosures where either average-for-the-year or end-of-the-year constant dollars may be used. Furthermore, if only the minimum disclosures are made, the enterprise need only report information for the *current* fiscal year. Therefore, it is not necessary to roll forward data from last year as was done in the comprehensive example.

FIGURE 2.5
MR Corporation
Statement of Income on an Historical Cost/Constant Dollar Basis
(Statement Format)
For the Year Ended December 31, 19X9

	As Reported in Primary Financial Statements	Adjusted for General Inflation
Sales	$4,000,000	$4,000,000
Cost of Goods Sold (see Schedule 2.14)	2,600,000	2,652,026
Gross Profit	1,400,000	$1,347,974
Operating Expenses (excluding depreciation)	$ 480,000	$ 480,000
Depreciation (see Schedule 2.15)	76,000	103,570
Provision for Income Taxes	295,400	295,400
Income from Continuing Operations	$ 548,600	$ 469,004
Purchasing Power Loss (see Schedule 2.16)		$ (32,570)

FIGURE 2.6
MR Corporation
Statement of Income on an Historical Cost/Constant Dollar Basis
(Reconciliation Format)
For the Year Ended December 31, 19X9

Income from Continuing Operations	$548,600
Adjustments to Restate Costs for the Effect of General Inflation—	
Cost of Goods Sold	(52,026)
Depreciation	(27,570)
Income from Continuing Operations Adjusted for the Effects of General Inflation	$469,004
Purchasing Power Loss	$ (32,570)

Schedule 2.14 depicts the steps necessary to adjust the cost of goods sold when FIFO is used to cost the inventories. First, the beginning inventories must be restated to average-for-the-year constant dollars. Notice that the CPI used is 217.1—the average CPI for 19X9—rather than the year-end CPI. The beginning inventories restated in terms of average-for-the-year purchases amount to $450,282.

In Schedule 2.14, purchases for 19X9 are not restated. Purchases will not have to be restated when adjusting to average-for-the-year constant dollars and there is no seasonality. This is true when both conditions are met because the purchases will have been made evenly throughout the year. Therefore, the "average" purchase will have been made at the average-for-the-year purchasing power. If seasonality is present, purchases will have to be restated. The effects of seasonality on the restatement of revenues and expenses are discussed with other computational problems in the following section.

Next, the ending inventories must be rolled back to average-for-the-year purchasing power. The ending inventories are currently stated in terms of November-December purchasing power. As such, the ending inventories are restated in terms of average-for-the-year constant dollars. The restated ending inventories are $458,256.

SCHEDULE 2.14

Cost of goods sold is restated on an historical cost/constant dollar basis when minimum disclosures are made as follows:

For 19X9 Cost of Goods Sold—

Step 1. Restate 19X9 beginning inventories to average-for-the-year 19X9 constant dollars:
Beginning Inventories (historical cost) × (19X9 average CPI/ Nov.–Dec. 19X8 CPI) = Beginning Inventories Restated to 19X9 Constant Dollars
$420,000 × (217.1/202.5) = $450,282

Step 2. Purchases need not be restated in the absence of significant seasonal trends.

Step 3. Restate 19X9 ending inventories to average-for-the-year 19X9 constant dollars:
Ending Inventories (historical cost) × (19X9 average CPI/Nov.– Dec. 19X9 CPI) = Ending Inventories Restated to 19X9 Constant Dollars
$480,000 × (217.1/227.4) = $458,256

Step 4. Compute 19X9 cost of goods sold restated to average-for-the-year 19X9 constant dollars:
Restated Beginning Inventories + Restated Purchases − Restated Ending Inventories = Cost of Goods Sold Restated to 19X9 Constant Dollars
$450,282 + $2,660,000 − $458,256 = $2,652,026

At that point, the beginning inventories, purchases, and ending inventories are all stated in average-for-the-year constant dollars. Therefore, cost of goods sold in average-for-the-year constant dollars is computed by adding the restated beginning inventories to the purchases and then subtracting the restated ending inventories. The resulting cost of goods sold figure of $2,652,026 differs from the historical cost amount by $52,026. This is the amount by which income from continuing operations is adjusted in the reconciliation format (Figure 2.6). In the statement format (Figure 2.5), the constant dollar cost of goods sold figure is used in place of the historical cost of goods sold amount.

MR Corporation is using FIFO to cost its inventories. If it had been using LIFO, cost of goods sold would not have needed adjustment in 19X9. A shortcut is provided when LIFO is used and there is no depletion of the LIFO base. If both conditions are met, the historical cost of goods sold may be used since it will closely approximate the constant dollar amount. (This simplifying assumption may not always be used by manufacturing enterprises—see Chapter 10.) If there is a depletion of the LIFO base, the historical cost of goods sold need only be adjusted for the effects of the depletion of the LIFO base. These computations are illustrated in the following section.

The computational procedure to adjust the depreciation expense is identical to that used in the comprehensive illustration presented earlier. Again notice that a difference arises because the depreciation is adjusted to average-for-the-year constant dollars rather than end-of-the-year constant dollars. The difference does *not* result because the computational procedure differs. The adjustment of depreciation expense to average-for-the-year constant dollars is shown in Schedule 2.15. Also, in the minimum disclosures, only the 19X9 depreciation expense need be adjusted.

SCHEDULE 2.15

Depreciation expense is restated on an historical cost/constant dollar basis when minimum disclosures are made as follows:

For 19X9 Depreciation Expense—

Step 1. Determine fixed asset layers (see Schedule 2.5).

Step 2. Determine historical cost depreciation (see Schedule 2.5).

Step 3. Determine CPI associated with acquisition dates (see Schedule 2.5).

Step 4. Restate 19X9 depreciation expense to average-for-the-year 19X9 constant dollars:

Depreciation Expense (historical cost) × (19X9 average CPI/base CPI) = Depreciation Expense Restated to 19X9 Constant Dollars

a. Building	$12,500 × (217.1/155.4) =	$ 17,464
b. Equipment	52,500 × (217.1/155.4) =	73,348
c. Equipment	11,000 × (217.1/187.2) =	12,758
Total		$103,570

The 19X9 depreciation expense stated in average-for-the-year 19X9 constant dollars is $103,570. This exceeds the historical cost amount by $27,570. In the reconciliation format (Figure 2.6), the historical cost income from continuing operations is adjusted for the increased constant dollar depreciation. In the statement format (Figure 2.5), the constant dollar amount of $103,570 is used in place of the historical cost amount. The enterprise may use either reporting format (the enterprise will use one or the other format, not both).

The minimum disclosures include the purchasing power gain or loss from holding net monetary items. As in the comprehensive example used earlier in this chapter, MR Corporation held net monetary assets during a period of inflation. This will give rise to a purchasing power loss. The purchasing power loss is computed in Schedule 2.16. Monetary items are restated in terms of average-for-the-year constant dollars. This means that monetary items held at year-end are rolled back to average-for-the-year constant dollars. The sources and uses of monetary items from operations (sales, purchases, operating expenses, and provision for income taxes) are not restated for the same reason that purchases were not restated in computing cost of goods sold on a constant dollar basis. If seasonality were present, these items would be adjusted to reflect their seasonal nature. The computations needed when seasonal patterns exist are discussed in the section on computational problems.

MR Corporation experienced a purchasing power loss of $32,570 when monetary items were restated to average-for-the-year 19X9 constant dollars. This amount is *not* used in computing income from continuing operations on a constant dollar basis. In both the statement format (Figure 2.5) and the reconciliation format (Figure 2.6), the purchasing power loss is disclosed *after* income from continuing operations on a constant dollar basis is computed.

SCHEDULE 2.16

Purchasing power gain or loss is computed as follows:

For 19X9 Purchasing Power Gain or Loss—
Compute purchasing power gain or loss for 19X9:

Item	Historical Cost Amount ×	Conversion Factor =	Restated to 19X9 Constant Dollars
Net Monetary Assets, December 31, 19X8	$310,430	217.1/202.9	$332,160
Add: Sources of Net Monetary Items— Sales	4,000,000	217.1/217.1	4,000,000
Less: Uses of Net Monetary Items— Purchases	(2,660,000)	217.1/217.1	(2,660,000)
Operating Expenses (excluding depreciation)	(480,000)	217.1/217.1	(480,000)

SCHEDULE 2.16 (continued)

Provision for			
Income Taxes	(295,400)	217.1/217.1	(295,400)
Dividends declared	(219,440)	217.1/228.4	(208,600)
Net Monetary Assets, December 31, 19X9 Restated			$688,160
Net Monetary Assets, December 31, 19X9	$655,590		655,590
Purchasing Power Gain (Loss)			$(32,570)

This section has described the minimum constant dollar disclosures required by SFAS No. 33. In developing the constant dollar information, there are certain problems that complicate the computation procedures. Those problems, along with their solutions, are presented and discussed in the following section.

Computational Problems in Developing Constant Dollar Disclosures

The comprehensive and minimum disclosures presented in this chapter do not reflect the special computational problems that can occur for certain enterprises. There are four factors that can cause problems and complicate the constant dollar adjustments. These factors are: (1) using LIFO to cost inventories, (2) recoverable amounts less than cost, (3) determining fixed asset layers, and (4) seasonality.

Each of these factors affects the conversion factor which is needed to make the constant dollar adjustments. Therefore, it is important to know what effect each factor will have on the constant dollar adjustments and how to determine the appropriate conversion factor in each case. This section will describe the procedures needed when these factors are present.

Determining Layers of LIFO-Base Inventories

When an enterprise uses LIFO to cost its inventories, a problem is created which does not exist when FIFO is used. LIFO-costed inventories consist of cost layers, which is not the case for FIFO-costed inventories. Therefore, an index is needed for each layer.

If LIFO is used to cost inventories, the enterprise must determine whether there has been a depletion of the LIFO-base in the current year, i.e., a decline in the number of units on hand at year-end. If there has been a depletion of the LIFO-base, the enterprise must determine which layer(s) has been depleted and the extent of the depletion. By determining the extent to which existing layers have been depleted, the enterprise can then assess which layers remain for purposes of restating the ending inventories on a constant dollar basis.

In the case used earlier in this chapter, MR Corporation used FIFO to cost its inventories. If LIFO were being used, the constant dollar adjustments would differ for both cost of goods sold and ending inventories. In order to illustrate how the results would differ, the LIFO layers must first be determined. Assume that the increase in the cost of inventories is identical to the increase in the general price-level as measured by the CPI. Under that assumption, the LIFO layers can be computed. Recall that since the inventory turns over approximately six times per year, the appropriate base CPI for adjusting the FIFO ending inventories is the November-December average for each year. Schedule 2.17 presents the LIFO layers for MR Corporation.

SCHEDULE 2.17—Restating LIFO Inventories

Step 1. Determine appropriate CPI for each year:

Year	CPI
19X4	155.4
19X5	166.0
19X6	174.1
19X7	185.8
19X8	202.5
19X9	227.4

Step 2. Determine LIFO layers for 19X4:
Since 19X4 is the inception of MR Corporation, the inventories are $300,000 regardless of the costing method chosen. Therefore, the first layer is $300,000.

Step 3. Determine LIFO layers for 19X5:
Roll ending FIFO inventories back to base price-level—
Ending Inventories × (19X4 CPI/19X5 CPI) = 19X5 Ending Inventories in Base (19X4) Constant Dollars
$260,000 × (155.4/166.0) = $243,412
Since the 19X4 ending inventories consisted of only one layer, the decline in inventory is peeled off of 19X4 ending inventories, leaving $243,412 in the first layer.

SCHEDULE 2.17 (continued)

Step 4. Determine LIFO layers for 19X6:
   a. Roll ending FIFO inventories back to base price-level—
      Ending Inventories $\times$ (19X4 CPI/19X6 CPI) = 19X6 Ending
      Inventories in Base (19X4) Constant Dollars
      $300,000 $\times$ (155.4/174.1) = $267,780
   b. Determine whether inventories increased or decreased—
      Beginning Base Inventories — 19X6 Ending Inventories Re-
      stated = (Increase) Decrease
      $243,412 — $267,780 = ($24,368)
   c. Determine layers and appropriate CPI in order to calculate
      LIFO ending inventories—

Year of Layer	Base Amount	$\times$	CPI for Layer	$\div$	Base CPI	=	Inflated Layer
19X4	$243,412		155.4		155.4		$243,412
19X6	24,368		174.1		155.4		27,302

Base Inventories $267,780   LIFO Inventories $270,714

Step 5. Determine LIFO layers for 19X7:
   a. Roll ending FIFO inventories back to base price-level—
      Ending Inventories $\times$ (19X4 CPI/19X7 CPI) = 19X7 Ending
      Inventories in Base (19X4) Constant Dollars
      $400,000 $\times$ (155.4/185.8) = $334,560
   b. Determine whether inventories increased or decreased—
      Beginning Base Inventories — 19X7 Ending Inventories Re-
      stated = (Increase) Decrease
      $267,780 — $334,560 = ($66,780)
   c. Determine layers and appropriate CPI in order to calculate
      LIFO ending inventories—

Year of Layer	Base Amount	$\times$	CPI for Layer	$\div$	Base CPI	=	Inflated Layer
19X4	$243,412		155.4		155.4		$243,412
19X6	24,368		174.1		155.4		27,302
19X7	66,780		185.8		155.4		79,849

Base Inventories $334,560   LIFO Inventories $350,563

Step 6. Determine LIFO Layers for 19X8:
   a. Roll ending FIFO inventories back to base price-level—
      Ending Inventories $\times$ (19X4 CPI/19X8 CPI) = 19X8 Ending
      Inventories in Base (19X4) Constant Dollars
      $420,000 $\times$ (155.4/202.5) = $322,308

SCHEDULE 2.17 (continued)

> b. Determine whether inventories increased or decreased—
> Beginning Base Inventories — 19X8 Ending Inventories
> Restated = (Increase) Decrease
> $334,560 — $322,308 = $12,252
> c. Determine layers and appropriate CPI in order to calculate
> LIFO ending inventories—

Year of Layer	Base Amount ×	CPI for Layer	÷ Base CPI =	Inflated Layer
19X4	$243,412	155.4	155.4	$243,412
19X6	24,368	174.1	155.4	27,302
19X7	54,528	185.8	155.4	65,199

Base Inventories $322,308   LIFO Inventories $344,290

Step 7. Determine LIFO layers for 19X9:
> a. Roll ending FIFO inventories back to base price-level—
> Ending Inventories × (19X4 CPI/19X9 CPI) = 19X9 Ending
> Inventories in Base (19X4) Constant Dollars
> $480,000 × (155.4/227.4) = $328,032
> b. Determine whether inventories increased or decreased—
> Beginning Base Inventories — 19X9 Ending Inventories Re-
> stated = (Increase) Decrease
> $322,308 — $328;032 = ($5,724)
> c. Determine layers and appropriate CPI in order to calculate
> LIFO ending inventories—

Year of Layer	Base Amount ×	CPI for Layer	÷ Base CPI =	Inflated Layer
19X4	$243,412	155.4	155.4	$243,412
19X6	24,368	174.1	155.4	27,302
19X7	54,528	185.8	155.4	65,199
19X9	5,724	227.4	155.4	8,377

Base Inventories $328,032   LIFO Inventories $344,290

As can be seen from Schedule 2.17, MR Corporation had a decline in the quantity of inventories on hand at the end of 19X8 and an increase of inventories on hand at the end of 19X9. The figures labeled "Base Inventories" refer to the inventories stated in end-of-the-year 19X4 constant dollars, whereas the figures labeled "LIFO Inventories" indicate the amount of ending inventories that would be recorded each year if LIFO were used to cost ending inventories in place of FIFO. End-of-the-year 19X4 constant dollars are used as the base because MR Corporation began operations on December 31, 19X4. Therefore, that is the base period for all LIFO inventory layers. (Each enterprise must determine the earliest layer in its LIFO inventory; that then becomes the base period for its LIFO layers.)

Now that the LIFO layers have been determined for MR Corporation, the difference in the constant dollar adjustment between FIFO and LIFO can be illustrated. First the adjustment for cost of goods sold will be illustrated. These computations are made in Schedule 2.18. SFAS No. 33 provides a shortcut method when LIFO is used in the primary financial statements. If LIFO is used, the constant dollar cost of goods sold needs only to be adjusted for any depletion of the LIFO base. If inventories increase, historical cost of goods sold may be used to approximate the constant dollar cost of goods sold amount.

In 19X8, ending inventories declined from the beginning level. Therefore, an adjustment must be made for the depletion of the LIFO base. As illustrated in step 2 of Schedule 2.18, the historical cost of goods sold is adjusted upward by the amount that the LIFO layer(s) is depleted. In 19X8, ending inventories declined by $12,252 in 19X4 constant dollars. The decline in 19X4 constant dollars (base period) must be rolled forward to end-of-the year 19X8 constant dollars. The depletion in this example is assumed to be from the 19X7 layer. The CPI for November-December 19X7 is 185.8. The depletion of the 19X7 layer is rolled forward by multiplying the depleted amount by the ratio of the 19X8 year-end CPI to the 19X7 CPI (November–December average). This results in an adjustment to the 19X8 cost of goods sold of $13,379. For purposes of presenting the restated 19X8 cost of goods sold with the 19X9 restated cost of goods sold on a comparative basis, the 19X8 restated cost of goods sold is then rolled forward to end-of-the-year 19X9 constant dollars. If the enterprise opts for the minimum disclosures, 19X8 restated cost of goods sold is not required to be disclosed.

The 19X9 ending inventories increased. This means that the constant dollar cost of goods sold can be approximated by the historical cost of goods sold. Therefore, the 19X9 cost of goods sold figure would not have to be restated if MR Corporation were using LIFO to cost its ending inventories. All that would be required for presenting the 19X9 figures on a comparative basis with 19X0 would be to roll forward the 19X9 historical cost figure to end-of-the-year 19X0 constant dollars.

SCHEDULE 2.18

Cost of goods sold is restated on an historical cost/constant dollar basis when LIFO is used as follows:

For 19X8 Cost of Goods Sold—

Step 1. Determine decrease in ending inventories (see Schedule 2.17): Decrease in end-of-the-year 19X9 constant dollars $12,252

Step 2. Adjust historical cost of goods sold for depletion of LIFO base: Cost of Goods Sold (historical cost) + [Depleted Base × (19X8 CPI/base CPI)] = Cost of Goods Sold Restated to 19X8 Constant Dollars
$2,080,000 + [$12,252 × (202.9/185.8)] = $2,093,379

Step 3. Roll forward 19X8 restated cost of goods sold to end-of-the-year 19X9 constant dollars:
19X8 Restated Cost of Goods Sold × (19X9 year-end CPI/19X8 year-end CPI) = Cost of Goods Sold Restated to 19X9 Constant Dollars
$2,093,379 × (228.4/202.9) = $2,356,307

For 19X9 Cost of Goods Sold—

Step 4. Determine decrease in ending inventories (see Schedule 2.17): Ending inventories increased, therefore cost of goods sold on an historical cost/constant dollar basis may be approximated by using the cost of goods sold from the primary financial statements.

If the inventory turned over less frequently than six times per year, the only change in the adjustments would be the use of a different CPI. If, for example, the inventory turned over only twice per year, the appropriate index would be the average for the last six months of the year. Likewise, a turnover of four times per year would make the average for the last three months of the year the appropriate CPI.

If MR Corporation experienced turnover of two times per year, the adjustment to the 19X8 historical cost of goods sold would differ because the base period would be changed. The adjustment for 19X8 (step 2 of Schedule 2.18) would be

$$\$12,252 \times (202.9/184.3) = \$13,488$$

where 184.3 is the average CPI for the last six months of 19X7, since it is the 19X7 layer that was depleted. No adjustment would be needed for 19X9, however, since ending inventories increased in 19X9.

The use of LIFO for costing inventories becomes a more acute problem when comprehensive statements are prepared than if the minimum disclosures are used. If the minimum disclosures are all that an enterprise chooses to make, no adjustments to the ending inventories must be made. If, however, the enterprise chooses to make a comprehensive constant dollar disclosure, each layer of the ending LIFO inventories must be rolled forward. This is illustrated in Schedule 2.19 assuming an inventory turnover of six times. With an inventory turnover of six, the appropriate base CPI is the average for November-December for each layer.

SCHEDULE 2.19

Ending inventories are restated on an historical cost/constant dollar basis when LIFO is used as follows:

For 19X8 Ending Inventories—

Step 1. Determine the layers and CPI associated with each layer (see Schedule 2.17):

Year of Layer	Base Amount	CPI for Layer
19X4	$243,412	155.4
19X6	24,368	174.1
19X7	54,528	185.8

Step 2. Restate the ending inventories to end-of-the-year 19X8 constant dollars:

Base Amount × (19X8 year-end CPI/CPI for layer) = Inventory Layers Restated to 19X8 Constant Dollars

19X4	243,412 × (202.9/155.4) =	$317,799
19X6	24,368 × (202.9/174.1) =	28,398
19X7	54,528 × (202.9/185.8) =	59,545
		$405,742

Step 3. Roll forward 19X8 restated ending inventories to end-of-the-year 19X9 constant dollars:

19X8 Restated Ending Inventories × (19X9 year-end CPI/19X8 year-end CPI) = Ending Inventories Restated to 19X9 Constant Dollars

$405,742 × (228.4/202.9) = $456,735

For 19X9 Ending Inventories—

Step 4. Determine the layers and CPI associated with each layer (see Schedule 2.17):

SCHEDULE 2.19 (continued)

Year of Layer	Base Amount	CPI for Layer
19X4	$243,412	155.4
19X6	24,368	174.1
19X7	54,528	185.8
19X9	5,724	227.4

Step 5. Restate the ending inventories to end-of-the-year 19X9 constant dollars:

Base Amount × (19X9 year-end CPI/CPI for layer) = Inventory Layers Restated to 19X9 Constant Dollars

19X4	$243,412 × (228.4/155.4) =	$357,743
19X6	24,368 × (228.4/174.1) =	31,966
19X7	54,528 × (228.4/185.8) =	67,026
19X9	5,724 × (228.4/227.4) =	5,749
		$462,484

For the 19X8 ending inventories, three layers must be rolled forward to end-of-the-year 19X9 constant dollars. Once the layers have been identified (step 6, Schedule 2.17), each should be restated to end-of-the-year 19X8 constant dollars. The 19X8 ending inventories in end-of-the-year 19X8 constant dollars is $405,742 as compared to the historical cost LIFO amount of $344,290 (step 6, Schedule 2.17). The restated ending inventories are then rolled forward to end-of-the-year 19X9 constant dollars.

The 19X9 ending LIFO inventories consist of four layers. For comprehensive disclosures, each layer must be rolled forward to end-of-the-year 19X9 constant dollars. The process of restating each layer is demonstrated in step 5 of Schedule 2.19. However, recall that in 19X9 inventory quantities increased. When LIFO is used to cost the ending inventories, an increase in the inventory quantity means that a new layer is added to the beginning inventory amount. When inventories increase and LIFO is used, a short-cut is available. Rather than restating each layer individually, MR Corporation needs only to roll forward the beginning inventories and restate the new layer. This is simplified since the beginning inventories for 19X9 are identical to the ending inventories for 19X8. That amount is rolled forward in step 3 of Schedule 2.19 ($456,735). The new layer is restated as $5,749 (step 5, Schedule 2.19). Adding these two amounts together ($456,735 + $5,749) yields the 19X9 ending inventories restated in end-of-the-year 19X9 constant dollars ($462,484).

Once again, these figures can be easily adjusted if the inventory turnover differs. An inventory turnover of four would require using the average CPI for the last three months of each year in place of the November-December average. An inventory turnover of 12 would mean that the December CPI would be appropriate for each year.

In summary, the use of LIFO costing of inventories requires that the inventory layers be properly identified, as to both amount and time period. The time period is important in order to determine the proper CPI which should be used to restate each layer. In comprehensive statements, each layer must be rolled forward to the current year constant dollars. The cost of goods sold amount, however, will need adjustment only for the amount of the LIFO base which has been depleted.

Adjustments for Recoverable Amounts

SFAS No. 33 requires enterprises to disclose, as a component of the constant dollar income from continuing operations, the reductions of the historical cost amounts of inventory, property, plant, and equipment to lower recoverable amounts. The recoverable amount represents the net realizable value of the inventories and the value the enterprise derives from using its property, plant and equipment.

This is similar to making a lower of cost or market determination for ending inventories for the primary financial statements. Unfortunately, it is not quite as straightforward as the standard lower of cost or market determination. In the determination of lower of cost or market for the primary financial statements, the enterprise compares the historically costed ending inventories with the replacement cost of the inventories, choosing the lower amount. However, for the constant dollar disclosures, the enterprise must compare the *constant dollar* adjusted amounts of inventories and property, plant, and equipment with their recoverable amounts, and then choose the lower of those two amounts. This means that the recoverable amount might be required to be used even when the net realizable value of the inventories is increasing.

MR Corporation has ending FIFO inventories for 19X9 of $480,000. Assume that MR Corporation sells its inventories at 5% above cost. Using this assumption, as the cost of the inventories to MR Corporation increases so does its selling price and hence its net realizable value. Furthermore, under this assumption, the recoverable amount of MR Corporation's inventory will always exceed its cost. However, SFAS No. 33 requires reporting enterprises to compare the constant dollar amounts with the recoverable amounts.

MR Corporation's constant dollar ending inventories for 19X9 amount to $482,064 (see Schedule 2.11). The recoverable amount of its ending inventories would be $504,000 ($480,000 × 105%). As we can see, the recoverable amount exceeds the constant dollar amount. Therefore, no adjustment would be needed for the constant dollar amount.

However, if MR Corporation had an inventory turnover of one rather than six, the appropriate CPI would have been the 19X9 average-for-the-year (217.1) rather than the November-December average (227.4). In this case, the constant dollar ending inventories would be $504,960 ($480,000 × 228.4/217.1). The recoverable amount would still be $504,000. Now, the recoverable amount is *less* than the constant dollar amount and an adjustment would be required. The constant dollar income from continuing operations would now be reduced by $960 to reflect the lower recoverable amount and the inventory would be stated at $504,000 in the constant dollar balance sheet.

Under what circumstances is the recoverable amount likely to be less than the constant dollar amount? There are two factors that make this likely to occur. The first is that the enterprise has a low turnover rate. The second is that the recoverable amounts are increasing at a *lower rate* than the general price-level. The combination of these two factors can cause the recoverable amount to be less than the constant dollar amount. This can be seen in the second case above where the inventory turnover was only one and the general price-level was increasing by 5.2%.

As can be seen, the constant dollar adjustments can be further complicated when recoverable amounts are less than constant dollar amounts. In these circumstances, an additional loss must be charged against the constant dollar income from continuing operations, and when comprehensive disclosures are being made, the recoverable amounts must be used in the balance sheet.

Determining Fixed Asset Layers

Perhaps the most difficult problem in making the constant dollar adjustments for the first time is determining the layers of fixed assets the enterprise owns. Theoretically, each fixed asset should be associated with the CPI that existed on the date the asset was acquired. However, there may be problems in determining the appropriate CPI to use. It should be emphasized that this problem will be most prevalent the first time the enterprise makes the constant dollar disclosures. In subsequent periods, the enterprise can adjust the data compiled in the first period.

If the enterprise has not kept adequate records of acquisitions and disposals of fixed assets, it will be difficult to determine the proper CPI. In large enterprises—and the enterprises *required* to make these disclosures are large ones—it may be impractical or impossible to reconstruct the records by specifically identifying each asset and its acquisition date.

A similar problem can result when a pooling-of-interests combination is effected. In this situation the historical cost amounts and acquisition dates should be carried forward.

The best solution is to reconstruct the records so that they accurately reflect purchase dates. However, when this is impractical, a substitute method must be used. While the FASB has not sanctioned any method for the CPIs which should be used, one alternative would seem to result in reasonable results for purposes of the constant dollar disclosures.

The enterprise must first separate the fixed assets into identifiable categories, i.e., land, factory buildings, factory equipment, office equipment, etc. Then, a flow assumption must be adopted for each category. FIFO may be appropriate in many situations where the enterprise replaces its oldest assets first. Under this assumption, the enterprise will then identify its most recent purchases for purposes of layering its fixed assets.

Suppose, for example, the MR Corporation could not identify the acquisition dates of its equipment. Assume that MR Corporation had made the following acquisitions and disposals of equipment:

Acquisition (Disposal) Amount	Date	CPI
$100,000	January 19X9	204.7
120,000	November 19X8	202.0
(50,000)	September 19X8	199.3
300,000	April 19X8	191.5
75,000	February 19X7	177.1
(215,000)	December 19X5	166.3
200,000	December 19X4	155.4

MR Corporation has a total of $530,000 in gross equipment on December 31, 19X9. If MR Corporation assumed a FIFO flow of its equipment, then the ending 19X9 equipment would be assumed to consist of the most recent $530,000 of acquisitions. Under that assumption, the fixed asset layers at December 31, 19X9 would be:

Layer Amount	CPI
$100,000	204.7
120,000	202.0
300,000	191.5
10,000	177.1
$530,000	

This would give a constant dollar figure of $617,918 (see Schedule 2.20). This method will closely approximate the "true" constant dollar amounts if two requirements are met: (1) the flow assumption adopted approximates the enterprise's replacement pattern with regard to the asset category, and (2) the increase in the price of the assets is approximately equal to the general price-level increase.

SCHEDULE 2.20—Fixed Asset Layers Assuming FIFO

Layer Amount × (19X9 year-end CPI/base CPI) = Fixed Asset Layers Restated to 19X9 Constant Dollars

$$
\begin{aligned}
\$100,000 \times (228.4/204.7) &= \$111,570 \\
120,000 \times (228.4/202.0) &= 135,672 \\
300,000 \times (228.4/191.5) &= 357,780 \\
10,000 \times (228.4/177.1) &= 12,896 \\
&\ \ \overline{\$617,918}
\end{aligned}
$$

These approximations should not be used as a substitute if it is possible to determine the fixed asset layers; however, when it is impractical to do so, the enterprise can approximate the layers in this way. For this to be successful, the enterprise must carefully categorize the assets and carefully evaluate the flow pattern used in replacing the assets.

The Effect of Seasonality

SFAS No. 33 states that sales and operating expenses (exclusive of depreciation) need not be adjusted when the minimum disclosures are being made. Likewise, these items can be adjusted using the average-for-the-year as the base when the comprehensive disclosures are made and the end-of-the-year is used as the constant dollar. However, this is true only when there is no significant seasonality in the business patterns of the reporting enterprise. If significant seasonal patterns do exist, they must be reflected in the constant dollar adjustments.

Schedule 2.21 illustrates how seasonality would be reflected in the adjustment of sales to reflect 19X9 constant dollars. For purposes of Schedule 2.21, assume that MR Corporation has the following seasonal pattern, where 100 equals average sales with no seasonality.

Quarter	Seasonal Index
First	120
Second	110
Third	80
Fourth	90

As Schedule 2.21 shows, the average CPI for 19X8 now becomes 194.7 for 19X8 rather than 195.4 which was the case where no seasonality was present. This results in a larger constant dollar sales amount. This occurs because MR Corporation's seasonal pattern means it made more sales during the early part of the year. Thus, more sales were made with the stronger dollars of the first half of the year. MR Corporation would also have to reflect the seasonal pattern when adjusting the 19X9 sales on a constant dollar basis.

SCHEDULE 2.21

The effects of seasonality on historical cost/constant dollar adjustments:

For 19X8 Sales—

Step 1. Determine new base CPI:

a. Quarter	Average CPI	X	Seasonal Index	=	Weighted Index
First	188.5		120		226.2
Second	193.4		110		212.7
Third	197.9		80		158.3
Fourth	201.9		90		181.7
					778.9

b. Divide weighted index by four:
Weighted Index/Four = Base CPI
778.9/4 = 194.7

Step 2. Restate 19X8 sales to end-of-the-year 19X8 constant dollars:
Sales × (19X8 year-end CPI/base CPI) = Sales Restated to 19X8 Constant Dollars
$3,200,000 × (202.9/194.7) = $3,334,720

Step 3. Roll forward 19X8 sales to end-of-the-year 19X9 constant dollars:
Restated Sales × (19X9 year-end CPI/19X8 year-end CPI) = Sales Restated to 19X9 Constant Dollars
$3,334,720 × (228.4/202.9) = $3,753,561

Also, an enterprise should give consideration to the effect that seasonal fluctuations would have on its operating expenses. Some operating expenses will not be affected by seasonal fluctuations (e.g., rent of the office building). Other operating expenses will be affected by the seasonal nature of the business (e.g., wages paid to store clerks by department stores). In these situations, both the sales and the appropriate operating expenses should be adjusted to reflect the seasonal pattern of the business.

Summary

The FASB, through the disclosure requirements of SFAS No. 33, now stipulates that supplementary constant dollar information be presented in annual reports of certain enterprises. Enterprises affected are those with inventories and property, plant, and equipment amounting to more than $125 million or total assets aggregating to more than $1 billion.

This chapter has examined and illustrated the steps necessary to develop these required constant dollar disclosures. Alternative formats for implementing the disclosure requirements were presented so that enterprises may select from among the alternatives the one that is most appropriate to the reporting enterprise.

APPENDIX

ASSETS

	Monetary	Nonmonetary
Cash on hand and demand bank deposits (U.S. dollars)	X	
Time deposits (U.S. dollars)	X	
Foreign currency on hand and claims to foreign currency	X	
Securities:		
Common stocks (not accounted for on the equity method)		X
Common stocks represent residual interest in the underlying net assets and earnings of the issuer.		
Preferred stock (convertible or participating)		
Circumstances may indicate that such stock is either monetary or nonmonetary. See convertible bonds.	(see discussion)	
Preferred stock (nonconvertible, nonparticipating)		
Future cash receipts are likely to be substantially unaffected by changes in specific prices.	X	
Convertible bonds		
If the market values the security primarily as a bond, it is monetary; if it values the security primarily as a stock, it is nonmonetary.	(see discussion)	
Bonds (other than convertibles)	X	
Accounts and notes receivable	X	
Allowance for doubtful accounts and notes receivable	X	
Variable rate mortgage loans	X	
The terms of such loans do not link them directly to the rate of inflation. Also, there are practical reasons for classifying all loans as monetary.		

75

	Monetary	Nonmonetary
Inventories used on contracts		
They are, in substance, rights to receive sums of money if the future cash receipts on the contracts will not vary due to future changes in specific prices. (Goods used on contracts to be priced at market upon delivery are nonmonetary.)	(see discussion)	
Inventories (other than inventories used on contracts)		X
Loans to employees	X	
Prepaid insurance, advertising, rent, and other prepayments.		
Claims to future services are non-monetary. Prepayments that are deposits, advance payments or receivables are monetary because the prepayment does not obtain a given quantity of future services, but rather is a fixed money offset.	(see discussion)	
Long-term receivables	X	
Refundable deposits	X	
Advances to unconsolidated subsidiaries	X	
Equity investment in unconsolidated subsidiaries or other investees		X
Pension, sinking, and other funds under an enterprise's control		
The specific assets in the fund should be classified as monetary or non-monetary. (See listings under securities above.)	(see discussion)	
Property, plant, and equipment		X
Accumulated depreciation of property, plant and equipment		X
Cash surrender value of life insurance	X	
Purchase commitments—portion paid on fixed price contracts		X
An advance on a fixed price contract is the portion of the purchaser's claim to nonmonetary goods or services that is recognized in the accounts; it is not right to receive money.		

	Monetary	Nonmonetary
Advances to supplier—not on fixed price contract	X	
A right to receive credit for a sum of money; not a claim to a specified quantity of goods or services.		
Deferred income tax charges	X	
Offsets to prospective monetary liabilitites.		
Patents, trademarks, licenses and formulas		X
Goodwill		X
Deferred life insurance policy acquisition costs	X	
The portion of future cash receipts for premiums that is recognized in the accounts. Alternatively, viewed as an offset to the policy reserve.		
Deferred property and casualty insurance policy acquisition costs related to unearned premiums.		X
Other intangible assets and deferred charges		X

LIABILITIES

	Monetary	Nonmonetary
Accounts and notes payable	X	
Accrued expenses payable (wages, etc.)	X	
Accrued vacation pay		
Nonmonetary if it is paid at the wage rates as of the vacation dates and if those rates may vary.	(see discussion)	
Cash dividends payable	X	
Obligations payable in foreign currency	X	
Sales commitments—portion collected on fixed price contracts		X
An advance received on a fixed price contract is the portion of the seller's obligation to deliver goods or services that is recognized in the accounts; it is not an obligation to pay money.		

	Monetary	Nonmonetary
Advanced from customers—not on a fixed price contract	X	
Equivalent of a loan from the customer; not an obligation to furnish a specified quantity of goods or services.		
Accrued losses on firm purchase commitments	X	
In essence, these are accounts payable.		
Deferred revenue		
Nonmonetary if an obligation to furnish goods or services is involved. Certain "deferred income" items of savings and loan associations are monetary.	(see discussion)	
Refundable deposits	X	
Bonds payable and other long-term debt	X	
Unamortized premium or discount and prepaid interest on bonds or notes payable	X	
Inseparable from the debt to which it relates—a monetary item.		
Convertible bonds payable	X	
Until converted these are obligations to pay sums of money.		
Accrued pension obligations		
Fixed amounts payable to a fund are monetary; all other amounts are nonmonetary.	(see discussion)	
Obligations under warranties		X
These are nonmonetary because they oblige the enterprise to furnish goods or services or their future price.		
Deferred income tax credits	X	
Cash requirements will not vary materially due to changes in specific prices.		
Deferred investment tax credits		X
Not to be settled by payment of cash; associated with nonmonetary assets.		

	Monetary	Nonmonetary
Life insurance policy reserves	X	
Portions of policies face values that are now deemed liabilities		
Property and casualty insurance loss reserves	X	
Unearned property and casualty insurance premiums		X
These are nonmonetary because they are principally obligations to furnish insurance coverage. The dollar amount of payments to be made under that coverage might vary materially due to changes in specific prices.		
Deposit liabilities of financial institutions	X	

CHAPTER 3

Implementing Current Cost Accounting for External Reporting

■□■□■□■□■□■□■

With the issuance of Statement of Financial Accounting Standards (SFAS) No. 33, "Financial Reporting and Changing Prices," the Financial Accounting Standards Board (FASB) presented the business community in general and the accounting profession in particular with the unenviable task of cultivating disclosures of current cost information for published financial reports. While the Securities and Exchange Commission (SEC) previously had required certain replacement cost disclosures to be made by its registrants, no accounting standard-setting body in the private sector ever has *required* current cost disclosures in general-purpose financial reports until the FASB issued SFAS No. 33. Chapter 2 presented the historical cost/constant dollar disclosure requirements of SFAS No. 33, and this chapter will discuss and exemplify the current cost disclosure requirements of the standard.

Enterprises Required to Disclose Current Cost Information

The historical cost/constant dollar disclosures, discussed in the previous chapter, must be made by certain large, publicly traded enterprises in their annual financial statements for fiscal periods ending on or after December 25, 1979. But, while the FASB encourages disclosure of current cost information in these financial statements, enterprises were given a year of adaptation for the current cost disclosures since the reporting mechanics are so radically different from those of the traditional historical cost model. As a result, the current cost disclosures required in SFAS No. 33 need not be made until annual reports are issued for fiscal years ending on or after December 25, 1980.

The SEC recently deleted its replacement cost disclosure requirements for enterprises who elect to implement the SFAS No. 33 current cost disclosures immediately. Thus, many enterprises have elected to implement currently the SFAS No. 33 disclosures since, even if an enterprise utilizes the "grandfather provision" in SFAS No. 33, when these disclosures are made for fiscal years ending on or after December 25, 1980, they must be made retroactive for fiscal years ending on or after December 25, 1979. Since this provision, in essence, must be applied for current annual reports, many enterprises are deciding to make the disclosures on a timely basis.

The enterprises subject to these current cost disclosures are the same ones subject to the historical cost/constant dollar disclosures discussed in Chapter 2. To reiterate briefly, enterprises required to make these current cost disclosures are public enterprises that prepare their primary annual financial statements (SFAS No. 33 does not apply to interim reports) in U.S. dollars and in accordance with U.S. generally accepted accounting principles (GAAP) and that have, at the beginning of the fiscal year to which the financial statements relate, either:

1. inventories and property, plant, and equipment (before deducting accumulated depreciation, depletion, and amortization) amounting in the aggregate to more than $125 million, or
2. total assets amounting to more than $1 billion (after deducting accumulated depreciation).

Required Supplementary Disclosures on a Current Cost Basis

Disclosure Requirements

Enterprises subject to making the current cost disclosures under SFAS No. 33 are required to disclose, at a minimum,

1. information on income from continuing operations for the current fiscal year on a current cost basis;
2. the current cost amounts of inventory and property, plant, and equipment at the end of the current fiscal year; and

3. increases or decreases for the current fiscal year in the current cost amounts of inventory and property, plant, and equipment, net of inflation. These increases or decreases in current cost amounts should not be included in income from continuing operations.

Since the historical cost/constant dollar disclosures discussed in the previous chapter are based on the principles of historical costing with changes being made in the *measuring unit* from the historical dollar to a general purchasing power dollar and these current cost disclosures change the *attributes being measured* from historical costs to current costs, rarely will these separately determined measures be identical. However, in certain circumstances, there may be no material difference between the amount of income from continuing operations determined on an historical cost/constant dollar basis and a current cost basis. In these cases, the current cost disclosures enumerated above need not be made for the current fiscal year but the reporting enterprise should state, in a note to the supplementary disclosures, the reason for omitting the current cost information.

The required current cost disclosures may be presented in either a statement format (see Figure 3.5) or a reconciliation format (see Figure 3.6). Regardless of the format selected, disclosures should include material amounts of or adjustments to cost of goods sold, depreciation, depletion, and amortization expense.

In these disclosures, inventories should be measured at current cost or lower recoverable amount at the measurement date. Current cost of inventories owned by an enterprise is the current cost to purchase the goods or the current cost of resources required to produce the goods, whichever is appropriate to the reporting enterprise. In determining cost to produce inventories, an allowance for current overhead costs according to allocation bases used under GAAP should be included. The recoverable amount of inventories means the current worth of the net amount of cash expected to be recoverable from use or sale of the assets. Recoverable amounts should be measured in one of the following ways:

1. Net realizable value, which is the amount of cash (or its equivalent) expected to be derived from the sale of an asset net of costs required to be incurred as a result of the sale. Net realizable values should be considered as a measurement alternative only when the asset being valued is about to be sold.
2. Value in use, which is the net present value of future cash flows (including ultimate proceeds of disposal) expected to be derived from the use of an asset by the enterprise. Value in use should be

considered as a measurement alternative only when immediate sale of the asset being valued is not intended. Value in use should be estimated by discounting expected cash flows at an appropriate discount rate that allows for risk of activities concerned.

Recoverable amounts of inventories need not be ascertained by considering individual items unless those items are used independently of other assets.

Property, plant, and equipment (excluding income-producing real estate properties and unprocessed natural resources) should be measured at current cost or lower recoverable amount (determined the same as with inventories) of the assets' remaining service potential at the measurement date. SFAS No. 33 does not contain provisions for the current cost measurement of income-producing real estate properties, unprocessed natural resources, and related depreciation, depletion, and amortization expense. Note should be taken that historical cost/constant dollar disclosures for these properties are not exempted; rather, only the current cost disclosures are delayed until the FASB concludes further studies to provide a basis for decisions concerning applicability of the current cost information to these special assets and expenses. (See Chapter 10.) If an enterprise presents the current cost disclosures of SFAS No. 33 in annual reports for a fiscal year ended before December 25, 1980, these special assets and expenses may be measured at their historical cost/constant dollar amounts or by reference to an appropriate index of specific price changes.

The current cost of property, plant, and equipment owned by an enterprise is the current cost of acquiring the same service potential (indicated by operating costs and physical output capacity) as embodied by the asset currently owned. Sources of information used in determining current cost of property, plant, and equipment should reflect a method of acquisition currently considered appropriate for the reporting enterprise. There are three ways to measure the current cost of a used asset:

1. Measuring the current cost of a new asset that has the same service potential as the used asset had when it was new and deducting a depreciation allowance.
2. Measuring the current cost of a used asset of the same age and in the same condition as the currently owned asset.
3. Measuring the current cost of a new asset with a different service potential and adjusting that cost for the value of differences in service potential due to increases in life, output, capacity, nature of service, and operating costs.

In measuring the current cost of inventory and property, plant, and equipment, if current cost is measured in terms of a foreign currency, that foreign currency amount should be translated into U.S. dollars at the current exchange rate. This rate is the exchange rate at the date of use, sale, or commitment to a specific contract (for depreciation and cost of goods sold) or the rate at the balance sheet date (for inventory and property, plant, and equipment).

In determining the current cost, enterprises are expected to utilize the types of information appropriate to their particular circumstances. Examples of information that may be used include the following:

1. Indexation
   (a) Externally generated price indices for the class of goods or services being measured, or
   (b) Internally generated price indices for the class of goods or services being measured.
2. Direct Pricing
   (a) Current invoice prices,
   (b) Vendors' price lists or other quotations or estimates, or
   (c) Standard manufacturing costs that reflect current costs.

It should be noted that cost of goods sold measured on a last in, first out (LIFO) basis may provide an acceptable approximation of current cost of goods sold, provided that the effect of any decreases in inventory layers is excluded. Further, there is a presumption that the same methods and estimates used for historical cost/constant dollar and historical cost determination of depreciation expense are utilized in the calculation of current cost depreciation. However, different methods and estimates may be used in current cost and historical cost/constant dollar calculations if the methods and estimates used in the historical cost financial statements have been selected partly to allow for expected price changes.

Enterprises that present the *minimum* disclosures required by SFAS No. 33 relating to current cost income from continuing operations should measure cost of goods sold at current cost or lower recoverable amount (as discussed above) at the date of sale or at the date on which resources are used or committed to a specific contract. Depreciation and amortization expense should be measured on the basis of average current cost or lower recoverable amount (as discussed above) of the assets' service potential during the period of use. Other revenues, expenses, gains, and losses may be measured at the amounts included in the primary financial statements. Enterprises electing to present *comprehensive* current cost/constant dollar disclosures may measure the components of such statements either in terms of average-for-the-year or end-of-the-year constant dollars, as discussed in the preceding chapter.

The income tax provision in computations of current cost income from continuing operations should be the same as the provision used in the primary financial statements. No adjustments to the tax provision should be made for any timing differences that may be assumed to arise between amounts determined at current cost and historical cost measurements. Further, the income tax provision should *not* be allocated between income from continuing operations and increases or decreases in the current cost of inventory and property, plant, and equipment.

The increases or decreases in the current cost of inventory and property, plant, and equipment represent the differences between asset measures at the beginning of the year or dates of acquisition (whichever is applicable) and asset measures at the end of the year or the dates of use, sale, or commitment to a specific contract (whichever is applicable). These increases should be disclosed both before and after eliminating the effects of general inflation. When comprehensive current cost/constant dollar financial statements are prepared, enterprises may measure these increases or decreases in average-for-the-year or end-of-the-year constant dollars.

Illustration of Current Cost/Constant Dollar Financial Statements Prepared on a Comprehensive Basis

The following illustrations are based on the same primary financial statement information for MR Corporation that was used in determining the historical cost/constant dollar disclosures in the previous chapter. For ease of reference, these comparative historical cost statements are presented again in Figures 3.1 and 3.2. The same underlying assumptions exist for these statements as existed in Chapter 2. Checklist 3.1 should be used as an overview of the restatement process from historical cost to current cost.

FIGURE 3.1
MR Corporation
Comparative Balance Sheets
December 31, 19X4—19X9

	December 31					
	19X4	19X5	19X6	19X7	19X8	19X9
ASSETS						
Cash	$ 100,000	$ 176,250	$ 282,500	$ 398,750	$ 410,250	$ 514,250
Receivables (net)	300,000	528,750	847,500	1,196,250	1,230,750	1,542,750
Inventories (FIFO)	300,000	260,000	300,000	400,000	420,000	480,000
Land	80,000	80,000	80,000	80,000	80,000	80,000
Buildings	500,000	500,000	500,000	500,000	500,000	500,000
Accumulated Depreciation—Buildings	-0-	(12,500)	(25,000)	(37,500)	(50,000)	(62,500)
Equipment	420,000	420,000	420,000	420,000	530,000	530,000
Accumulated Depreciation—Equipment	-0-	(52,500)	(105,000)	(157,500)	(221,000)	(284,500)
Total Assets	$ 1,700,000	$ 1,900,000	$ 2,300,000	$ 2,800,000	$ 2,900,000	$ 3,300,000
LIABILITIES AND STOCKHOLDER'S EQUITY						
Current Liabilities	$ 160,000	$ 154,943	$ 192,234	$ 242,891	$ 215,793	$ 227,532
Long-term Liabilities	700,000	774,715	961,167	1,214,456	1,078,963	1,137,657
Deferred Taxes	-0-	14,292	24,499	30,623	35,814	36,221
Capital Stock ($10 par value)	280,000	280,000	280,000	280,000	280,000	280,000
Additional Paid-In Capital	560,000	560,000	560,000	560,000	560,000	560,000
Retained Earnings	-0-	116,050	282,100	472,030	729,430	1,058,590
Total Liabilities and Stockholder's Equity	$ 1,700,000	$ 1,900,000	$ 2,300,000	$ 2,800,000	$ 2,900,000	$ 3,300,000

FIGURE 3.2
MR Corporation
Comparative Statements of Income and Retained Earnings
For the Years Ended December 31, 19X5–19X9
For the Year Ended December 31

	19X5	19X6	19X7	19X8	19X9
Sales (net)	$1,600,000	$2,000,000	$2,400,000	$3,200,000	$4,000,000
Cost of Goods Sold:					
Beginning Inventories	$ 300,000	$ 260,000	$ 300,000	$ 400,000	$ 420,000
Purchases (net)	1,000,000	1,340,000	1,660,000	2,100,000	2,660,000
Goods Available for Sale	$1,300,000	$1,600,000	$1,960,000	$2,500,000	$3,080,000
Ending Inventories	260,000	300,000	400,000	420,000	480,000
Cost of Goods Sold	$1,040,000	$1,300,000	$1,560,000	$2,080,000	$2,600,000
Gross Profit	$ 560,000	$ 700,000	$ 840,000	$1,120,000	$1,400,000
Operating Expenses (Excluding Depreciation)	$ 192,000	$ 240,000	$ 288,000	$ 384,000	$ 480,000
Depreciation Expense	65,000	65,000	65,000	76,000	76,000
Total Operating Expense	$ 257,000	$ 305,000	$ 353,000	$ 460,000	$ 556,000
Income before Income Taxes	$ 303,000	$ 395,000	$ 487,000	$ 660,000	$ 844,000
Provision for Income Taxes	106,050	138,250	170,450	231,000	295,400
Net Income	$ 196,950	$ 256,750	$ 316,550	$ 429,000	$ 548,600
Beginning Retained Earnings	-0-	116,050	282,100	472,030	729,430
	$ 196,950	$ 372,800	$ 598,650	$ 901,030	$1,278,030
Less: Dividends	80,900	90,700	126,620	171,600	219,440
Ending Retained Earnings	$ 116,050	$ 282,100	$ 472,030	$ 729,430	$1,058,590

CHECKLIST 3.1

Computational Guidance for Comprehensive Current Cost Disclosures
(Paragraph numbers refer to SFAS No. 33.)

1. Determine Current Cost of Inventories.
   a. Determine current cost of purchasing inventories or current cost of resources required to produce inventories, whichever is applicable. (par. 57)
   b. Determine recoverable amounts of inventories, i.e., the current net amount of cash expected to be recoverable from the sale of the inventories. (par. 62–63)
   c. Inventories should be measured at the lower of their current cost (a) or their recoverable amounts (b). (par. 62)
2. Determine Current Cost of Property, Plant, and Equipment.
   a. Determine current cost of acquiring property, plant, and equipment with the same service potential as embodied by the asset currently owned. (par. 58)
   b. Determine recoverable amounts of property, plant, and equipment, i.e., the current net amount of cash expected to be recoverable from the use or sale, whichever is appropriate, of the property, plant, and equipment. (par. 62–63)
   c. Property, plant, and equipment should be measured at the lower of their current cost (a) or their recoverable amounts (b). (par. 62)
3. Determine Purchasing Power Gain or Loss.
   a. Segregate financial statement elements into monetary and nonmonetary categories. (par. 23,50)
   b. Restate beginning net monetary items to average-for-the-year constant dollars or end-of-the-year constant dollars as appropriate. (par. 50,232)
   c. Restate increases and decreases in net monetary items to average-for-the-year constant dollars or end-of-the-year constant dollars as appropriate. (par. 50,232)
   d. Restate ending net monetary items to average-for-the-year constant dollars or end-of-the-year constant dollars as appropriate. (When end-of-the-year constant dollars are used, the restatement conversion factor is 1.00 since ending net monetary items are stated in terms of end-of-the-year purchasing power.) (par. 50,232)
   e. Purchasing power gain (loss) equals beginning net monetary items restated (b) plus increases in net monetary items restated minus decreases in net monetary items restated (c) minus ending net monetary items (d). (par. 50,232)
4. Determine Holding Gain or Loss for Inventories and Property, Plant and Equipment.

CHECKLIST 3.1 (continued)

    a. Gross holding gain or loss equals current cost of inventories and property, plant, and equipment at year-end plus (minus) increases (decreases) in current cost amounts during the period minus current cost of inventories and property, plant, and equipment at beginning of year. (par. 56)

    b. Restate beginning, ending and changes in current cost to average-for-the-year or end-of-the-year constant dollars as appropriate. (par. 233)

    c. Net holding gain or loss equals restated current cost of inventories and property, plant, and equipment at year-end plus (minus) increases (decreases) in restated current cost minus restated current cost of inventories and property, plant, and equipment at beginning of year. (par. 56)

    d. Inflation component of gross holding gain or loss equals gross holding gain or loss (a) minus net holding gain or loss (c). (par. 234)

5. Steps to Prepare Current Cost/Constant Dollar Income Statement. When using end-of-the-year constant dollars—

    a. Restate operating revenues to end-of-the-year constant dollars. (par. 210)

    b. Restate operating expenses (exclusive of cost of goods sold and depreciation) to end-of-the-year constant dollars. (par. 210)

    c. Restate cost of goods sold and depreciation to current cost in end-of-the-year constant dollars. (When LIFO method of inventory costing is used, cost of goods sold may be approximated by historical cost of goods sold adjusted to end-of-the-year constant dollars unless a LIFO layer has been depleted. In this case, costs associated with a depleted LIFO layer should be restated.) (par. 52)

    d. Restate the provision for income taxes to end-of-the-year constant dollars. (par. 210)

    e. Income from continuing operations equals operating revenues (a) minus operating expenses (b,c) minus provision for income taxes (d). (par. 52)

    f. Add (deduct) purchasing power gain (loss) (3,e). (par. 29)

    g. Add (deduct) net holding gain (loss) (4,c). (par. 55–56)

6. Steps to Prepare Current Cost/Constant Dollar Income Statement. When using average-for-the-year constant dollars—

    a. Operating revenues may be historical cost operating revenues (consideration should be given to seasonal fluctuations in the generation of revenues). (par. 210)

    b. Operating expenses (exclusive of cost of goods sold and depreciation) may be historical cost operating expenses (considerations should be given to seasonal fluctuations in the incurrence of expenses). (par. 210)

CHECKLIST 3.1 (continued)

    c. Restate cost of goods sold and depreciation to current cost. (When LIFO method of inventory costing is used, cost of goods sold may be approximated by historical cost of goods sold unless a LIFO layer has been depleted. In this case, costs associated with a depleted LIFO layer should be restated.) (par. 52)

    d. The provision for income taxes should be the historical cost provision for income taxes, all of which is included in the determination of income from continuing operations. (par. 54)

    e. Income from continuing operations equals operating revenues (a) minus operating expenses (b,c) minus provision for income taxes (d). (par. 52)

    f. Add (deduct) purchasing power gain (loss) (3,e). (par. 29)

    g. Add (deduct) net holding gain (loss) (4,c). (par. 55–56)

7. Steps to Prepare Current Cost/Constant Dollar Balance Sheet. When using end-of-the-year constant dollars—

    a. Monetary items are historical cost monetary items since they are stated in end-of-the-year constant dollars.

    b. Restate nonmonetary items to current cost amounts in end-of-the-year constant dollars.

8. Steps to Prepare Current Cost/Constant Dollar Balance Sheet. When using average-for-the-year constant dollars—

    a. Roll back monetary items to average-for-the-year constant dollars.

    b. Restate nonmonetary items to current cost amounts in average-for-the-year constant dollars.

9. Step to Prepare Comparative Current Cost/Constant Dollar Statements. Roll forward all financial statement elements from previous current cost/constant dollar statements to average-for-the-current-year or end-of-the-current-year constant dollars as appropriate.

Figures 3.3 and 3.4 and related schedules represent the restatement process applicable to converting the financial statement elements from their historical cost measurements to current cost/constant dollar amounts (hereafter, current cost). In this example, end-of-the-year constant dollars are utilized since average-for-the-year constant dollars are used in developing the minimum required disclosures in the next section of this chapter. It should be noted, however, that enterprises electing to make comprehensive disclosures under SFAS No. 33 may choose either end-of-the-year or average-for-the-year constant dollars in formulating the disclosures. The Consumer Price Indices (CPI) used in developing these current cost statements are shown in Schedule 3.1.

FIGURE 3.3
MR Corporation
Comparative Balance Sheets on a Current Cost/Constant Dollar Basis
December 31, 19X8 and 19X9

	19X8	19X9
ASSETS		
Cash (see Schedule 3.13)	$ 461,818	$ 514,250
Receivables (net) (see Schedule 3.13)	1,385,455	1,542,750
Inventories (FIFO) (see Schedule 3.14)	480,664	485,000
Land (see Schedule 3.15)	130,967	126,243
Building (see Schedule 3.15)	845,791	794,390
Accumulated Depreciation—Building (see Schedule 3.15)	(84,579)	(99,299)
Equipment (see Schedule 3.15)	798,318	756,949
Accumulated Depreciation—Equipment (see Schedule 3.15)	(345,731)	(419,268)
Total Assets	$3,672,703	$3,701,015
LIABILITIES AND STOCKHOLDERS' EQUITIES		
Current Liabilities (see Schedule 3.13)	$ 242,918	$ 227,532
Long-term Liabilities (see Schedule 3.13)	1,214,589	1,137,657
Deferred Taxes (see Schedule 3.13)	40,316	36,221
Capital Stock ($10 par value) (see Schedule 3.16)	411,551	411,551
Additional Paid-In Capital (see Schedule 3.16)	823,102	823,102
Retained Earnings (see Schedule 3.16)	940,227	1,064,952
Total Liabilities and Stockholders' Equities	$3,672,703	$3,701,015

FIGURE 3.4
MR Corporation
Comparative Statements of Income and Retained Earnings
Restated on a Current Cost/Constant Dollar Basis
For the Years Ended December 31, 19X8 and 19X9

	For the Year Ended December 31	
	19X8	19X9
Sales (net) (see Schedule 3.2)	$ 3,740,566	$ 4,208,400
Current Cost of Goods Sold (see Schedule 3.3)	2,471,851	2,795,066
Gross Profit	$ 1,268,715	$ 1,413,334
Operating Expenses (Excluding Depreciation) (see Schedule 3.4)	$ 448,868	$ 505,008
Depreciation Expense (see Schedule 3.6)	117,595	111,313
Total Operating Expenses	$ 566,463	$ 616,321
Income before Income Taxes	$ 702,252	$ 797,013
Provision for Income Taxes (see Schedule 3.7)	270,022	310,790
Income from Continuing Operations	$ 432,230	$ 486,223
Purchasing Power Loss (see Schedule 3.10)	$ (21,456)	$ (68,437)
Increase in Current Cost of Inventories (see Schedule 3.8):		
Gross Increase	$ 132,693	$ 193,066
Less: Effect of Inflation	(131,886)	$ (192,116)
Excess of Increase in Specific Prices over General Price Level	$ 807	$ 950
Increase in Current Cost of Property, Plant and Equipment (see Schedule 3.9):		
Gross Increase	$ 165,458	$ 75,567
Less: Effect of Inflation	(116,279)	(150,138)
Excess of Increase in Specific Prices over General Price Level	$ 49,179	$ (74,571)
Net Income	$ 460,760	$ 344,165
Beginning Retained Earnings (see Schedule 3.11)	672,637	940,227
	$ 1,133,397	$ 1,284,392
Less Dividends (see Schedule 3.12)	(193,170)	(219,440)
Ending Retained Earnings (see Schedule 3.11)	$ 940,227	$ 1,064,952

SCHEDULE 3.1

The Consumer Price Index for all urban consumers is presented below.

Year	Jan.	Feb.	Mar.	Apr.	May	June	July	Aug.	Sept.	Oct.	Nov.	Dec.	Avg.
19X4	139.7	141.5	143.1	143.9	145.5	146.9	148.0	149.9	151.7	153.0	154.3	155.4	147.7
19X5	156.1	157.2	157.8	158.6	159.3	160.6	162.3	162.8	163.6	164.6	165.6	166.3	161.2
19X6	166.7	167.1	167.5	168.2	169.2	170.1	171.1	171.9	172.6	173.3	173.8	174.3	170.5
19X7	175.3	177.1	178.2	179.6	180.6	181.8	182.6	183.3	184.0	184.5	185.4	186.1	181.5
19X8	187.2	188.4	189.8	191.5	193.3	195.3	196.7	197.8	199.3	200.9	202.0	202.9	195.4
19X9	204.7	207.1	209.1	211.5	214.1	216.6	218.9	221.1	223.4	224.1	226.3	228.4	217.1

Schedule 3.2 presents the restatement of sales from the historical cost statements to the current cost statements. It will be apparent at the outset that much of the restatement process to current cost will be the same as the restatement to historical cost/constant dollars in the previous chapter. This commonality exists from the FASB's conscious effort in SFAS No. 33 to make the disclosure requirements meaningful yet as simplistic as possible. Thus, in restating sales for the current cost disclosure, the identical steps used in Chapter 2 once again will be utilized. The 19X8 sales first are restated to the end of 19X8; then are rolled forward to the end of 19X9 for inclusion in the comparative statements.

Since this example includes an inherent assumption that sales are being generated evenly throughout the year, any seasonality problems are ignored. However, for an approach to handling any sales seasonality, refer back to Chapter 2. Based on this evenly generated sales assumption, the 19X9 sales restatement is based on the relationship of the end-of-the-year and average-for-the-year 19X9 CPI.

Schedule 3.3 is an analysis of the cost of goods sold restatement when inventories are accounted for on a first in, first out (FIFO) basis. As mentioned earlier in this chapter, when cost of goods sold is measured on a LIFO basis, the historical cost measurement may serve as an acceptable approximation of current cost of goods sold. Therefore, the more complicated FIFO assumption is utilized in this example. The current cost of goods sold determined in Schedule 3.3 utilizes the assumption that suppliers' price lists were used to determine ending inventories for each year on a current cost basis as follows: 19X4 = $300,000, 19X5 = $265,000, 19X6 = $310,000, 19X7 = $405,000, 19X8 = $427,000 and 19X9 = $485,000.

SCHEDULE 3.2

Sales are restated on a current cost/constant dollar basis when comprehensive disclosures are made as follows:

For 19X8 Sales—

Step 1. Restate 19X8 sales to end-of-the-year 19X8 constant dollars:
Sales (historical cost) × (19X8 year-end CPI/19X8 average CPI) = Sales Restated to 19X8 Constant Dollars
$3,200,000 × (202.9/195.4) = $3,322,880

Step 2. Roll forward sales as restated for 19X8 to end-of-the-year 19X9 constant dollars:
Restated 19X8 Sales × (19X9 year-end CPI/19X8 year-end CPI) = Sales Restated to 19X9 Constant Dollars
$3,322,880 × (228.4/202.9) = $3,740,566

For 19X9 Sales—

Step 3. Restate 19X9 sales to end-of-the-year 19X9 constant dollars:
Sales (historical cost) × (19X9 year-end CPI/19X9 average CPI) = Sales Restated to 19X9 Constant Dollars
$4,000,000 × (228.4/217.1) = $4,208,400

SCHEDULE 3.3

Cost of goods sold is restated on a current cost/constant dollar basis when comprehensive disclosures are made as follows:

For 19X8 Cost of Goods Sold—

Step 1. Restate 19X8 current cost/nominal dollar beginning inventories to end-of-the-year 19X8 constant dollars:
Beginning Inventories (current cost/nominal dollars) × (19X8 year-end CPI/Nov.–Dec. 19X7 CPI) = Beginning Inventories Restated to 19X8 Constant Dollars
$405,000 × (202.9/185.8) = $442,274

Step 2. Restate 19X8 purchases to end-of-the-year 19X8 constant dollars:
Purchases (historical cost) × (19X8 year-end CPI/19X8 average CPI) = Purchases Restated to 19X8 Constant Dollars
$2,100,000 × (202.9/195.4) = $2,180,604

SCHEDULE 3.3 (continued)

Step 3. Determine 19X8 current cost ending inventories (see narrative accompanying this schedule):
Current Cost Ending Inventories $427,000

Step 4. Compute 19X8 cost of goods sold restated to end-of-the-year 19X8 constant dollars:
Restated Beginning Inventories + Restated Purchases − Restated Ending Inventories = Current Cost of Goods Sold Restated to 19X8 Constant Dollars
$442,274 + $2,180,604 − $427,000 = $2,195,878

Step 5. Roll forward current cost of goods sold as restated for 19X8 to end-of-the-year 19X9 constant dollars:
Restated 19X8 Current Cost of Goods Sold × (19X9 year-end CPI/19X8 year-end CPI) = Current Cost of Goods Sold Restated to 19X9 Constant Dollars
$2,195,878 × (228.4/202.9) = $2,471,851

For 19X9 Cost of Goods Sold—

Step 6. Restate 19X9 current cost/nominal dollar beginning inventories to end-of-the-year 19X9 constant dollars:
Beginning Inventories (current cost/nominal dollars) × (19X9 year-end CPI/Nov.–Dec. 19X8 CPI) = Beginning Inventories Restated to 19X9 Constant Dollars
$427,000 × (228.4/202.5) = $481,614

Step 7. Restate 19X9 purchases to end-of-the-year 19X9 constant dollars:
Purchases (historical cost) × (19X9 year-end CPI/19X9 average CPI) = Purchases Restated to 19X9 Constant Dollars
$2,660,000 × (228.4/217.1) = $2,798,452

Step 8. Determine 19X9 current cost ending inventories (see narrative accompanying this schedule):
Current Cost Ending Inventories $485,000

Step 9. Compute 19X9 current cost of goods sold restated to end-of-the-year 19X9 constant dollars:
Restated Beginning Inventories + Restated Purchases − Restated Ending Inventories = Current Cost of Goods Sold Restated to 19X9 Constant Dollars
$481,614 + $2,798,452 − $485,000 = $2,795,066

The cost of goods sold restatement is a very complicated process, involving determinations of both changes in the general price level (the constant dollar adjustment) and increases or decreases in the current cost of inventories. Except for the fact that inventory restatements and roll-forwards involve these two components instead of the single constant dollar element, as illustrated in Chapter 2, the current cost of goods sold determination essentially is the same as the historical cost/constant dollar adjustments. Inventories are assumed to turn over about six times per year so that purchases are restated using the average CPI for the period and ending inventories are restated using an average index of the last two months of the period.

Schedule 3.4 represents the restatement of operating expenses (exclusive of depreciation) which are assumed to have been incurred evenly throughout the year in proportion to sales. SFAS No. 33 prescribes no unique current cost restatement procedures for such expenses and, therefore, this restatement is the same as the one used in the preparation of the historical cost/constant dollar statements, i.e., the 19X8 and 19X9 operating expenses are rolled forward and restated in terms of end-of-the-year 19X9 constant dollars.

Schedule 3.5 presents a tabular summation of CPIs specifically associated with machinery and equipment, buildings, and land (property, plant, and equipment per SFAS No. 33). These indices are utilized in Schedule 3.6 in ascertaining the current cost depreciation expense of property, plant, and equipment. This process involves layering fixed assets at acquisition dates and determining historical cost depreciation as utilized in the primary financial statements. Then, specific indices related to the property, plant, and equipment items must be ascertained as reflected in Schedule 3.5 (these indices were derived from the Producer Price Indices by Major Commodity Groups). The restatement process in Schedule 3.6, using these specific indices to determine depreciation expense each year, then essentially is no different from the constant dollar restatement and roll-forward techniques except that specific as opposed to general indices are utilized.

SCHEDULE 3.4

Operating expenses (exclusive of depreciation) are restated on a current cost/constant dollar basis when comprehensive disclosures are made as follows:

For 19X8 Operating Expenses—

Step 1. Restate 19X8 operating expenses to end-of-the-year 19X8 constant dollars:
Operating Expenses (historical cost) × (19X8 year-end CPI/19X8 average CPI) = Operating Expenses Restated to 19X8 Constant Dollars
$384,000 × (202.9/195.4) = $398,746

Step 2. Roll forward operating expenses as restated for 19X8 to end-of-the-year 19X9 constant dollars:
Restated 19X8 Operating Expenses × (19X9 year-end CPI/19X8 year-end CPI) = Operating Expenses Restated to 19X9 Constant Dollars
$398,746 × (228.4/202.9) = $448,868

For 19X9 Operating Expenses—

Step 3. Restate 19X9 operating expenses to end-of-the-year 19X9 constant dollars:
Operating Expenses (historical cost) × (19X9 year-end CPI/19X9 average CPI) = Operating Expenses Restated to 19X9 Constant Dollars
$480,000 × (228.4/217.1) = $505,008

SCHEDULE 3.5

The Consumer Price Indices for machinery and equipment, buildings, and land are presented below.

Date	Machinery and Equipment	Buildings	Land
Dec. 31, 19X4–Jan. 1, 19X5	139.4	183.6	153.2
Dec. 31, 19X5–Jan. 1, 19X6	161.4	176.9	174.0
Dec. 31, 19X6–Jan. 1, 19X7	171.0	205.6	186.3
Dec. 31, 19X7–Jan. 1, 19X8	181.7	236.3	200.5
Dec. 31, 19X8–Jan. 1, 19X9	196.0	275.9	222.8
Dec. 31, 19X9–Jan. 1, 19X0	209.2	291.7	241.5

SCHEDULE 3.6

Depreciation expense is restated on a current cost/constant dollar basis when comprehensive disclosures are made as follows:

For 19X8 Depreciation Expense—

Step 1. Determine fixed asset layers:

	Asset	Historical Cost	Acquisition Date	Depreciation Method
a.	Building	$500,000	December 31, 19X4	Straight-line (40 years)
b.	Equipment	420,000	December 31, 19X4	Straight-line (8 years)
c.	Equipment	110,000	January 1, 19X8	Straight-line (10 years)

Step 2. Determine historical cost depreciation expense:

	Asset	Depreciation Expense
a.	Building	$12,500
b.	Equipment	52,500
c.	Equipment	11,000

Step 3. Determine Index associated with acquisition dates:

	Asset	Base Index
a.	Building	183.6
b.	Equipment	139.4
c.	Equipment	181.7

Step 4. Determine 19X8 current cost depreciation expense:
Depreciation Expense (historical cost) × (19X8 year-end index/ base index) = Current Cost Depreciation Expense

a.	Building	$12,500 × (275.9/183.6) =	$18,784
b.	Equipment	$52,500 × (196.0/139.4) =	73,816
c.	Equipment	$11,000 × (196.0/181.7) =	11,866
	Total		$104,466

Step 5. Roll forward current cost depreciation expense for 19X8 to end-of-the-year 19X9 constant dollars:
Current Cost Depreciation Expense × (19X9 year-end index/ 19X8 year-end index) = Current Cost Depreciation Expense Restated to 19X9 Constant Dollars
$104,466 × (228.4/202.9) = $117,595

For 19X9 Depreciation Expense—

Step 6. Determine layers and associated index for any new acquisitions: No acquisitions or disposals in 19X9.

SCHEDULE 3.6 (continued)

Step 7. Determine 19X9 current cost depreciation expense:
Depreciation expense (historical cost) $\times$ (19X9 year-end index/ base index) = Current Cost Depreciation Expense for 19X9

a. Building $12,500 $\times$ (291.7/183.6) = $19,860
b. Equipment $52,500 $\times$ (209.2/139.4) =   78,788
c. Equipment $11,000 $\times$ (209.2/181.7) =   12,665
Total $111,313

     Schedule 3.7 involves the steps necessary to restate the provision for income taxes for the current cost comprehensive disclosures. As was discussed in Chapter 2, the FASB concluded in SFAS No. 33 that the provision for income taxes in the restated historical cost/constant dollar and current cost disclosures should equate the provision used in the primary financial statements. However, as was discussed earlier, since this comprehensive current cost restatement is being based on end-of-the-year constant dollars, and since *all* other components of income from continuing operations are being restated to such constant dollars, it seems only logical that the provision for income taxes also should be restated. Therefore, in these disclosures, the tax provision is restated similar to other expenses.

SCHEDULE 3.7

Provisions for income taxes are restated on a current cost/constant dollar basis when comprehensive disclosures are made as follows:

For 19X8 Provision for Income Taxes—

Step 1. Restate 19X8 provision for income taxes to end-of-the-year 19X8 constant dollars:
Provision for Income Taxes (historical cost) $\times$ (19X8 year-end CPI/19X8 average CPI) = Provision for Income Taxes Restated to 19X8 Constant Dollars
$231,000 $\times$ (202.9/195.4) = $239,870

Step 2. Roll forward provision for income taxes as restated for 19X8 to end-of-the-year 19X9 constant dollars:

SCHEDULE 3.7 (continued)

> Restated 19X8 Provision for Income Taxes × (19X9 year-end CPI/19X8 year-end CPI) = Provision for Income Taxes Restated to 19X9 Constant Dollars
> $239,870 × (228.4/202.9) = $270,022

For 19X9 Provision for Income Taxes—

Step 3. Restate 19X9 provision for income taxes to end-of-the-year 19X9 constant dollars:
> Provision for Income Taxes (historical cost) × (19X9 year-end CPI/19X9 average CPI) = Provision for Income Taxes Restated to 19X9 Constant Dollars
> $295,400 × (228.4/217.1) = $310,790

Schedule 3.8 represents the determination of the required disclosure related to the increase or decrease in the current cost of inventories, while Schedule 3.9 shows a similar calculation for property, plant, and equipment. While these iterative determinations appear complex, they actually represent the computation of two interrelated numbers: the increase or decrease in the current cost of inventory and property, plant, and equipment due to changes in the general price level and the increase or decrease due to specific price changes related to the assets concerned. As such, and as can be seen in Schedules 3.8 and 3.9, the inflation component applicable to inventory and property, plant, and equipment should be determined by restating and rolling forward for constant dollar adjustments the current cost of these assets at the measurement date.

Schedule 3.10 shows the calculations involved in determining the purchasing power gain or loss on net monetary assets/liabilities. This schedule is identical to Schedule 2.7 in Chapter 2 when the purchasing power gain or loss was determined for inclusion in the historical cost/ constant dollar disclosures. Since MR Corporation held net monetary assets in both 19X8 and 19X9, a purchasing power loss results in each year since the conversion of these amounts to cash (or other final use) will result in a net receipt of dollars with a lower purchasing power in a period of rising prices. Notice that the 19X8 purchasing power loss must be rolled forward to end-of-the-year 19X9 constant dollars when the 19X8 amounts are included in the 19X9 financial statements for comparative purposes.

Schedule 3.11 discusses the determination of the retained earnings balances for the current cost financial statements. In the first year of restatements to current cost, the retained earnings amount will be "plugged" as the difference between restated assets and restated equities other than retained earnings. Thereafter, the retained earnings balance may be determined directly by adjusting the original (or updated) amount for any increases, e.g., current cost income, or decreases, e.g., current cost dividends, in retained earnings. In this example, the retained earnings balance is determined on a combined statement of income and retained earnings.

SCHEDULE 3.8

Increase in current cost of inventories is determined as follows:

For 19X8 Increase in Current Cost of Inventories—

Step 1. Compute increase in current cost of inventories for 19X8:

	Current Cost/ Nominal Dollars $\times$	Conversion Factor $=$	Current Cost/ End-of-the- Year 19X8 Constant Dollars
Balance, January 1, 19X8	$ 405,000	202.9/186.1	$ 441,561
Purchases	2,100,000	202.9/195.4	2,180,604
Cost of Goods Sold	(2,195,878)	202.9/202.9	(2,195,878)
Balance, December 31, 19X8	(427,000)	202.9/202.9	(427,000)
Increase (decrease) in current cost of inventories	$ 117,878		$ 713
Increase in current cost (nominal dollars)			$ 117,878
Increase in current cost (constant dollars)			713
Inflation component			$ 117,165

Step 2. Roll forward 19X8 increase in current cost of inventories to end-of-the-year 19X9 constant dollars:
Increase in current cost $\times$ (19X9 year-end CPI/19X8 year-end CPI) = Increase in current cost restated to 19X9 constant dollars.

Nominal dollars	$117,878 $\times$ (228.4/202.9) = $132,693
Constant dollars	713 $\times$ (228.4/202.9) = 807
Inflation component	117,165 $\times$ (228.4/202.9) = 131,886

SCHEDULE 3.8 (continued)

For 19X9 Increase in Current Cost of Inventories—

Step 3. Compute increase in current cost of inventories for 19X9:

	Current Cost/ Nominal Dollars	×	Conversion Factor	=	Current Cost/ End-of-the- Year 19X9 Constant Dollars
Balance, January 1, 19X9	$ 427,000		228.4/202.9		$ 480,664
Purchases	2,660,000		228.4/217.1		2,798,452
Cost of Goods Sold	(2,795,066)		228.4/228.4		(2,795,066)
Balance, December 31, 19X9	(485,000)		228.4/228.4		(485,000)
Increase (decrease) in current cost of inventories	$ 193,066				$ 950
Increase in current cost (nominal dollars)					$ 193,066
Increase in current cost (constant dollars)					950
Inflation component					$ 192,116

SCHEDULE 3.9

Increase in current cost of property, plant, and equipment is determined as follows:

For 19X8 Increase in Current Cost of Property, Plant, and Equipment—

Step 1. Compute increase in current cost of property, plant, and equipment for 19X8:

	Current Cost/ Nominal Dollars	×	Conversion Factor	=	Current Cost/ End-of-the- year 19X8 Constant Dollars
Balance, January 1, 19X8	$1,042,109		202.9/186.1		$1,136,184
Additions	110,000		202.9/187.2		119,225
Depreciation Expense	(104,466)		202.9/202.9		(104,466)
Balance, December 31, 19X8	(1,194,628)		202.9/202.9		(1,194,628)

SCHEDULE 3.9 (continued)

Increase (decrease) in current cost of property, plant, and equipment	$ 146,985	$ 43,685

Increase in current cost (nominal dollars)	$ 146,985
Increase in current cost (constant dollars)	43,685
Inflation component	$ 103,300

Step 2. Roll forward 19X8 increase in current cost of property, plant, and equipment to end-of-the-year 19X9 constant dollars:

Increase in Current Cost × (19X9 year-end CPI/19X8 year-end CPI) = Increase in Current Cost Restated to 19X9 Constant Dollars

Nominal dollars	$146,985 × (228.4/202.9) = $165,458
Constant dollars	43,685 × (228.4/202.9) = 49,179
Inflation component	103,300 × (228.4/202.9) = 116,279

For 19X9 Increase in Current Cost of Property, Plant, and Equipment—

Step 3. Compute increase in current cost of property, plant, and equipment for 19X9:

	Current Cost/ Nominal Dollars	×	Conversion Factor	=	Current Cost/ End-of-the year 19X9 Constant Dollars
Balance, January 1, 19X9	$1,194,628		228.4/202.9		$1,344,766
Additions	—				
Depreciation Expense	(111,313)		228.4/228.4		(111,313)
Balance, December 31, 19X9	(1,158,882)		228.4/228.4		(1,158,882)
Increase (decrease) in current cost of property, plant, and equipment	$ 75,567				$ (74,571)

Increase in current cost (nominal dollars)	$ 75,567
Decrease in current cost (constant dollars)	(74,571)
Inflation component	$ 150,138

SCHEDULE 3.10

Purchasing power gain or loss is determined as follows:

For 19X8 Purchasing Power Gain or Loss—

Step 1. Compute purchasing power gain or loss for 19X8:

Item	Historical Cost Amounts	$\times$ Conversion Factor	= Restated to 19X8 Constant Dollars
Net Monetary Assets, December 31, 19X7	$ 107,030	202.9/186.1	$116,695
Add: Sources of Net Monetary Items—			
Sales	3,200,000	202.9/195.4	3,322,880
Less: Uses of Net Monetary Items—			
Purchases	(2,100,000)	202.9/195.4	(2,180,640)
Operating Expenses (excluding depreciation)	(384,000)	202.9/195.4	(398,746)
Provision for Income Taxes	(231,000)	202.9/195.4	(239,870)
Dividends Declared	(171,600)	202.9/202.9	(171,600)
Purchase of Equipment	(110,000)	202.9/187.2	(119,229)
Net Monetary Assets, December 31, 19X8 Restated			$ 329,490
Net Monetary Assets, December 31, 19X8	$ 310,430		310,430
Purchasing Power Gain (Loss)			$ (19,060)

Step 2. Roll forward 19X8 purchasing power loss to end-of-the-year 19X9 constant dollars:

Purchasing Power Loss $\times$ (19X9 year-end CPI/19X8 year-end CPI) = Purchasing Power Loss Restated to 19X9 Constant Dollars

$(19,060) \times (228.4/202.9) = $(21,456)

For 19X9 purchasing power gain or loss—

Step 3. Compute purchasing power gain or loss for 19X9:

SCHEDULE 3.10 (continued)

Item	Historical Cost Amounts	×	Conversion Factor	=	Restated to 19X9 Con- stant Dollars
Net Monetary Assets, December 31, 19X8	$ 310,430		228.4/202.9		$ 349,451
Add: Sources of Net Monetary Items— Sales	4,000,000		228.4/217.1		4,208,400
Less: Uses of Net Monetary Items— Purchases	(2,660,000)		228.4/217.1		(2,798,586)
Operating Expenses (excluding depreciation)	(480,000)		228.4/217.1		(505,008)
Provision for Income Taxes	(295,400)		228.4/217.1		(310,790)
Dividends Declared	(219,440)		228.4/228.4		(219,440)
Net Monetary Assets, December 31, 19X9 Restated					$ 724,027
Net Monetary Assets, December 31, 19X9	$ 655,590				655,590
Purchasing Power Gain (Loss)					$ (68,437)

SCHEDULE 3.11—Restatement of Retained Earnings

For 19X8 Retained Earnings—

Step 1. In the first year of restatement, ending retained earnings is the balancing figure, i.e., the difference between restated assets and restated equities other than retained earnings.

Step 2. Determine beginning retained earnings:
Ending Retained Earnings + Dividends − Net Income = Beginning Retained Earnings
$940,227 + $193,170 − $460,760 = $672,637

For 19X9 Retained Earnings—

Step 3. Retained earnings amounts for 19X9 are computed on the statement of income and retained earnings.

Schedule 3.12 represents the current cost restatement of dividends which, in this case, is simple since dividends are assumed declared at or near year-end, and therefore the dividend amounts measured in historical costs are reflective of current cost dividends at the measurement date. In the event dividends are declared at some other time or multiple times during the year, these amounts should be restated to end-of-the-year constant dollars based on the relationship of the end-of-the-year CPI to the CPI in effect when the dividends are declared.

The restatement of monetary items in Schedule 3.13 is identical to the Chapter 2 restatement for constant dollars in Schedule 2.10. Current year monetary items need not be restated since these items already are measured in terms of their end-of-the-year monetary equivalent. The 19X8 numbers presented for comparative purposes should be rolled forward to reflect end-of-the-year 19X9 constant dollars.

Schedule 3.14 represents a current cost determination of ending amounts of inventory. These balance sheet amounts tie back to Schedule 3.3 where the inventory amounts used in the computation of cost of goods sold were determined.

The restatement of fixed assets in Schedule 3.15 follows the same rationale as the restatement of related depreciation in Schedule 3.6. The final steps in the current cost restatement of fixed assets involve layering the assets into acquisition periods and determining the associated base indices. The historical amounts should then be restated, using the relationship of the end-of-the-year specific index for the current reporting period to the index in effect at the acquisition dates of the assets. The same logic applies in restating any accumulated depreciation, amortization, or depletion associated with these assets.

SCHEDULE 3.12

Dividends are restated on current cost/constant dollar basis when comprehensive disclosures are made as follows:

For 19X8 Dividends—

Step 1. It is assumed that dividends are declared at or near year-end. Therefore, the dividends declared already are stated at end-of-the-year constant dollars. If dividends are declared during the year, these amounts should be restated to end-of-the-year constant dollars using the CPI in effect at the date of declaration.

Step 2. Roll forward dividends for 19X8 to end-of-the-year 19X9 constant dollars:
Dividends $\times$ (19X9 year-end CPI/19X8 year-end CPI) = Dividends Restated to 19X9 Constant Dollars
$171,600 $\times$ (228.4/202.9) = $193,170

For 19X9 Dividends—

Step 3. Procedure is the same as step 1.

SCHEDULE 3.13—Restatement of Monetary Items

For 19X8 Monetary Items—

Step 1. Roll forward 19X8 monetary items to end-of-the-year 19X9 constant dollars:
Monetary Item $\times$ (19X9 year-end CPI/19X8 year-end CPI) = Monetary Item Restated to 19X9 Constant Dollars

a. Cash	$ 410,250 $\times$ (228.4/202.9) =	$ 461,818
b. Receivables	1,230,750 $\times$ (228.4/202.9) =	1,385,455
c. Current Liabilities	215,793 $\times$ (228.4/202.9) =	242,918
d. Long-term Liabilities	1,078,963 $\times$ (228.4/202.9) =	1,214,589
e. Deferred Taxes	35,814 $\times$ (228.4/202.9) =	40,316

For 19X9 Monetary Items—

Step 2. Monetary items for 19X9 are stated in end-of-the-year 19X9 constant dollars. Therefore no restatement is necessary.

SCHEDULE 3.14—Restatement of Inventories

For 19X8 Inventories—

Step 1. Determine 19X8 current cost ending inventories (see Schedule 3.3):
Current cost amount $427,000

Step 2. Roll forward 19X8 restated ending inventories to end-of-the-year 19X9 constant dollars:
Restated Ending Inventories × (19X9 year-end CPI/19X8 year-end CPI) = Ending Inventories Restated to 19X9 Constant Dollars
$427,000 × (228.4/202.9) = $480,664

Step 3. Determine 19X9 current cost ending inventories (see narrative accompanying Schedule 3.3):
Current cost amount $485,000

SCHEDULE 3.15—Restatement of Fixed Assets

For 19X8 Fixed Assets—

Step 1. Determine fixed asset layers:

Asset	Historical Cost	Acquisition Date
a. Land	$ 80,000	December 31, 19X4
b. Building	500,000	December 31, 19X4
c. Equipment	420,000	December 31, 19X4
d. Equipment	110,000	January 1, 19X8

Step 2. Determine Index associated with acquisition dates:

Asset	Base Index
a. Land	153.2
b. Building	183.6
c. Equipment	139.4
d. Equipment	181.7

Step 3. Determined current cost of fixed assets for 19X8:
Fixed Asset (historical cost) × (19X8 year-end index/base index) = Current Cost of Fixed Asset

SCHEDULE 3.15 (continued)

a. Land $80,000 × (222.8/153.2) = $116,345
b. Building   500,000 × (275.9/183.6) = 751,362
c. Equipment   420,000 × (196.0/139.4) = 590,531
d. Equipment   110,000 × (196.0/181.7) = 118,657

Step 4. Roll forward 19X8 current cost of fixed assets to end-of-the-year 19X9 constant dollars:
Current Cost of Fixed Asset × (19X9 year-end CPI/19X8 year-end CPI) = Current Cost of Fixed Assets Restated to 19X9 Constant Dollars

a. Land $116,345 × (228.4/202.9) = $130,967
b. Building   751,362 × (228.4/202.9) = 845,791
c. Equipment   590,531 × (228.4/202.9) = 664,748
d. Equipment   118,657 × (228.4/202.9) = 133,570

Step 5. Determine percentage of asset which has been depreciated at December 31, 19X8:
Accumulated Depreciation (historical cost)/Fixed Asset (historical cost) = Percentage Depreciated

b. Building $50,000/$500,000 = 10%
c. Equipment   210,000/420,000 = 50%
d. Equipment   11,000/110,000 = 10%

Step 6. Determine current cost accumulated depreciation in end-of-the-year 19X9 constant dollars:
Current Cost of Fixed Asset Restated (step 4) × Percentage Depreciated (step 5) = Current Cost of Accumulated Depreciation Restated to 19X9 Constant Dollars

b. Building $845,791 × 10% = $84,579
c. Equipment   664,748 × 50% = 332,374
d. Equipment   133,570 × 10% = 13,357

For 19X9 Fixed Assets—

Step 7. Determine current cost of fixed assets for 19X9:
Fixed Asset (historical cost) × (19X9 year-end index/base index) = Current Cost of Fixed Assets in 19X9 Constant Dollars

a. Land $80,000 × (241.5/153.2) = $126,243
b. Building   500,000 × (291.7/183.6) = 794,390
c. Equipment   420,000 × (209.2/139.4) = 630,301
d. Equipment   110,000 × (209.2/181.7) = 126,648

SCHEDULE 3.15 (continued)

Step 8. Determine percentage of asset which has been depreciated at December 31, 19X9:

Accumulated Depreciation (historical cost)/Fixed Asset (historical cost) = Percentage Depreciated

b. Building $62,500/$500,000 = 12.5%
c. Equipment   262,500/420,000 = 62.5%
d. Equipment   22,000/110,000 = 20.0%

Step 9. Determine current cost accumulated depreciation in end-of-the-year 19X9 constant dollars:

Current Cost of Fixed Assets (step 7) × Percentage Depreciated (step 8) = Current Cost of Accumulated Depreciation in 19X9 Constant Dollars

b. Building $794,390 × 12.5% = $99,299
c. Equipment   630,301 × 62.5% = 393,938
d. Equipment   126,648 × 20.0% = 25,330

The paid-in capital restatement in Schedule 3.16 is very similar to the fixed asset restatement in Schedule 3.15 since the amounts all represent nonmonetary items. The major difference in the restatement process is that for paid-in capital amounts general, rather than specific, CPIs are used such that the current cost paid-in capital restatement is identical to the historical cost/constant dollar restatement in Schedule 2.13 of Chapter 2. After layers and appropriate indices are determined for paid-in capital, these amounts should be restated to end-of-the-year constant dollars using the relationship of the end-of-the-year CPI to the CPI in effect when the paid-in capital was generated.

While these comprehensive disclosures are not required in SFAS No. 33, they are permitted and should provide a thorough knowledge of how the minimum disclosures should be generated. The next section of this chapter formulates an example of the required minimum disclosures under SFAS No. 33.

SCHEDULE 3.16—Restatement of Paid-In Capital

For 19X8 Paid-In Capital—

Step 1. Determine appropriate layers for paid-in capital:

Paid-In Capital	Amount	Issue Date
a. Capital Stock	$280,000	December 31, 19X4
b. Additional Paid-In Capital	560,000	December 31, 19X4

Step 2. Determine appropriate CPI:

Paid-In Capital	Base CPI
a. Capital Stock	155.4
b. Additional Paid-In Capital	155.4

Step 3. Restate paid-in capital to end-of-the-year 19X8 constant dollars:
Paid-In Capital (historical cost) $\times$ (19X8 year-end CPI/base CPI)
= Paid-In Capital Restated to 19X8 Constant Dollars

a. Capital Stock $280,000 $\times$ (202.9/155.4) = $365,596
b. Additional Paid-In Capital   560,000 $\times$ (202.9/155.4) =   731,192

Step 4. Roll forward 19X8 paid-in capital as restated to end-of-the-year 19X9 constant dollars:
Restated Paid-In Capital $\times$ (19X9 year-end CPI/19X8 year-end CPI) = Paid-In Capital Restated to 19X9 Constant Dollars

a. Capital Stock $365,596 $\times$ (228.4/202.9) = $411,551
b. Additional Paid-In Capital   731,192 $\times$ (228.4/202.9) =   823,102

For 19X9 Paid-In Capital—

Step 5. Determine layers and associated CPI for any additional issuances: No additional issuances in 19X9

Step 6. Restate paid-in capital to end-of-the-year constant dollars:
Paid-In Capital (historical cost) $\times$ (19X9 year-end CPI/base CPI)
= Paid-In Capital Restated to 19X9 Constant Dollars

a. Capital Stock $280,000 $\times$ (228.4/155.4) = $411,551
b. Additional Paid-In Capital   560,000 $\times$ (228.4/155.4) =   823,102

Illustration of Minimum Current Cost Disclosure Requirements

SFAS No. 33 requires that reporting enterprises report, as a minimum, the following information on a current cost basis:

1. Income from continuing operations;
2. Inventory and property, plant, and equipment at the end of the current fiscal year; and
3. Increases or decreases for the current fiscal year in inventory and property, plant, and equipment.

Checklist 3.2 provides an overview to the computational steps required to make the minimum current cost disclosures.

CHECKLIST 3.2
Computational Guidance for Minimum Current Cost Disclosures
(Paragraph numbers refer to SFAS No. 33.)

1. Determine Current Cost of Inventories.
   a. Determine current cost of purchasing inventories or current cost of resources required to produce inventories, whichever is applicable (par. 57)
   b. Determine recoverable amounts of inventories, i.e., the current net amount of cash expected to be recoverable from the sale of the inventories. (par. 62–63)
   c. Inventories should be measured at the lower of their current cost (a) or their recoverable amounts (b). (par. 62)
2. Determine Current Cost of Property, Plant, and Equipment.
   a. Determine current cost of acquiring property, plant and equipment with the same service potential as embodied by the asset currently owned. (par. 58)
   b. Determine recoverable amounts of property, plant and equipment, i.e., the current net amount of cash expected to be recoverable from the use or sale, whichever is appropriate, of the property, plant and equipment. (par. 62–63)
   c. Property, plant and equipment should be measured at the lower of their current cost (a) or their recoverable amounts (b). (par. 62)
3. Determine Purchasing Power Gain or Loss.
   a. Segregate financial statement elements into monetary and nonmonetary categorizations. (par. 23, 50)
   b. Restate beginning net monetary items to average-for-the-year constant dollars. (par. 50, 232)

CHECKLIST 3.2 (continued)

     c. Restate increases and decreases in net monetary items to average-for-the-year constant dollars (par. 50, 232)

     d. Restate ending net monetary items to average-for-the-year constant dollars. (par. 50, 232)

     e. Purchasing power gain (loss) equals beginning net monetary items restated (b) plus increases in net monetary items restated minus decreases in net monetary items restated (c) minus ending net monetary items restated (d). (par. 50, 232)

4. Determine Holding Gain or Loss for Inventories and Property, Plant and Equipment.

     a. Gross holding gain or loss equals current cost of inventories and property, plant, and equipment at year-end plus (minus) increases (decreases) in current cost amounts during the period minus current cost of inventories and property, plant, and equipment at beginning of year. (par. 56)

     b. Restate beginning, ending and changes in current cost to average-for-the-year constant dollars. (par. 233)

     c. Net holding gain or loss equals restated current cost of inventories and property, plant, and equipment at year end plus (minus) increases (decreases) in restated current cost amounts during period minus restated current cost of inventories and property, plant, and equipment at beginning of year. (par. 56)

     d. Inflation component of gross holding gain or loss equals gross holding gain or loss (a) minus net holding gain or loss (c). (par. 234)

5. Steps to Prepare Current Cost Income Statement. When using average-for-the-year constant dollars—

     a. Operating revenues may be historical cost operating revenues (consideration should be given to seasonal fluctuations in the generation of revenues). (par. 210)

     b. Operating expenses (exclusive of cost of goods sold and depreciation) may be historical cost operating expenses (consideration should be given to seasonal fluctuations in the incurrence of expenses). (par. 210)

     c. Restate cost of goods sold and depreciation expense. (When LIFO method of inventory costing is used, restated cost of goods sold may be approximated by historical cost of goods sold unless a LIFO layer has been depleted. In this case, costs associated with a depleted LIFO layer should be restated.) (par. 212, 223–227)

     d. The provision for income taxes should be the historical cost provision for income taxes. (par. 210)

CHECKLIST 3.2 (continued)

   e. Income from continuing operations equals operating revenues (a) minus operating expenses (b,c) minus provision for income taxes (d). (par. 70)

   f. Disclose purchasing power gain (loss) (1,e). (par. 29)

   g. Disclose gross holding gain (loss) (4,a). (par. 55–56)

   h. Disclose net holding gain (loss) (4,c). (par. 55–56)

The reporting enterprise may make the required disclosures in either of two formats. The disclosures may be made using a statement format (see Figure 3.5) or a reconciliation format (see Figure 3.6). In either case, the enterprise must adjust income to reflect the current cost of goods sold and depreciation, depletion, and amortization expense.

When an enterprise elects to make the minimum current cost disclosures under SFAS No. 33, average-for-the-year constant dollars (as opposed to end-of-the-year constant dollars) are required to be used in formulating the disclosures. This approach will be used in developing the example of the required minimum disclosures.

Schedule 3.17 depicts the steps necessary to adjust cost of goods sold to current cost when FIFO inventory costing is used. As previously mentioned, the amount of cost of goods sold determined using LIFO inventory costing for the primary financial statements may serve as a viable alternative to these FIFO adjustments. Assuming a FIFO adjustment is necessary, the current cost of beginning inventories first should be restated to average-for-the-year constant dollars. Notice in Schedule 3.17 that purchases need not be restated when average-for-the-year constant dollars are used in the absence of significant seasonality (see Chapter 2). Next, the current cost of ending inventories should be rolled back to average-for-the-year purchasing power. At this point, all components of current cost of goods sold are stated in terms of average-for-the-year constant dollars such that the current cost of goods sold is determined by the simple additive process shown in step 4 of Schedule 3.17.

116 CURRENT COST ACCOUNTING FOR EXTERNAL REPORTING

FIGURE 3.5
MR Corporation
Statement of Income on a Current Cost/Constant Dollar Basis
(Statement Format)
For the Year Ended December 31, 19X9

	As Reported in Primary Financial Statements	Adjusted for General Inflation	Adjusted for Changes in Specific Prices (Current Costs)
Sales	$ 4,000,000	$ 4,000,000	$ 4,000,000
Cost of Goods Sold (see Schedule 3.17)	2,600,000	2,652,026	2,656,781
Gross Profit	$ 1,400,000	$ 1,347,974	$ 1,343,219
Operating Expenses (Excluding Depreciation)	$ 480,000	$ 480,000	$ 480,000
Depreciation (see Schedule 3.18)	76,000	103,570	107,889
Provision for Income Taxes	295,400	295,400	295,400
Income from Continuing Operations	$ 548,600	$ 469,004	$ 459,930
Purchasing Power Loss (see Schedule 3.19)		$ (32,570)	$ (32,570)
Increase in Specific Prices of Inventories and Property, Plant, and Equipment Held during the Year (see Schedules 3.20 and 3.21)			$ 126,924
Effect of Increase in General Price Level			(194,820)
Excess of Increase in General Price Level over Increase in Specific Prices			$ (67,896)

FIGURE 3.6
MR Corporation
Statement of Income on a Current Cost/Constant Dollar Basis
(Reconciliation Format)
For the Year Ended December 31, 19X9

Income from Continuing Operations		$ 548,600
Adjustments to restate costs for the Effect of General Inflation—		
Cost of Goods Sold	$ (52,026)	
Depreciation	(27,570)	(79,596)
Income from Continuing Operations Adjusted for the Effects of General Inflation		$ 469,004
Adjustment to Reflect the Difference between General Inflation and Changes in Specific Prices:		
Cost of Goods Sold	$ (4,755)	
Depreciation	(4,319)	(9,074)
Income from Continuing Operations Adjusted for Specific Price Changes		$ 459,930
Purchasing Power Loss		$ (32,570)
Increase in Specific Prices of Inventories and Property, Plant, and Equipment held during the year		$ 126,924
Effect of Increase in General Price Level		(194,820)
Excess of Increase in Geneal Price Level over Increase in Specific Prices		$ (67,896)

SCHEDULE 3.17

Cost of goods sold is restated on a current cost/constant dollar basis when minimum disclosures are made as follows:

For 19X9 Cost of Goods Sold—

Step 1. Restate 19X9 current cost beginning inventories to average-for-the-year 19X9 constant dollars:
Beginning Inventories (current cost) × 19X9 average CPI/Nov.–Dec. 19X8 CPI) = Current Cost Beginning Inventories Restated to 19X9 Constant Dollars
$427,000 × (217.1/202.5) = $457,786

Step 2. Purchases need not be restated in the absence of significant seasonal trends.

Step 3. Restate 19X9 current cost ending inventories to average-for-the-year 19X9 constant dollars:
Ending Inventories (current cost) × (19X9 average CPI/year-end 19X9 CPI) = Current Cost Inventories Restated to 19X9 Constant Dollars
$485,000 × (217.1/228.4) = $461,005

Step 4. Compute 19X9 current cost of goods sold restated to average-for-the-year 19X9 constant dollars:
Restated Current Cost Beginning Inventories + Restated Purchases − Restated Current Cost Ending Inventories = Current Cost of Goods Sold Restated to 19X9 Constant Dollars
$457,786 + $2,660,000 − $461,005 = $2,656,781

The computational procedures to adjust depreciation expense to reflect current cost depreciation for the minimum disclosures are identical to the procedures used for the comprehensive disclosures, except that average-for-the-year constant dollars are utilized and depreciation for prior years need not be rolled forward. Schedule 3.18 reflects the restatement of depreciation expense for the minimum disclosures.

The purchasing power gain or loss for disclosure in current cost amounts is computed in Schedule 3.19. As in the comprehensive example used earlier in this chapter, MR Corporation held net monetary assets during a period of rising prices such that a purchasing power loss results. In the minimum disclosure computations, monetary items held at year-end must be restated in terms of average-for-the-year constant dollars. Sources and uses of monetary items from operations are not restated for the same reason that purchases were not restated earlier in the determination of cost of goods sold; in the absence of significant seasonality, these amounts already reflect average-for-the-year purchasing power. Note should be made that this purchasing power loss ($32,570) is the same amount used in the minimum historical cost/constant dollar disclosures in Schedule 2.16 of Chapter 2.

SCHEDULE 3.18

Depreciation expense is restated on a current cost/constant dollar basis when minimum disclosures are made as follows:

For 19X9 Depreciation Expense—

Step 1. Determine average current cost of fixed assets for the period (see Schedule 3.15):

	Current Cost		
Asset	Beginning	Ending	Average-for-the-year
b. Building	$751,362	$794,390	$772,876
c. Equipment	590,531	630,301	610,416
d. Equipment	118,657	126,648	122,653

Step 2. Determine historical cost annual depreciation rate:

Asset	Depreciation Expense ÷	Historical Depreciable Amount =	Annual Depreciable Rate
b. Building	$12,500	$500,000	2.5%
c. Equipment	52,500	420,000	12.5%
d. Equipment	11,000	110,000	10.0%

Step 3. Calculate current cost depreciation expense:

Asset	Average Current Cost ×	Annual Depreciation Rate =	Current Cost Depreciation Expense
b. Building	$772,876	2.5%	$ 19,322
c. Equipment	610,416	12.5%	76,302
d. Equipment	122,653	10.0%	12,265
			$107,889

SCHEDULE 3.19

Purchasing power gain or loss is computed as follows:

For 19X9 Purchasing Power Gain or Loss—

Compute purchasing power gain or loss for 19X9:

Item	Historical Cost Amount	× Conversion Factor =	Restated to 19X9 Constant Dollars
Net Monetary Assets, December 31, 19X8	$ 310,430	217.1/202.9	$ 332,160
Add: Sources of Net Monetary Items— Sales	4,000,000	217.1/217.1	4,000,000
Less: Uses of Net Monetary Items— Purchases	(2,660,000)	217.1/217.1	(2,660,000)
Operating Expenses (excluding depreciation)	(480,000)	217.1/217.1	(480,000)
Provision for income taxes	(295,400)	217.1/217.1	(295,400)
Dividends declared	(219,440)	217.1/228.4	(208,600)
Net Monetary Assets, December 31, 19X9 Restated			$ 688,160
Net Monetary Assets, December 31, 19X9	$ 655,590		655,590
Purchasing Power Gain (Loss)			$ (32,570)

The final computations necessary to develop the current cost minimum disclosures involve a determination of any increases or decreases in the current cost amounts of inventories and property, plant, and equipment. These determinations are shown in Schedules 3.20 and 3.21. These computations are identical to the ones made in Schedules 3.8 and 3.9 of this chapter for the comprehensive disclosures except that average-for-the-year constant dollars are used and prior year increases or decreases may be ignored.

This section has described the minimum current cost disclosures required under SFAS No. 33. Used in conjunction with the previous chapter and the comprehensive current cost illustration in this chapter, the computation problems of developing these disclosures should be more fully understood.

SCHEDULE 3.20

Increase in current cost of inventories when the minimum disclosures are made is determined as follows:

For 19X9 Increase in Current Cost of Inventories—

	Current Cost/ Nominal Dollars $\times$	Conversion Factor $=$	Current Cost/Aver-age-for-the-year 19X9 Constant Dollars
Balance, January 1, 19X9	$ 427,000	217.1/202.9	$ 456,884
Purchases	2,660,000	217.1/217.1	2,660,000
Cost of Goods Sold	(2,656,781)	217.1/217.1	(2,656,781)
Balance, December 31, 19X9	(485,000)	217.1/228.4	(461,005)
Increase (decrease) in current costs of inventories	$ 54,781		$ 902
Increase in current cost (nominal dollars)			$ 54,781
Increase in current cost (constant dollars)			902
Inflation component			$ 53,879

SCHEDULE 3.21

Increase in current cost of property, plant, and equipment when the minimum disclosures are made is determined as follows:

For 19X9 Increase in Current Cost of Property, Plant and Equipment—

	Current Cost/ Nominal Dollars ×	Conversion Factor =	Current Cost/Average-for-theyear 19X9 Constant Dollars
Balance, January 1, 19X9	$1,194,628	217.1/202.9	$1,278,234
Additions	. . . . .		. . . . .
Depreciation Expense	(107,889)	217.1/217.1	(107,889)
Balance, December 31, 19X9	(1,158,882)	217.1/228.4	(1,101,547)
Increase (decrease) in current costs of property, plant, and equipment	$ 72,143		$ (68,798)

Increase in current cost (nominal dollars)	$72,143
Decrease in current cost (constant dollars)	(68,798)
Inflation component	$ 140,941

Summary

The FASB, through the issuance of SFAS No. 33, now requires certain large, publicly traded enterprises to formulate supplementary financial statement disclosures prepared on a current cost basis. Enterprises affected are those with inventories and property, plant, and equipment amounting to more than $125 million or total assets aggregating more than $1 billion.

This chapter has examined and illustrated the steps necessary to develop these required current cost disclosures. Alternative formats for implementing the disclosure requirements were presented so that enterprises may select from among alternatives the one that is most appropriate to the reporting enterprise.

CHAPTER 4

Key Methods for External Reporting of Constant Dollar and Current Cost Accounting

□□□□□□□□□□□□□

In Chapters 2 and 3 of this *Handbook,* the mechanics of restating the historical cost/constant dollar information contained in the primary financial statements to reflect constant dollar and current cost adjustments were emphasized. The purpose of this chapter is to provide operational guidance to reporting the information developed in previous chapters. Presented here are a discussion of the five-year summary of selected financial information and management's discussion of the disclosures required by the Financial Accounting Standards Board (FASB) in Statement of Financial Accounting Standards (SFAS) No. 33 entitled "Financial Reporting and Changing Prices." Further, a discussion of some reporting subtleties included in SFAS No. 33, e.g., what earnings per share (EPS) disclosures are required, comparisons with the previous disclosures required under Accounting Series Release (ASR) No. 190 entitled "Notice of Adoption of Amendments to Regulation S-X—Required Disclosures of Certain Replacement Cost Data," audit report implications, and a comprehensive compliance checklist should enable readers of this book to synthesize the overall reporting requirements of SFAS No. 33. The Appendix to this chapter contains the complete financial reporting package required by SFAS No. 33.

The Five-Year Summary of Selected Financial Data

In addition to the historical cost/constant dollar and current cost disclosures discussed in the preceding two chapters, SFAS No. 33 also requires applicable enterprises to disclose the following information for each of the five most recent fiscal years:

1. Net Sales and Other Operating Revenues
2. Historical Cost/Constant Dollar Information
   (a) Income from continuing operations
   (b) Income per share from continuing operations
   (c) Net assets at fiscal year-end
3. Current Cost Information (except for individual years in which the information was excluded from current year disclosures because there was no material difference between income from continuing operations on an historical cost/constant dollar basis and on a current cost basis)
   (a) Income from continuing operations
   (b) Income per common share from continuing operations
   (c) Net assets at fiscal year-end
   (d) Increases or decreases in the current cost amounts of inventory and property, plant, and equipment, net of inflation
4. Other Information
   (a) Purchasing power gain or loss on net monetary items
   (b) Cash dividends declared per common share
   (c) Market price per share at fiscal year-end

A note to the five-year summary should disclose the average-for-the-year or end-of-the-year Consumer Price Index (CPI), whichever is used for the measurement of income from continuing operations. If the reporting enterprise elects to state net assets in the five-year summary at amounts computed from comprehensive financial statements prepared on an historical cost/constant dollar or on a current cost/constant dollar basis, this fact should be disclosed in a note to the five-year summary.

The information in the five-year summary is to be stated either in:

1. average-for-the-year constant dollars or end-of-the-year constant dollars (whichever is used for the measurement of income from continuing operations) as measured by the CPI for the current fiscal year, or

2. dollars having a purchasing power equal to that of dollars of the base period used by the Bureau of Labor Statistics in calculating the CPI (currently 1967).

Companies that present this information in current year dollars must roll forward prior year information each reporting period to reflect the current CPI. Companies that utilize base year dollars avoid this annual roll-forward procedure (since restatement would be necessary only as the base year changes), but would show different amounts of income from continuing operations in the five-year summary and in current year disclosures (which must be in current year constant dollars). This latter result could be extremely confusing to users of these disclosures. And, since investors typically analyze the purchasing power of the dollar in terms of the most recent time period, the use of current year constant dollars seems to be preferable.

If an enterprise presents the minimum information required by SFAS No. 33, net assets (i.e., stockholders' equity) should be measured, for purposes of the five-year summary, in one of the following two ways:

1. On an historical cost/constant dollar basis at the amount reported in its primary financial statements adjusted for the difference between the historical cost and the historical cost/constant dollar amounts or lower recoverable amounts of inventories and property, plant, and equipment.

2. On a current cost basis at the amount reported in the primary financial statements adjusted for the difference between the historical cost amounts and the current cost or lower recoverable amounts of inventories and property, plant, and equipment and restated in terms of constant dollars to the current or base year.

In an effort to simplify transition to the reporting requirements of SFAS No. 33, the FASB requires that only sales, cash dividends per share, market price per share, and the CPI utilized be presented for fiscal years ending prior to December 25, 1979. A complete five-year summary of other disclosures is not required until 1983. The FASB, however, does encourage disclosure of the other information in the five-year summary on a retroactive basis during this transition period.

An enterprise that first applies the provisions of SFAS No. 33 for a fiscal year ended after December 24, 1980 (e.g., because the enterprise becomes a public company) is required to disclose for earlier years in the five-year summary only sales, dividends, market price, and CPI information. For example, an enterprise that becomes subject to the provisions of

SFAS No. 33 in 1983 would not have to present the historical cost/constant dollar disclosures (including the purchasing power gain or loss) or the current cost disclosures for 1982 and prior years.

Illustrative Example of Five-Year Summary Disclosures Using End-of-the-Year and Average-for-the-Year Constant Dollars

As previously mentioned, the five-year summary disclosures should be made above and beyond the historical cost/constant dollar and current cost disclosures discussed in the two previous chapters of this book. For continuity, the five-year summaries developed in this section are derived from the same historical cost numbers of MR Corporation utilized in these previous chapters and, where appropriate, reference back to the figures and schedules developed in prior chapters will be made.

Figure 4.1 represents the required five-year summary presentation when end-of-the-year constant dollars are used in developing the historical cost/constant dollar and current cost disclosures, i.e., when comprehensive disclosures are made *and* the reporting enterprise elects to restate amounts in terms of end-of-the-year constant dollars. Figure 4.2 is a similar presentation based on average-for-the-year constant dollars, i.e., appropriate if elected in making comprehensive disclosures and required for minimum disclosures. The following discussion relates to the schedules that derive the numbers utilized in the five-year summary; the reporting format is that used in SFAS No. 33.

Schedules 4.1 through 4.9 contain the restatement mechanics applicable to Figure 4.1 where end-of-the-year constant dollars are used. Notice in Figure 4.1 and related schedules that the amounts included in the five-year summary for *the current year (19X9) and all prior years presented are restated in terms of end-of-the-year 19X9 constant dollars.* Since comprehensive restatement is assumed in Figure 4.1, *all* numbers included in the summary are restated and rolled forward; this methodology will change for the minimum disclosures on average-for-the-year dollars as presented later in this section and represented in Figure 4.2.

Schedule 4.1 represents the restatement and roll-forward technique for net sales and other operating revenues. Since the historical cost model utilized in these examples assumes that revenues are generated evenly throughout the year, the restatement and roll-forward process involves ascertaining the CPI at the end of 19X9 (228.4) and the average CPI for the time periods involved in the generation of revenue and rolling these historical amounts forward to reflect end-of-the-year 19X9 constant dollars.

FIGURE 4.1
MR Corporation
Five-Year Comparison of Selected Supplementary
Financial Data Adjusted for Effects of
Changing Prices
(In End-of-the Year 19X9 Constant Dollars)

	19X5	19X6	19X7	19X8	19X9
Net Sales and Other Operating Revenues (see Schedule 4.1)	$2,266,998	$2,679,179	$3,020,165	$3,740,566	$4,208,400
Historical Cost Information Adjusted for General Inflation:					
Income from Continuing Operations (see Figure 2.4)					493,450
Income per Common Share from Continuing Operations (see Schedule 4.2)					17.62
Net Assets at Year-End (see Schedule 4.3)					2,237,228
Current Cost Information:					
Income from Continuing Operations (see Figure 3.4)					486,223
Income per Common Share from Continuing Operations (see Schedule 4.4)					17.37
Net Assets at Year-End (see Schedule 4.5)					2,299,605
Excess of Increase in Specific Prices over Increase in General Price Level (see Schedule 4.6)					(73,621)
Other Information:					
Purchasing Power Gain (Loss) on Net Monetary Items (see Figure 4.4, Chapter 2)					(68,437)
Cash Dividends Declared per Common Share (see Schedule 4.7)	3.97	4.25	5.55	6.90	7.84
Market Price per Common Share at Year-End (see Schedule 4.8)	27.47	34.07	38.05	33.77	35.00
Year-End CPI	166.3	174.3	186.1	202.9	228.4

Figure 4.2
MR Corporation
Five-Year Comparison of Selected Supplementary Financial Data
Adjusted for Effects of Changing Prices
(In Average-for-the-Year 19X9 Constant Dollars)

	19X5	19X6	19X7	19X8	19X9
Net Sales and Operating Revenues (see Schedule 4.9)	$2,154,839	$2,546,628	$2,870,744	$3,555,374	$4,000,000
Historical Cost Information Adjusted for General Inflation:					
Income from Continuing Operations (see Figure 2.5, Chapter 2)					469,004
Income per Common Share from Continuing Operations (see Schedule 4.10)					16.75
Net Assets at Year-End (see Schedule 4.11)					2,126,469
Current Cost Information:					
Income from Continuing Operations (see Figure 3.5, Chapter 3)					459,930
Income per Common Share from Continuing Operations (see Schedule 4.12)					16.43
Net Assets at Year-End (see Schedule 4.13)					2,255,976
Excess of Increase in Specific Prices over Increase in General Price Level (see Figure 3.5, Chapter 3)					(67,896)
Other Information:					
Purchasing Power Gain (loss) on Net Monetary Items (see Figure 2.5, Chapter 2)					(32,570)
Cash Dividends Declared per Common Share (see Schedule 4.14)	3.77	4.04	5.27	6.56	7.45
Market Price per Common Share at Year-End (see Schedule 4.15)	26.11	32.38	36.16	32.10	33.27
Average-for-the-Year CPI	161.2	170.5	181.5	195.4	217.1

SCHEDULE 4.1

Net sales and other operating revenues are adjusted as follows:
Adjust sales from each year to end-of-the-year 19X9 constant dollars—
Sales (historical cost) × (19X9 year-end CPI/average CPI for the year) =
   Sales Adjusted to 19X9 Constant Dollars

19X5	$1,600,000 × (228.4/161.2)	= $2,266,998
19X6	$2,000,000 × (228.4/170.5)	= $2,679,179
19X7	$2,400,000 × (228.4/181.5)	= $3,020,165
19X8	$3,200,000 × (228.4/195.4)	= $3,740,566
19X9	$4,000,000 × (228.4/217.1)	= $4,208,400

Schedule 4.2 is the computation of income per common share as determined on an historical cost/constant dollar basis. The provisions of Accounting Principles Board Opinion (APBO) No. 15, entitled "Earnings Per Share," should be followed in determining the EPS numbers to be used in the supplemental disclosures required by SFAS No. 33. Accordingly, the number of shares used in calculating these per-share numbers should be the same as the number of shares used in determining the disclosures for the primary financial statements. While SFAS No. 33 does not indicate that this supplementary per-share data should be presented on both a primary and a fully diluted basis, the staff of the FASB has indicated that, as a minimum, primary per-share data should be disclosed, and additional disclosure on a fully diluted basis is encouraged.[1] Thus, in making EPS disclosures for the historical cost/constant dollar and current cost disclosures, enterprises simply use the number of shares of stock used in developing the disclosures in the primary financial statements.

The computations reflected in Schedule 4.2 to determine EPS for 1979 are relatively simplistic since, in the case of MR Corporation, 28,000 shares of stock are presumed outstanding for the entire fiscal year 1979. Increasing the complexity of EPS computations is not a result of implementing SFAS No. 33; therefore, no complexities need to be introduced to this reporting scheme. Remember, EPS disclosures need not be made in the five-year summary for fiscal years ending prior to December 25, 1979.

Schedule 4.3 is the determination of net assets to be reported in the five-year summary. The numbers derived in this schedule were abstracted from Figure 2.3 in Chapter 2 which is the presentation of MR Corporation's comparative balance sheets on a current cost/constant dollar basis.

---

[1]Deloitte Haskins & Sells, *Financial Reporting and Changing Prices* (New York: Deloitte Haskins & Sells, 1979) p. 45.

Total assets minus all liabilities and deferred credits of **MR** Corporation results in the net assets number for 1979. This number also need not be reported for fiscal years ending prior to December 25, 1979.

SCHEDULE 4.2

Income from continuing operations per common share on an historical cost/ constant dollar basis is computed as follows:

Step 1. Compute weighted average shares of common stock outstanding for 19X9: Since 28,000 shares were outstanding for the entire year, 28,000 shares is the weighted average shares of common stock outstanding.

Step 2. Compute income from continuing operations per common share: Income from Continuing Operations (historical cost/constant dollar)/Weighted Average Shares Outstanding = Income from Continuing Operations per Common Share.
$493,450/28,000 shares = $17.62 per common share

SCHEDULE 4.3

Net assets at year-end on an historical cost/constant dollar basis is computed as follows:

From Figure 2.3, Chapter 2—

Total Assets — Current Liabilities — Long-Term Liabilities — Deferred Taxes = Net Assets
$3,638,638 — $227,532 — $1,137,657 — $36,221 = $2,237,228

Schedule 4.4 shows the calculation of income per common share on a current cost basis. As in Schedule 4.2 for the historical cost/constant dollar number, each enterprise simply should utilize the number of common shares used in computing EPS in the primary financial statements and divide that number of shares into the current cost income from continuing operations.

As in Schedule 4.3, the net assets determined on a current cost basis for 19X9 in Schedule 4.5 are determined from reference back to Figure

3.3 in Chapter 3 where comparative balance sheets for MR Corporation are presented on a current cost/constant dollar basis. A simple deduction of liabilities and deferred credits from total assets results in the net assets number to be used in the five-year summary.

Recall that in generating the current cost disclosures, any increases or decreases in the current cost of inventories and property, plant, and equipment should be segregated into two components: the increase or decrease due to general changes in purchasing power and any excess increase or decrease in specific prices over changes in the general price level. Schedule 4.6 develops this latter number from Figure 3.4 in Chapter 3 which is a presentation of current cost/constant dollar comparative statements of income and retained earnings for MR Corporation. Notice that this increase or decrease need not be disclosed for fiscal years ending prior to December 25, 1979.

Cash dividends per share must be disclosed in all five years of the summary regardless of the initial year SFAS No. 33 is applied. In the case of MR Corporation, dividends of each year are divided by the 28,000 common shares assumed outstanding each year and then rolled forward to end-of-the-year 19X9 constant dollars. Schedule 4.7 iterates this restatement and roll-forward process. Recall that in the case of MR Corporation, all dividends were assumed to be declared at or near year-end. If this is not the case, e.g., multiple dividend declarations are made, cash dividends must be restated to end-of-the year constant dollars by multiplying amounts declared per share by the end-of-the year CPI and dividing that result by the CPI present at the declaration date.

SCHEDULE 4.4

Income from continuing operations per common share on a current cost basis is computed as follows:

> Step 1. Compute weighted average shares of common stock outstanding for 19X9 (See Schedule 4.2, step 1)
>
> > 28,000 Weighted Average Shares
>
> Step 2. Compute income from continuing operations per common share:
>
> Income from continuing operations (current cost)/weighted average shares outstanding = Income from continuing operations per common share.
>
> > $486,223/28,000 shares = $17.37 per common share

SCHEDULE 4.5

Net assets at year-end on a current cost basis is computed as follows:

From Figure 3.3, Chapter 3—

Total Assets − Current Liabilities − Long-Term Liabilities − Deferred Taxes = Net Assets

$3,701,015 − $227,532 − $1,137,657 − $36,221 = $2,299,605

SCHEDULE 4.6

Excess of increase in specific prices over increase in general price level is computed as follows:

From Figure 3.4, Chapter 3—

Excess of Increase in Specific Price over General Price Level for Inventories	+	Excess of Increase in Specific Prices over General Price Level for Property, Plant, and Equipment	=	Excess of Increase in Specific Price over General Price Level
$950	+	$(74,571)	=	$(73,621)

SCHEDULE 4.7

Cash dividends declared per common share is determined as follows:

Step 1. Determine dividends declared per common share each year— Dividends Declared/Common Shares Outstanding = Dividends Declared per Common Share

19X5	$80,900/28,000 shares	= $2.89
19X6	$90,700/28,000 shares	= $3.24
19X7	$126,620/28,000 shares	= $4.52
19X8	$171,600/28,000 shares	= $6.13
19X9	$219,440/28,000 shares	= $7.84

Step 2. Roll forward dividends declared per share to end-of-the-year 19X9 constant dollars (assume all dividends were declared at year-end)—

SCHEDULE 4.7 (continued)

Dividends Declared per Common Share × (19X9 year-end CPI/year-end CPI) = Dividends Declared per Common Share in 19X9 Constant Dollars

19X5	$2.89 × (228.4/166.3)	= $3.97
19X6	$3.24 × (228.4/174.3)	= $4.25
19X7	$4.52 × (228.4/186.1)	= $5.55
19X8	$6.13 × (228.4/202.9)	= $6.90
19X9	$7.84 × (228.4/228.4)	= $7.84

Schedule 4.8 reflects the market price per common share restatement and roll-forward process necessary since this data must be disclosed in all five years of the summary regardless of the initial application period of SFAS No. 33. In developing this schedule, the following year-end market prices on a nominal dollar basis are assumed: 19X5=$20, 19X6=$26, 19X7=$31, 19X8=$30, and 19X9=$35. For inclusion in the five-year summary, these numbers simply are rolled forward to the end-of-the-year 19X9 constant dollars by using the relationship of the end-of-the-year CPI for each year to the end-of-the-year 1979 CPI.

SCHEDULE 4.8

Market price per common share is computed as follows:

Market Price per Common Share × (19X9 year-end CPI/year-end CPI) = Market Price per Common Share in 19X9 Constant Dollars

19X5	$20 × (228.4/166.3)	=	$27.47
19X6	26 × (228.4/174.3)	=	34.07
19X7	31 × (228.4/186.1)	=	38.05
19X8	30 × (228.4/202.9)	=	33.77
19X9	35 × (228.4/228.4)	=	35.00

Schedules 4.9 through 4.15 relate to the minimum disclosure requirements in terms of average-for-the-year constant dollars as reflected in Figure 4.2. Notice that the only difference in Schedule 4.9 referring to restatement of sales and other operating revenues from Schedule 4.1 (where end-of-the-year constant dollars were used) is that these numbers are restated and rolled forward in terms of average-for-the-year 19X9 constant dollars. Otherwise, the operational mechanics are identical. The same logic applies to Schedule 4.10 where income per common share on an historical cost/constant dollar basis is computed using income determined on average-for-the-year constant dollars.

SCHEDULE 4.9

Net sales and other operating revenues are adjusted as follows:

Adjust sales from each year to average-for-the-year 19X9 constant dollars—

Sales (historical cost) $\times$ (Average 19X9 CPI/Average CPI for the Year) = Sales Adjusted to 19X9 Constant Dollars

19X5	$1,600,000 $\times$ (217.1/161.2)	=	$2,154,839
19X6	2,000,000 $\times$ (217.1/170.5)	=	2,546,628
19X7	2,400,000 $\times$ (217.1/181.5)	=	2,870,744
19X8	3,200,000 $\times$ (217.1/195.4)	=	3,555,374
19X9	4,000,000 $\times$ (217.1/217.1)	=	4,000,000

SCHEDULE 4.10

Income from continuing operations per common share on an historical cost/ constant dollar basis is computed as follows:

Step 1. Compute weighted average shares of common stock for 19X9 (see step 1, Schedule 4.2):

28,000 Weighted Average Shares

Step 2. Compute income from continuing operations per common share:

Income from Continuing Operations (historical cost/constant dollar)/ Weighted Average Shares Outstanding = Income from Continuing Operations per Common Share.

$469,004/28,000 shares   = $16.75 per common share

The determination of net assets restated in terms of average-for-the-year constant dollars requires some calculations as shown in Schedule 4.11 since this number was not generated in a set of complete financial statements; remember that in the comprehensive restatement allowed under SFAS No. 33, MR Corporation elected to use end-of-the-year constant dollars. The first step in this process is to *roll back* to average-for-the-year constant dollars net monetary items on hand at year-end. These items must be rolled back since, in historical cost terms, they are reflective of end-of-the-year constant dollars. The next step in this process is to restate ending inventories to average-for-the year constant dollars as in step 3 of Schedule 2.14 in Chapter 2. Similarly, property, plant, and equipment must be restated by multiplying the historical amounts of these assets by a conversion factor derived by dividing the average CPI of the current year by the base index in effect when the assets were purchased. Finally, as in step 4 of Schedule 4.11, net assets at year-end are determined by summing the restated *net* monetary assets, the restated ending inventories, and the restated property, plant, and equipment. Notice that net monetary assets are utilized in Schedule 4.11 and, since all liabilities of MR Corporation are monetary, no deduction for liabilities in ascertaining net assets is necessary.

SCHEDULE 4.11

Net assets at year-end on an historical cost/constant dollar basis is computed as follows:

Step 1. Roll back net monetary items to average-for-the-year 19X9 constant dollars

Net Monetary Assets $\times$ (average 19X9 CPI/year-end 19X9 CPI) = Net Monetary Assets in 19X9 Constant dollars

$$\$655,590 \times (217.1/228.4) = \$623,155$$

Step 2. Restate ending inventories to average-for-the-year 19X9 constant dollars (see step 3, Schedule 2.14, Chapter 2):

Restated Ending Inventories $458,256

Step 3. Restate property, plant, and equipment to average-for-the-year 19X9 constant dollars (see Schedule 2.5, Chapter 2 for base indices):

Property, Plant, and Equipment (historical cost) $\times$ (average 19X9 CPI/ Base CPI) = Property, Plant, and Equipment Restated to 19X9 Constant Dollars

a.	Land	$ 80,000 $\times$ (217.1/155.4)	=	$111,763
b.	Buildings (net)	437,500 $\times$ (217.1/155.4)	=	611,205
c.	Equipment (net)	157,500 $\times$ (217.1/155.4)	=	220,034
d.	Equipment (net)	88,000 $\times$ (217.1/187.2)	=	102,056
				$1,045,058

Step 4. Determine net assets at year-end:

Restated Net Monetary Assets + Restated Ending Inventories + Restated Property, Plant, and Equipment = Net Assets in 19X9 Constant dollars

$623,155 + $458,256 + $1,045,058 = $2,126,469

In Schedule 4.12, the current cost income per share is calculated. Notice that the only difference in Schedule 4.12 and Schedule 4.4 is that current cost income from continuing operations was determined using average-for-the-year constant dollars in the former case and end-of-the-year constant dollars in the latter.

Schedule 4.13 involves the determination of net assets at year-end on a current cost basis. Net monetary items still need to be rolled back to average-for-the-year constant dollars as in step 1 of Schedule 4.11. The average current cost of inventories may be determined using a two-point average since purchases were assumed to have been made evenly throughout the year by MR Corporation. The same approach is followed in restating the property, plant, and equipment in step 3 of Schedule 4.13. And, as in Schedule 4.11, the determination of the current cost of net assets at year-end stated in terms of average-for-the-year constant dollars involves simply adding the restated net monetary assets to the current cost of inventories and the current cost of property, plant, and equipment.

The restatement of cash dividends per share on an average purchasing power basis involves the same mechanics as the restatement for end-of-the-year purchasing power (see Schedule 4.7). Schedule 4.14 presents this restatement and roll-forward process that involves multiplying the dividends declared at the end of each year by a conversion factor determined through dividing the 19X9 average CPI by the end-of-the-year CPI for each year restated and rolled forward. If dividends are declared evenly throughout the year, historical amounts should reflect reasonable approximation of average-for-the-year constant dollars. The same restatement and roll-forward process is used in Schedule 4.15 where the market price per share at the end of each year is adjusted using the relationship of the 19X9 average-for-the-year CPI and the end-of-the-year CPI for each year included in the five-year summary.

SCHEDULE 4.12

Income from continuing operations per common share on a current cost basis is computed as follows:

Step 1. Compute weighted average shares of common stock outstanding for 19X9 (see Schedule 4.2, step 1):

28,000 Weighted Average Shares

Step 2. Compute income from continuing operations per common share:

Income from Continuing Operations (current cost)/Weighted Average Shares Outstanding = Income from Continuing Operations per Common Share.

$459,930/28,000 shares = $16.43 per common share

SCHEDULE 4.13

Net assets at year-end on a current cost basis is computed as follows:

Step 1. Roll back net monetary items to average-for-the-year 19X9 constant dollars (see step 1, Schedule 4.11):

Restated Net Monetary Assets $623,155

Step 2. Determine average current cost inventories:

(Current Cost of Beginning Inventories + Current Cost of Ending Inventories)/2 = Average Current Cost of Inventories* (see Schedule 3.3, Chapter 3)

($427,000 + $485,000)/2 = $456,000

Step 3. Determine average net current cost of property, plant, and equipment:

(Net Current Cost of Beginning Property, Plant, and Equipment + Net Current Cost of Ending Property, Plant, and Equipment)/2 = Average Net Current Cost of Property, Plant, and Equipment* (see Schedule 3.15, Chapter 3)
($1,194,627 + $1,159,015)/2 = $1,176,821

Step 4. Determine net assets at year-end:

Restated Net Monetary Assets + Current Cost of Inventories + Net Current Cost of Property, Plant, and Equipment = Net Assets
$623,155 + $456,000 + $1,176,821 = $2,255,976

*These items need not be price level adjusted if no seasonality exists. Since this is the average current cost for the year, it is stated in average-for-the-year constant dollars.

SCHEDULE 4.14

Cash dividends declared per common share is determined as follows:

Step 1. Determine dividends declared per common share each year (see step 1, Schedule 4.7):

19X5	$2.89
19X6	3.24
19X7	4.52
19X8	6.13
19X9	7.84

Step 2. Roll forward dividends declared per common share to average-for-the-year 19X9 constant dollars (assume all dividends were declared at year-end):

Dividends Declared per Common Share $\times$ (average 19X9 CPI/year-end CPI) = Dividends Declared per Common Share in 19X9 Constant Dollars

19X5	$2.89	$\times$ (217.1/166.3)	=	$3.77
19X6	3.24	$\times$ (217.1/174.3)	=	4.04
19X7	4.52	$\times$ (217.1/186.1)	=	5.27
19X8	6.13	$\times$ (217.1/202.9)	=	6.56
19X9	7.84	$\times$ (217.1/228.4)	=	7.45

SCHEDULE 4.15

Market price per common share is computed as follows:

Market Price per Common Share $\times$ (average 19X9 CPI/year-end CPI) = Market Price per Common Share in 19X9 Constant Dollars

19X5	$20	$\times$ (217.1/166.3)	=	$26.11
19X6	26	$\times$ (217.1/174.3)	=	32.38
19X7	31	$\times$ (217.1/186.1)	=	36.16
19X8	30	$\times$ (217.1/202.9)	=	32.10
19X9	35	$\times$ (217.1/228.4)	=	33.27

A final note of emphasis is that this five-year summary data was prepared in current year constant dollars. But remember that SFAS No. 33 allows enterprises to roll back data in terms of base year (currently 1967) constant dollars. If the base year alternative is chosen, the mechanics of restatement are essentially the same except that amounts are rolled back to the base year as opposed to rolled forward to current year constant dollars. Since the base year alternative seems to be inferior to choosing the current year approach, the former is not illustrated in this book.

Comparing the Disclosure Requirements of
SFAS No. 33 with Those of ASR No. 190

The Securities and Exchange Commission (SEC) recently withdrew the reporting requirements of ASR No. 190 for those enterprises that comply with the current cost disclosure requirements of the FASB in SFAS No. 33. Since the ASR No. 190 disclosures no longer are applicable, no purpose would be served in illustrating the requirements of the document; but, since many enterprises affected by SFAS No. 33 previously have been reporting under, and have grown relatively accustomed to, ASR No. 190, a summary of the differences in the two sets of reporting requirements may help enterprises better understand SFAS No. 33.

Note should be made that ASR No. 190 required certain replacement cost disclosures but no adjustments on a constant dollar basis were required to be disclosed. Therefore, the following summary of differences reflects only changes from reporting under the SEC's replacement costing to the FASB's current costing and involves no mention of the historical cost/constant dollar disclosures required under SFAS No. 33.[2]

1. The disclosures required under SFAS No. 33 are more extensive than the disclosures required under ASR No. 190.
2. The requirements of SFAS No. 33 are applicable to public enterprises with inventories and gross property, plant, and equipment in excess of $125 million or with total assets in excess of $1 billion, whereas ASR No. 190 applied to public enterprises with inventories and gross property, plant, and equipment in excess of $100 million.
3. The only exclusions from the current cost disclosure requirements of SFAS No. 33 are income-producing real estate properties and unprocessed natural resources, whereas ASR No. 190 excluded land, assets not intended to be replaced, and construction in process from the replacement cost disclosures.
4. SFAS No. 33 requires current cost measurements for assets related to contracts and projects as of the date of use or commitment to the contract; current replacement cost measurements for such assets may or may not have been required under ASR No. 190 depending primarily on whether the contract or project was of a recurring nature.
5. SFAS No. 33 requires only disclosure of current cost *or* lower recoverable amount (net realizable value or value in use, as appro-

---

[2] Ibid., pp. 78–79.

        priate) in the current cost measurement of assets; ASR No. 190
required disclosure of replacement cost with separate disclosure
for net realizable value when lower than replacement cost.

6. SFAS No. 33 defines the current cost of an asset as the amount
of cash that would have to be paid to acquire *an identical asset*
currently. SEC Staff Accounting Bulletin No. 7 defines the replacement cost of an asset as the lowest amount that would have
to be paid in the normal course of business to obtain *a new asset*
of equivalent operating or productive capability.

7. Under the current cost basis utilized in SFAS No. 33, cost of
goods sold and inventories *should not* include expected cost savings from production and labor efficiencies resulting from
obtaining new facilities and equipment since there is not assumed
change in assets. ASR No. 190 allowed such adjustments.

8. SFAS No. 33 requires use of the same depreciation methods for
current cost purposes as are used for historical cost purposes in
the primary financial statements, unless the latter were chosen to
offset in part the effect of inflation. ASR No. 190 requires use of
straight-line depreciation when assets are being depreciated on
any time-expired basis in the historical cost financial statements.

Management Discussion of the
Supplementary Disclosures Required under
SFAS No. 33

The most difficult aspect of the SFAS No. 33 disclosure requirements
imposed on management of a reporting enterprise will be attempting to
explain and discuss the significance of these supplemental disclosures.
This discussion is required in paragraph 37 of SFAS No. 33 which states:

> Enterprises shall provide, in their financial reports, explanations of
> the information disclosed in accordance with this Statement and discus-
> sions of its significance in the circumstances of the enterprise.

The purpose of this section of this chapter is to present some guidance to
enterprises attempting to develop this management discussion.

Neither SFAS No. 33 nor any other document provides any standard
format for developing the management discussion. These explanations
could appear in a variety of places within the financial report, such as
footnotes to the supplemental data, the president's letter, a financial review section, or elsewhere. In any event, the president's letter probably
will contain some general commentary on the meaning of these supplemental disclosures.

An example of the type of explanation that might be included in financial reports follows:

> We use the LIFO method of accounting for cost of goods sold which charges current costs to the results of operations for both financial reporting and income tax purposes. Accordingly, no adjustment to cost of goods sold was necessary for the purpose of determining the supplemental inflation accounting data. Other companies in our industry use the FIFO method of accounting which generally results in higher income for financial reporting purposes. But these companies will show large adjustments to cost of goods sold in the inflation accounting information which are not deductible for tax purposes.

and

> Because the inflation adjustments to historical depreciation expense are not deductible for tax purposes, our effective tax rate in the supplemental current cost information has increased to 70% which is well in excess of the statutory rate of 46 percent.[3]

SFAS No. 33 identifies a number of advantages and disadvantages taken into account in deciding what supplementary disclosures were to be required. The following summary of various issues raised in SFAS No. 33 may be helpful to management in explaining and discussing the historical cost/constant dollar and current cost disclosures.[4]

1. Estimating future cash flows is an important objective of financial statement users. The supplementary information may provide additional means of estimating such cash flows as follows:
   (a) Current cost data may be considered a conservative estimate of net present value of future cash flow.
   (b) Current cost margin information together with current cost of inventory may be useful to assess cash flow, especially if selling prices reflect changes in costs.
   (c) Assets that are stated at lower recoverable amounts are by definition stated at the present value of management's estimate of future cash flow.
2. Current cost information may be useful in analyzing an enterprise's capability of maintaining its operating capacity without impairing its ability to declare dividends.
3. Alternately, constant dollar information may be useful in analyzing an enterprise's capacity for maintaining the purchasing power of the shareholders' investment and of sustaining an adequate return on that investment.
4. The use of a uniform unit of measure (constant dollars) should enhance the results of ratio analysis and other usual comparisons

---

[3] Ernst & Whinney, "Inflation Accounting," *Financial Reporting Developments* (Cleveland: Ernst & Whinney, December 1979) p. 5.
[4] Deloitte Haskins & Sells, op. cit., pp. 76–77.

of financial data. This uniformity also should enhance the significance of comparisons with other enterprises, both within the same industry and in other industries.

5. Inflation affects different prices in different ways. Therefore, presentation of holding gains or losses, both before and after deducting the effect of general inflation, highlights the specific effects of inflation on an enterprise's activities.

Users of annual financial reports will encounter a plethora of information that the FASB believes will prove useful in assessing the impact of inflation on the reporting enterprise. And management has a vested interest in explaining the significance of the inflation data since, unlike the SEC's replacement cost data, the FASB's disclosures must appear in annual reports to shareholders and will be very visible. Ernst & Whinney suggest a threefold challenge facing management in deriving these narrative explanations:

1. *To describe precisely what the data attempt to measure.* Management can best accomplish this objective with the matter-of-fact statements concerning the dual measurement issue (i.e., general inflation vs. specific price changes) and how the data was computed.

2. *To comment on the relevance of the required measurements to the effect of changing prices on the company.* Adequate descriptions of management views on the general relevance of the two measurement approaches and the significance of the various measurements to their company will contribute to achieving this objective.

3. *To provide additional information that will aid users in understanding the effects of inflation on the company.* Such additional information could be both quantitative and qualitative and often will depend on the individual circumstances of the company and the environment in which it operates.[5]

Audit Implications

As was the case with the replacement cost disclosures which certain SEC registrants were required to make, the current cost and constant dollar disclosures required by the FASB are supplemental in nature. Since the disclosures are supplemental and therefore outside of the financial statements, the independent auditor is not required to audit the supplemental disclosures. However, since the supplemental disclosures are in-

---

[5] Ernst & Whinney, op. cit., pp. 19–21.

cluded within the annual report which contains the auditor's report, there are audit implications to the supplemental current cost and constant dollar disclosures.

The supplemental disclosures are financial in nature and can be presented in statement form. Therefore, to avoid confusion on the part of the financial statement readers, the supplemental disclosures should clearly be labeled as "unaudited." No statements either in the auditor's report or in the management discussions should be made which would imply that the disclosures have been audited.

If the supplemental disclosures are not labeled "unaudited" or if management makes reference in its discussion to any procedures which the auditor has applied, the auditor's report on the audited financial statements should also include a paragraph stating that the supplementary disclosures have not been audited and that the auditor is disclaiming an opinion on the supplemental disclosures. The auditor should take care in the wording of this paragraph to avoid the misleading implication that (1) the supplemental disclosures have been audited or (2) the disclaimer of opinion applies to the audited financial statements.

The auditor must also apply limited procedures on the supplemental disclosures. The objective of limited procedures is to provide the auditor with a basis for assessing the reasonableness of the supplemental disclosures. Initially, the auditor should determine whether the enterprise is required to make the supplemental disclosures. If the enterprise is required by SFAS No. 33 to make the supplemental current cost and constant dollar disclosures and has not done so, the auditor should insist that the enterprise make the required disclosures. The auditor should then read the supplemental disclosures to insure that the minimum disclosure requirements have been made.

The auditor should then make certain inquiries of management. These inquiries are designed to provide the auditor with a basis of determining the reasonableness of the disclosures, not to render an opinion on the disclosures. The auditor should determine that the proper indices and base periods have been used in making the constant dollar adjustments to the historical cost data (see Chapter 2). The auditor should then inquire of management what procedures were used in determining the current cost amounts. If specific price indices have been used, the auditor should assure himself that the indices used were appropriate for the assets involved.

Inquiries should also be made of management as to the depreciation method used in computing the current cost and constant dollar income figures. Normally, the same depreciation method used in computing historical cost depreciation should be used on the current cost and constant dollar figures. Further, the auditor should make inquiries as to the recoverable amounts of the assets involved. The auditor should then ensure that assets have not been valued in excess of their recoverable amounts in either the current cost or the constant dollar disclosures.

The management discussion of the supplemental disclosures should also be read by the auditor. In reading the management discussion, the auditor should look for any inconsistencies between the discussion and management's responses to the auditor's inquiries. The auditor should also determine that the management discussion is consistent with the supplemental disclosures and is appropriate in light of the economic circumstances in which the enterprise operates.

If in the course of the auditor's review of the supplemental information he becomes aware of material misstatements, inconsistencies, or failures to comply with the reporting requirements of SFAS No. 33, the auditor should expand his scope in an effort to resolve the apparent inconsistencies. If further investigations lead the auditor to believe that the supplemental disclosures are inadequate or incorrect, he should request that management make appropriate modifications. If appropriate modifications are not made to the supplemental disclosures it may be necessary for the auditor to refer to them in his audit report.

In summary, the auditor must ensure that there are no references that would mislead the financial statement reader into believing the supplemental disclosures have been audited. The auditor should also see that the supplemental disclosures are reasonable in the circumstances and in compliance with SFAS No. 33.

Checklist of Compliance with Disclosure Requirements of SFAS No. 33

In this and the previous two chapters, a large amount of detailed financial reporting has been examined. What is presented in this section is a compliance checklist (checklist 4.1) that may be helpful to enterprises in attempting to analyze whether the provisions of SFAS No. 33, if applicable, have been applied properly. It should be examined for "no" answers which indicate a *possible* deficiency in applying SFAS No. 33. Items marked with an * need not be disclosed for fiscal years ending before December 25, 1979. And none of the current cost disclosures must be made in annual reports for fiscal years ending before December 25, 1980. Questions 1 and 2 relate to the required applicability of SFAS No. 33 to the reporting enterprise; subsequent questions assume that SFAS No. 33 is being applied. Paragraph references relate to SFAS No. 33.

CHECKLIST 4.1*

Question

1. Is the reporting enterprise a public enterprise that prepares its financial statements in U.S. dollars per U.S. GAAP? (para. 23)
2. Did the reporting enterprise have, at the beginning of the fiscal year, either (a) inventories and property, plant, and equipment (before depreciation, depletion, and amortization) in the aggregate in excess of $125 million, or (b) total assets in excess of $1 billion? (para. 23)
3. Does every published annual report contain the supplementary disclosures required in SFAS No. 33? (para. 27)

DO THE CURRENT YEAR DISCLOSURES INCLUDE (for questions 4-8):

4. Income from continuing operations on a historical cost/constant dollar basis? (para. 29(a))
5. The purchasing power gain or loss on net monetary items *outside* income from continuing operations? (para. 29(b))
6. Income from continuing operations on a current cost basis? (para. 30(a))
7. Current cost amounts of inventories and property, plant, and equipment? (para. 30(b))
8. Increases or decreases in current cost of inventories and property, plant, and equipment outside income from continuing operations? (para. 30(c))
9. Is the supplementary income from continuing operations disclosed in a statement format or reconciliation format? (para. 32)
10. Does the historical cost/constant dollar income from continuing operations include adjustments to or amounts for cost of goods sold, depreciation, depletion, amortization, and reductions of historical cost amounts to lower recoverable amounts? (para. 32)
11. Does the current cost income from continuing operations include adjustments to or amounts for cost of goods sold, depreciation, depletion, and amortization? (para. 32)

DO THE FIVE-YEAR SUMMARY DISCLOSURES INCLUDE (for questions 12-23):

12. Net sales and other operating revenues? (para. 35(a))
13. Historical cost/constant dollar income from continuing operations? (para. 35(b)(1))*

---

*This checklist is adapted from Thomas A. Ratcliffe and Paul Munter, "Auditors' Responsibility Regarding Supplementary Information," *The CPA Journal* (February 1981).

CHECKLIST 4.1 (continued)

14. Historical cost/constant dollar income per common share from continuing operations? (para. 35(b)(2))*
15. Historical cost/constant dollar net assets at fiscal year-end? (para. 35(b)(3))*
16. Current cost income from continuing operations? (para. 35(c)(1))*
17. Current cost income per common share from continuing operations? (para. 35(c)(2))*
18. Current cost net assets at fiscal year-end? (para. 35(c)(3))*
19. Increases or decreases in current cost amounts of inventories and property, plant, and equipment? (para. 35(c)(4))*
20. Purchasing power gain or loss on net monetary items? (para. 35(d)(1))*
21. Cash dividends declared per common share? (para. 35(d)(2))
22. Market price per common share at fiscal year-end? (para. 35(d)(3))
23. CPI used to restate supplementary information? (para. 35)

    DO THE NOTES TO THE SUPPLEMENTARY INFORMATION INCLUDE: (for questions 24-29):

24. Reasons for omitting current cost information for the current year when current cost and historical cost-constant dollar amounts are not materially different? (para. 31)
25. Aggregate current cost and historical cost-constant dollar depreciation expense if the expense is allocated among various categories in the supplementary disclosures? (para. 33)
26. Principal types of information used to calculate current cost of inventories, property, plant, and equipment, cost of goods sold, depreciation, depletion, and amortization? (para. 34(a))
27. Differences, if any, in methods and estimates used in computing historical cost/constant dollar and current cost depreciation from those used in determining historical cost depreciation? (para. 34(b))
28. The exclusion from supplementary information computations of any adjustments to or allocations of the amount of income tax expense in the primary financial statements? (para. 34(c))
29. The average level CPI or year-end CPI, whichever is used, for each year included in the five-year summary? (para. 35)
30. Do published financial reports include explanations of the supplementary information and discussions of its significance in the circumstances of the enterprise? (para. 37)

APPENDIX

MR Corporation
Statement of Income on a Current Cost/Constant Dollar Basis
(Statement Format)
for the Year Ended December 31, 19X9

	As Reported in Primary Financial Statements	Adjusted for General Inflation	Adjusted for Changes in Specific Prices (Current Costs)
Sales	$4,000,000	$4,000,000	$4,000,000
Cost of Goods Sold	2,600,000	2,652,026	2,656,781
Gross Profit	$1,400,000	$1,347,974	$1,343,219
Operating Expenses (excluding depreciation)	$ 480,000	$ 480,000	$ 480,000
Depreciation	76,000	103,570	107,889
Provision for Income Taxes	295,400	295,400	295,400
Income from Continuing Operations	$ 548,600	$ 469,004	$ 459,930
Purchasing power loss		$ (32,570)	$ (32,570)
Increase in specific prices of inventories and property, plant, and equipment held during the year			$ 126,924
Effect of increase in general price level			(194,820)
Excess of increase in general price level over increase in specific prices			$ (67,896)

149

MR Corporation

Five-Year Comparison of Selected Supplementary Financial Data
Adjusted for Effects of Changing Prices
(In Average-for-the-Year 19X9 Constant Dollars)

	19X5	19X6	19X7	19X8	19X9
Net Sales and Operating Revenues (see Schedule 4.9)	$2,154,839	$2,546,628	$2,870,744	$3,555,374	$4,000,000
Historical Cost Information Adjusted for General Inflation:					
Income from Continuing Operations					469,004
Income per Common Share from Continuing Operations					16.75
Net Assets at Year-End					2,126,469
Current Cost Information:					
Income from Continuing Operations					459,930
Income per Common Share from Continuing Operations					16.43
Net Assets at Year-End					2,255,976
Excess of Increase in Specific Prices over Increase in General Price Level					(67,896)
Other Information:					
Purchasing Power Gain (loss) on Net Monetary Items					(32,570)
Cash Dividends Declared per Common Share	3.77	4.04	5.27	6.56	7.45
Market Price per Common Share at Year-End	26.11	32.38	36.16	32.10	33.27
Average-for-the-Year CPI	161.2	170.5	181.5	195.4	217.1

CHAPTER 5

How to Use Cost Behavior Patterns in Inflationary Periods

▣▣▣▣▣▣▣▣▣▣▣▣

An understanding of cost behavior patterns is essential to informed decision-making concerning problems such as determining what products to manufacture, how much of a product to manufacture, what goods should be used in the manufacturing process, and when and how many goods should be purchased. Further, cost behavior analysis is useful in assessing operational performance and in estimating costs expected to be incurred in future operations. To facilitate cost behavior analysis, several statistical and nonstatistical methodologies are used in practice. Unfortunately, in the application of a particular strategy, many times the impact of inflation on the variables under consideration is ignored. The purpose of this chapter is to provide some operational guidance in introducing inflationary impacts into cost behavior analysis. Four widely used tools in assessing cost behavior patterns will be examined: (1) simple regression, (2) multiple regression, (3) high-low points, and (4) scatter diagrams. But first, an overview of statistical analysis is presented to acquaint the reader with the fundamental knowledge necessary to understand the examples that follow.

The Use of Statistical Analysis in Assessing Cost Behavior Patterns

In systems such as manufacturing processes, it typically is useful to examine what impact changes in certain variables have on other variables and/or the end result of the total system. For example, if an objective of management was to estimate overhead costs for a subsequent time period, an analysis of factors that comprise this type of costs should be useful. There may be a simple functional relationship between factors such as the number of direct labor hours worked and the total overhead cost incurred. But, in reality, any such assumption generally cannot be made, since most functional relationships are too difficult to assess in simple terms. When these complexities exist, functional relationships may be approximated by a simple mathematical function, e.g., a polynominal, which approximates the true relationship among variables within a defined range of activity.

One of the most common means of statistically analyzing relationships among data in business today is repression analysis. Use of this statistical tool requires identification of two types of variables: (1) *independent variables*, which either can be set to a desired value or amount (e.g., number of direct labor hours worked) or else may be observed but not controlled (e.g., inflation), and (2) *dependent variables*, which are affected by changes in independent variables (e.g., an increase in cost of a product).

Regression analysis attempts to measure the impact that changes in independent variables have on dependent variables. Changes in the independent variable may be controllable or uncontrollable. For example, the cost of manufacturing a product should increase as a result of a *controllable* change to the use of more expensive resource inputs. But this product cost also may increase simply due to an *uncontrollable* increase in the cost of goods due to inflation.

Regression analysis calculates the statistical relationship between the independent variable(s) and the dependent variable by minimizing the sum of squared error. For an in-depth discussion of regression analysis, the interested reader is referred to *Applied Regression Analysis* by Draper & Smith.[1] The following sections of this chapter discuss the use of regres-

---

[1]Draper, Norman and Smith, Harry, *Applied Regression Analysis* (New York: John Wiley & Sons, Inc., 1966).

sion analysis results in managerial decision-making. First simple regression analysis and then multiple regression analysis will be illustrated.

Use of Simple Regression in Cost Behavior Analysis

In time periods where inflation is not significant, cost-relationships that have existed in the past will yield reasonable approximations for predicting future cost patterns. However, as will be demonstrated in this section, persistent inflation can change the relationship between measures of activity and the costs related to such activity.

Based upon a study of its manufacturing operations, the management of MR Corporation believes that its manufacturing overhead costs are related to its manufacturing activity level. While management is uncertain as to how best to measure its activity level, the study of its operations has revealed that activity level can be measured by the following variables: Machine Hours, Direct Labor Hours, Indirect Labor Hours, and Idle Time Hours (designated as X_2, X_3, X_4, X_5 respectively in Table 5-1). MR Corporation collected data relative to its manufacturing operations and this data is presented in Table 5.1. If management has reason to believe that the use of one measure of activity level will yield predictive results of sufficient accuracy, a simple regression is all that needs to be used. A simple regression computes the statistical relationship between one independent variable (a measure of activity level) and a dependent variable (overhead costs). A multiple regression (to be discussed after the results of the simple regression analysis are presented) computes the statistical relationship between two or more independent variables and a dependent variable.

Table 5.2 presents the results of the four simple regressions. The F-values in the table are the ratios of the explained change in the dependent variable value to the unexplained change in the dependent variable value. The R^2 value indicates the percentage of the change in the dependent variable value which is explained (in a statistical sense) by changes in the independent variable. The probability of $R^2 = 0$ in the table indicates the chance that the computed R^2 value is a random (or accidental) result. The lower the probability, the more likely that the computed R^2 value is an accurate depiction of the relationship between the independent and dependent variables.

TABLE 5.1
List of Variables and Data
Used in Formulating the Regression Model

X_1 Time Period	X_2 Machine hours (in thousands)	X_3 Direct Labor Hours	X_4 Indirect Labor Hours	X_5 Idle Time Hours (in hundreds)	X_6 Overhead Costs (in thousands)
1	7,000	26,000	6,000	600	$78,500
2	1,000	29,000	15,000	520	74,300
3	11,000	56,000	8,000	200	104,300
4	11,000	31,000	8,000	470	87,600
5	7,000	52,000	6,000	330	95,900
6	11,000	55,000	9,000	220	109,200
7	3,000	71,000	17,000	60	102,700
8	1,000	31,000	22,000	440	72,500
9	2,000	54,000	18,000	220	93,100
10	21,000	47,000	4,000	260	115,900
11	1,000	40,000	23,000	340	83,800
12	11,000	66,000	9,000	120	113,300
13	10,000	68,000	8,000	120	109,400

154

TABLE 5.2
Results of Simple Regressions

Number of Observations in Each Regression: 13
Dependent Variable: X_6

Independent Variable	Overall F	R^2	Probability $R^2=0$	β Coefficient	Constant Term
X_2	12.602	53.39%	.0046	1.869	81.479
X_3	21.961	66.63%	.0007	.789	57.424
X_4	4.403	28.58%	.0598	−1.256	110.203
X_5	22.799	67.45%	.0006	− .738	117.568

An examination of Table 5.2 reveals that if management of MR Corporation believes that one predictive variable is sufficient, overhead costs can best be predicted with idle time hours as the independent (or predictive) variable. This can be seen by examining the R^2 value when each independent variable is regressed against overhead costs. Idle time hours has the highest R^2 (67.45%) when regressed against overhead costs. This is closely followed, however, by direct labor hours ($R^2 = 66.63\%$).

Before deciding to use idle time hours as the predictive variable, MR Corporation should determine if idle time hours can be estimated with reasonable accuracy. If significant problems exist in making this estimation and direct labor hours can be projected more accurately, MR Corporation may prefer to use direct labor hours as the prediction variable in attempting to predict overhead costs. This serves to illustrate the fact that budgeted figures cannot be any more accurate than the input used to budget the costs.

Use of Multiple Regression in
Cost Behavior Analysis

If the management of MR Corporation believes that much more meaningful results can be budgeted if two or more predictive variables are used, it can compute all possible multiple regressions with two or more of the independent variables regressed against overhead costs. The results of these regressions are presented in Table 5.3. It can be seen that the best predictive ability would appear to result when all four independent variables are used ($R^2 = 98.24\%$). However, a closer examination of the table indicates that using just two independent variables—either machine hours and idle time hours ($R^2 = 97.25\%$) or machine hours and direct labor hours ($R^2 = 97.86\%$) —yields nearly the same predictive ability.

TABLE 5.3
Results of Multiple Regressions

Number of Observations in Each Regression: 13
Dependent Variable: X_6

Independent Variable	Overall F	R^2	Probability $R^2=0$	β Coefficient for Each Independent Variable	Constant Term
X_2 X_3	229.504	97.86%	.0001	1.468, .662	52.577
X_2 X_4	6.066	54.82%	.0188	2.312, .494	72.349
X_2 X_5	176.627	97.25%	.0001	1.440, -.614	103.097
X_3 X_4	27.685	84.70%	.0001	.731, -1.008	72.075
X_3 X_5	10.628	68.01%	.0034	.311, -.457	94.160
X_4 X_5	72.267	93.53%	.0001	-1.200, -.725	131.282
X_2 X_3 X_4	166.346	98.23%	.0001	1.696, .651, .250	48.194
X_2 X_3 X_5	166.832	98.23%	.0001	1.452, .416, -.237	71.648
X_2 X_4 X_5	157.266	98.13%	.0001	1.052, -.410, -.643	111.684
X_3 X_4 X_5	107.374	97.28%	.0001	-.923, -1.448, -1.557	203.642
X_2 X_3 X_4 X_5	111.480	98.24%	.0001	1.551, .510, .102, -.144	62.405

How, then, can MR Corporation avoid computing all possible multiple regressions and still develop an accurate predictive model? One possible technique is to perform a stepwise multiple regression with the four independent variables. This technique is available in most statistical software packages. It, in essence, performs all possible regressions and chooses the best one, given cost-benefit constraints. MR Corporation can alter the cost-benefit relationship by setting the significance level for the variables to be entered into the stepwise multiple regression model. Table 5.4 presents the results when management uses a 5% level for variables to enter. This means that management has decided that it is cost efficient to include a variable in the predictive model only if there is a 95% probability (100%–5%) that the incoming variable will add to the predictive ability of the model. As Table 5.4 indicates, using this threshold, the stepwise multiple regression model has computed that the use of machine hours and idle time hours as independent variables will yield budgeted overhead cost figures that are sufficiently accurate to provide a basis for evaluating actual performance. Management can alter the variables by raising or lowering the 5% threshold. A lower threshold would result in more variables being used, but implementation costs also increase. Given the management decision to use a 5% threshold, machine hours and idle time hours will allow accurate budgeting of overhead costs. Management would then use the following formula to budget overhead costs:

$$X_6 = 103.1 + 1.4X_2 - .6X_5$$

where X_6 = overhead costs
X_2 = machine hours
X_5 = idle time hours

Therefore, if management anticipates an activity level of 10,000 machine hours and 500 idle time hours in the next month, the budgeted overhead cost would be \$114,100 ($X_6 = 103.1 + 1.4 * 10 - .6 * 5$).

TABLE 5.4
Results of Stepwise Regression—Using Variable X_2-X_6

Number of Observations: 13
Dependent Variable: X_6

Step	Independent Variable	Overall F	R^2	Probability $R^2 = 0$	β Coefficient for Each Independent Variable	Constant Term
1	X_5	22.801	67.45%	.0006	-.738	117.568
2	X_5 X_2	176.634	97.24%	.0001	-.614, 1.440	103.097

No other variable entered since none were significant at the 5% level of significance.

To this point, none of the regression models considered have accounted for inflation in the budgeting of overhead costs. Given the inflationary pattern which has persisted in the U.S. economy (and the economies of many developed countries), it is likely that the cost behavior patterns of the past may change. How can MR Corporation incorporate an inflation factor into its multiple regression model? Management could add an independent variable to the multiple regression which measures inflation such as the Consumer Price Index (CPI). However, if this were done, management would be in the position of having to predict the rate of increase in the CPI. There is another solution which does not require management to predict changes in the CPI. Management can add a time variable to the independent data set as a surrogate for the inflation factor. The time variable is incremented by one for each subsequent time period (see X_1 in Table 5.1). Perhaps it can be seen that the time variable is a surrogate for inflation by considering the results of a simple regression using time as the independent variable and inflation (as measured by the CPI) as the dependent variable. The slope of the line—as measured by the β Coefficient—is the predicted rate of inflation. Likewise, by inserting time as an independent variable in the multiple regression used to budget overhead costs, the β Coefficient of time is the best estimate of the rate of inflation. Using this approach, management needs only to increment time by one for each period rather than predicting the subsequent inflation rate.

Table 5.5 presents the results of the stepwise multiple regression when time is considered as an independent variable (again a 5% threshold is used to enhance comparability).

An examination of Table 5.5 yields an interesting result. Not only does it indicate that time—and hence inflation—is an important factor to consider in budgeting overhead costs, but it also shows that machine hours and direct labor hours—not idle time hours—should be used in conjunction with time. Using this new model, overhead costs would be budgeted using the following equation:

$$X_6 = 52.5 + .2X_1 + 1.5X_2 + .6X_3$$

where X_6 = overhead costs
X_1 = time period
X_2 = machine hours
X_3 = direct labor hours

Therefore, if management is budgeting 10,000 machine hours and 15,000 direct labor hours for the next month (time period 14, since 13 periods were used to develop the budget model), it would budget $79,300 in overhead costs (X_6 = 52.5 + .2 * 14 + 1.5 * 10 + .6 * 15). The coefficient attached to the time period (.2) indicates that overhead costs can be expected to increase by $200 each month due simply to the inflationary pattern which persists. This increase will continue—as long as these same cost behavior patterns remain unchanged—regardless of the changes in the activity level.

TABLE 5.5
Results of Stepwise Regression—Using Variables X_1–X_6

Number of Observations: 13
Dependent Variable: X_6

Step	Independent Variable	Overall F	R^2	Probability $R^2 = 0$	β Coefficient for Each Independent Variable	Constant Term
1	X_1	3.381	23.53%	.0930	1.873	82.308
2	X_1 X_2	10.841	68.43%	.0031	1.512, 1.730	71.926
3	X_1 X_2 X_3	145.520	97.98%	.0001	.155, 1.467, .641	52.527

No other variables entered since none were significant at the 5% level of significance.

An Examination of High-Low Points in Cost Behavior Analysis

An occasionally used, yet over-simplified, method of assessing cost behavior relationships is the high-low points method. This method requires the plotting of two costs representing the highest and lowest costs over a contemplated relevant range of activity.[2] The slope of the line connecting these two points is deemed representative of variable cost per unit of activity. But this plotting may or may not represent an acceptable approximation of the cost function contingent on the decision under analysis and on the behavior of the function over the entire relevant range.

The high-low points method is reflected in the following equation:

$$y' = a + bx$$

where $y' = $ estimate of overhead cost
$a = $ overhead cost at zero volume
$b = $ variable cost rate (slope of the line)
$x = $ measure of volume

In the case of MR Corporation, the overhead cost relationship for each prediction variable would be determined as follows (see Table 5-1 for cost amounts):

$$b = \frac{y_H - y_L}{x_H - x_L} = \frac{\text{change in overhead costs}}{\text{change in machine hours}}$$

$$b = \frac{\$115,900 - \$72,500}{21,000 - 1,000} = \frac{\$43,400}{20,000} = \$2.17 \text{ per machine hour}$$

and

$$b = \frac{y_H - y_L}{x_H - x_L} = \frac{\text{change in overhead costs}}{\text{change in direct labor hours}}$$

$$b = \frac{\$102,700 - \$78,500}{71,000 - 26,000} = \frac{\$24,200}{45,000} = \$.54 \text{ per direct labor hour}$$

and

$$b = \frac{y_H - y_L}{x_H - x_L} = \frac{\text{change in overhead costs}}{\text{change in indirect labor hours}}$$

---

[2]Horngren, Charles T., *Cost Accounting—A Managerial Emphasis*, 4th ed. (Englewood Cliffs, NJ: Prentice-Hall, Inc., 1977), pp. 232–233.

$$b = \frac{\$83,800 - \$115,900}{23,000 - \quad 4,000} = \frac{-\$32,100}{19,000} = -\$1.69 \text{ per indirect labor hour}$$

and

$$b = \frac{y_H - y_L}{x_H - x_L} = \frac{\text{change in overhead costs}}{\text{change in idle time hours}}$$

$$b = \frac{\$78,500 - \$102,700}{600 - 60} = \frac{\$24,200}{540} = -\$44.82 \text{ per idle time hour}$$

Exhibit 5.1 shows the plotting of overhead costs (x_6) against machine hours (x_2). Exhibit 5.2 graphically depicts the plotting of overhead costs (x_6) against direct labor hours (x_3). Exhibit 5.3 reflects the relationship between overhead costs (x_6) and indirect labor hours (x_4). And, Exhibit 5.4 represents the relationship between overhead costs (x_6) and idle time hours (x_5). These exhibits suggest an inherent weakness in using the high-low points method: the method is statistically inefficient. While 13 data points are available, the high-low points method utilizes only two points and thus disregards the other 11 observations. Because of this obvious weakness in utilizing the high-low points method, this approach is not recommended even in periods of relatively stable prices.

Since the budgeting of overhead costs entails estimates of expected future data, and since cost formulas should be modified to reflect anticipated changes in prices, efficiency, and other factors, the regression models presented in preceding sections of this chapter provide a much better means of approximating cost functions. This is especially true when significant inflation persists since in order to plot inflation-impacted amounts, the rate of inflation would have to be estimated, whereas in the regression models these inflationary trends have been incorporated directly into the budgeting process.

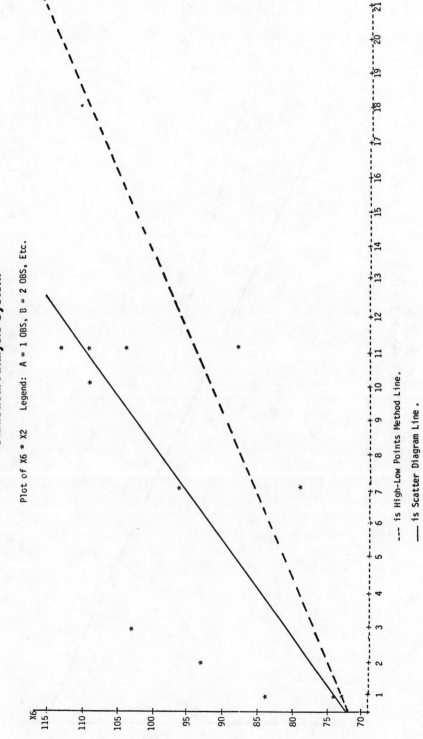

EXHIBIT 5.1
Statistical Analysis System

Plot of X6 * X2   Legend: A = 1 OBS, B = 2 OBS, Etc.

--- is High-Low Points Method Line.

——— is Scatter Diagram Line.

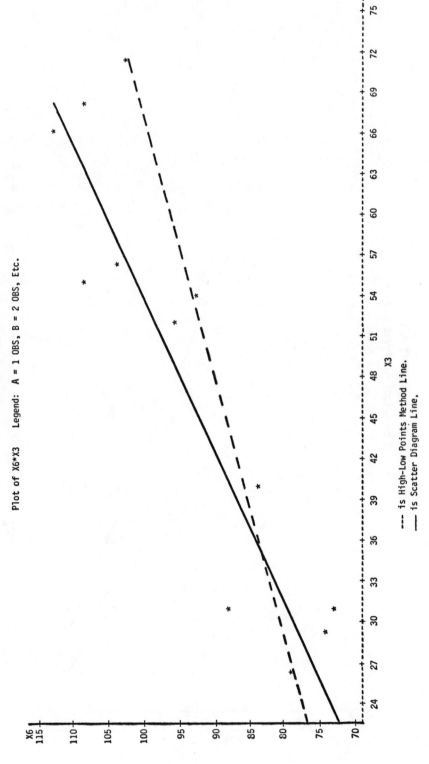

EXHIBIT 5.2
Statistical Analysis System

Plot of X6*X3   Legend: A = 1 OBS, B = 2 OBS, Etc.

--- is High-Low Points Method Line.
—— is Scatter Diagram Line.

EXHIBIT 5.3
Statistical Analysis System

Plot of X6*X4   Legend: A = 1 OBS, B = 2 OBS, Etc.

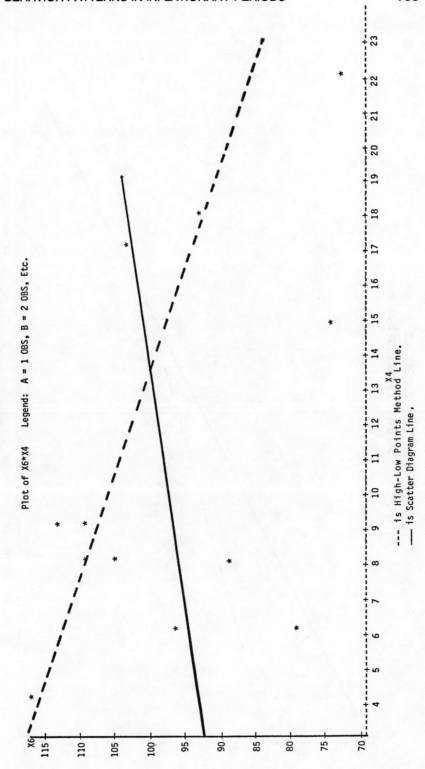

--- is High-Low Points Method Line.
—— is Scatter Diagram Line.

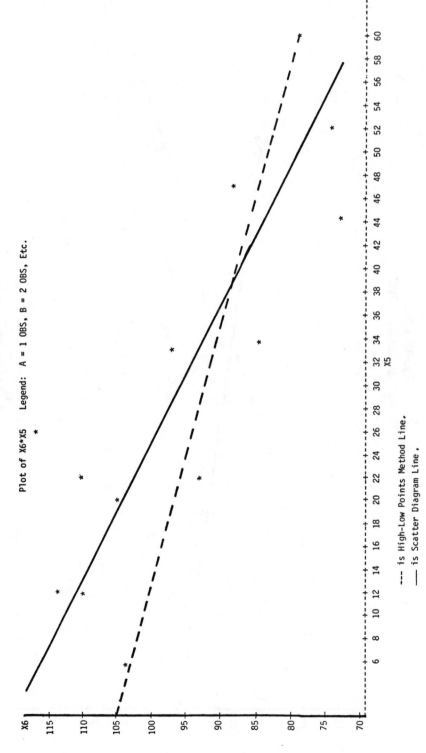

EXHIBIT 5.4
Statistical Analysis System

Plot of X6*X5　　　Legend:　A = 1 OBS, B = 2 OBS, Etc.

--- is High-Low Points Method Line,
—— is Scatter Diagram Line,

The Use of Scatter Diagrams in Cost Behavior Analysis

An often-used tool in analyzing cost behavior patterns is the scatter diagram. The scatter diagrams using each of the activity levels as the independent variable are depicted in Exhibits 5.1 through 5.4. An examination of the scatter points reveals the relationship between the specified independent variables and the dependent variables. A clear pattern of behavior points would indicate a high degree of correlation and, conversely, a widely dispersed arrangement of points would indicate a low degree of correlation.

If the points indicate that overhead costs are in fact following any of the predictive variables, a line is either visually located or statistically fitted among the points. This line should indicate the specific overhead costs to be incurred at varying activity levels, but if cost behavior patterns appear widely dispersed, the scatter diagram provides little useful data.

The scatter diagram approach incorporates the same data as does the simple regression method. The difference between the two methods is that, typically, if a scatter diagram is used, the line of fit will be plotted visually. The use of regression statistically determines the line of best fit. Since the scatter diagram method uses the same data that simple regression uses, it suffers from similar weaknesses. The most significant weakness is that the rate of inflation must be estimated; it cannot be input directly into the scatter diagram. In light of this fact, the use of scatter diagrams will yield dubious budgeted figures when inflation persists.

Summary

This chapter has discussed the use of four common methods used in budgeting manufacturing costs: (1) simple regression, (2) multiple regression, (3) high-low points, and (4) scatter diagrams. While these methods may yield reasonable approximations when inflation has little or no impact upon the cost structure of the enterprise, it has been shown that when inflation does have a significant impact upon the enterprise, these methods should be modified to reflect the inflationary trend. To incorporate inflation into the budgeting process when the enterprise uses either simple regression, high-low points, or scatter diagrams, the enterprise must estimate the rate of inflation for the budgeting time period. It has been shown in this chapter that the rate of inflation can be input directly into a multiple regression model by using a time variable. This allows the enterprise to budget costs during inflationary periods without having to predict the rate of inflation. Therefore, in most instances, the budgeted amounts will be much more accurate when inflation persists if the multiple regression approach demonstrated in this chapter is used.

CHAPTER 6

Effective Budgeting Operations during Inflationary Periods

□□□□□□□□□□□□

Well-developed and implemented budgeting processes can be seen in operation in most successful businesses, regardless of size. While the most sophisticated budgeting systems are found in larger companies, the need to budget effectively cannot be overemphasized in relation to any business. The purpose of this chapter is to analyze the impact of changing prices on formulating budgetary amounts. Budgeting for future time periods while using current or past prices—without introducing an inflation component into the system—can only lead to suboptimal forecasting. To illustrate how the impact of changing prices may be incorporated into budgets and planning processes in general, four managerial decisions will be focused upon: (1) developing the sales forecast, (2) determining standard costs, (3) planning and controlling inventory, and (4) allocating joint costs. But, first, an overview of operational budgeting is presented to acquaint the reader with the fundamental objectives attempting to be solved. Particular problems associated with capital budgeting decisions are the subject of Chapter 8 of this book.

Overview of Inflationary Impacts on Operational Budgeting

Budgets have been defined as:

> . . . a quantitative expression of a company's plan of action. It is the result of a process which translates the desired accomplishments of a business into quantitative terms. As such, the budget is an effective and indispensable aid to coordination and implementation of company goals.[1]

As such, budgets represent an attempt to project into subsequent time periods with reasonable accuracy, events and the impact these events have on a given company.

The basic approach to formulating an operational budget entails several steps that should have inflationary trends explicitly incorporated into the system. Table 6.1 provides a summary of the effect of inflation on operational budgeting procedures. The first step in formulating an operational budget is the projection of subsequent-period sales since estimated sales activity generally provides a good point of departure for estimating the level of related costs and expenses. While projected sales may be determined in a variety of ways, from discussions with sales staff to statistical forecasting models, this estimation process essentially should involve input as to anticipated inflation trends. The dollar amount of sale will vary from period to period if for no other reason than inflation. And the dollar amount of sales along with the number of units sold will increase or decrease according to the effects of inflation on the particular goods and services attempting to be marketed.

The second step in the operational budgeting process is the preparation of a production budget. Since the production budget typically is prepared in terms of *physical units* needed to meet sales needs and inventory needs, inflationary impacts are minimized in this step except to the extent the production budget is limited by the sales budget. Once the production budget is finalized, the third step in the budgeting process would be the assignment of projected costs to the physical units. This step involves the same complicating factors as the sales forecast in step one since the cost of goods purchased will increase or decrease with changes in the general (or specific) price level.

---

[1] Grant W. Newton, Thomas A. Ratcliffe, and Robin E. Taylor, "Behavioral Considerations in Present Budgeting Decisions," *Managerial Planning* (September/October 1977): 11.

The fourth budgetary objective would be to project labor and overhead costs through the budget period. Then, step five would entail estimating future selling and administrative expenses along with other expenses such as taxes. To be meaningful, all of these projections must encompass an inflationary component since these costs are tied largely to price level changes. And the formulation of a cash receipts and disbursements budget and an income statement and balance sheet is heavily dependent on all of these budgetary components. The remainder of this chapter attempts to provide some insight into how inflationary problems can be incorporated into the operational budgeting process.

TABLE 6.1
The Effects of Inflation on Operational Budgeting Decisions

Operational Budgeting Procedures	Effect of Inflation
1. Estimation of sales level	EFFECTED (Sales amounts in dollars will increase or decrease with general price level effects on sale price of goods and services.)
2. Preparation of production budget	NO EFFECT (Since the production budget is prepared in physical units, the impact of price level changes on the production budget is indirectly felt through its effect on sales in units.)
3. Estimation of cost of sales	EFFECTED (This step entails the assignment of dollar amounts to physical units determined above. As such, general and specific price level changes should be considered.)
4. Estimation of labor and overhead costs	EFFECTED (Labor costs and overhead costs tend to increase over time to allow for inflationary trends.)

TABLE 6.1 (continued)

5. Estimation of selling and administrative expenses	EFFECTED (These expenses increase or decrease with changes in the general price level.)
6. Preparation of cash budget	EFFECTED (Since the cash budget encompasses receipts and disbursements associated with previous steps, an inflation effect does exist.)
7. Preparation of financial statements	EFFECTED (Since the forecasted financial statements are derived from prior budgetary steps, an inflation effect does exist.)

Budgeting of Sales

The costs incurred by an enterprise are, in large part, a function of the level of activity maintained in the production process. The higher the level of production, the higher the costs associated with production. However, in most instances, an enterprise will have the physical capacity to produce more of its products than it can expect to sell. Therefore, the operational budgeting process should begin with its constraining factor—sales. Once the sales level has been budgeted, then the production level can be budgeted.

In preparing the sales budget, several factors must be considered—either explicitly or implicitly—by management. Among the most critical factors to be considered are: (1) sales volume of previous periods, (2) general economic conditions, (3) economic conditions of the industry(ies) in which the enterprise operates, (4) sales mix, and (5) overall corporate objectives.

There are many methods available to estimate sales. Perhaps the three most popular methods are: (1) estimates by the sales staff, (2) statistical approaches, e.g., trend analysis, and (3) top-level management estimates. Each method may be used either individually or in conjunction with the other methods.

Assume that MR Corporation uses the top-level management estimates to develop its sales budget. Table 6.2 shows the budgeted sales level and related costs for 19X0 for the corporation.

As Table 6.2 shows, the top-level management has budgeted a 27% increase in sales for 19X0. This budgeted figure is based upon the average sales increase of 26% which MR Corporation has experienced for the previous four years (see Schedule 6.1). Of the projected 27% increase in sales, the corporation anticipates that 10% of the increase will be attributable to price increases due to inflationary pressures. The remaining portion of the increase in sales is expected to come from an increase in the volume of sales.

TABLE 6.2
MR Corporation
Budget of Sales and Costs
for the Year 19X0

	Dollars	Percent Increase over 19X9	Percent Increase in Price	Percent Increase in Quantity
Sales	$5,100,000	27%	10%	17%
Cost of Goods Sold	3,315,000	27%	10%	17%
Gross Profit	1,785,000	27%	10%	17%
Operating Expenses	612,000	27%	10%	17%
Depreciation	76,000	-0-	-0-	-0-

SCHEDULE 6.1
Percentage Increase in Sales—Nominal Dollars

Year	Sales*	Percentage Increase
19X5	$1,600,000	—
19X6	2,000,000	25.0%
19X7	2,400,000	20.0%
19X8	3,200,000	33.3%
19X9	4,000,000	25.0%

Average Increase per Year   26.0%

*From Figure 2.2, Chapter 2.

However, the top-level management of MR Corporation developed its sales budget using nominal dollars—i.e., without adjusting for the impact of inflation. When the sales figures are adjusted for changes in the general price level—i.e., saies in real dollars—it becomes apparent that the average increase in sales has been only 16% rather than 26% (see Schedule 6.2). If the corporation is to maintain its real growth rate in 19X0, it would need to increase sales 16% above its 19X9 adjusted sales level of $4,208,000. As Schedule 6.3 shows, such an increase in real terms would result in a sales budget for 19X0 of $4,800,000, or $300,000 less than that projected using nominal dollars. This shows then that MR Corporation would not only have to maintain its real growth rate, but would actually need to increase real growth in order to meet is projected sales figure of $5,100,000.

SCHEDULE 6.2
Percentage Increase In Sales—Real Dollars

Year	Sales*		Adjustment Factor**		To End-of-the-Year 19X9 Dollars	Percentage Increase
19X5	$1,600,000	×	228.4/161.2	=	$2,267,200	—
19X6	2,000,000	×	228.4/170.5	=	2,680,000	18.2%
19X7	2,400,000	×	228.4/181.5	=	3,021,600	12.7%
19X8	3,200,000	×	228.4/195.4	=	3,740,800	23.8%
19X9	4,000,000	×	228.4/217.1	=	4,208,000	12.4%

Average Increase per Year.   16.7%

*From Figure 2.2, Chapter 2.
**From Schedule 2.1, Chapter 2.

SCHEDULE 6.3
Budgeted Sales and Costs—Real Dollars
19X0

	Dollars	Percent Increase for 19X9
Sales	$4,800,000	15%
Cost of Goods Sold	3,120,000	15%
Gross Profit	1,680,000	15%
Operating Expenses	576,000	15%
Depreciation	76,000	-0-

Budgeting of Inventory Costs

Before MR Corporation can develop its production budget, it must determine its inventory needs. It wishes to maintain a high inventory turnover level. Therefore, a relatively small amount of inventory is maintained. As can be seen from Table 6.3, MR Corporation plans to maintain an inventory level of $520,000.

TABLE 6.3
Budgeted MR Corporation
Production Costs for 19X0

Beginning Inventories*	$	480,000
Budgeted Cost of Goods Sold		
—see Table 6.2		3,315,000
Less: Budgeted Ending		
Inventories		(520,000)
Desired Production Level	$	3,355,000

*From Figure 2.1, Chapter 2

Once the sales level and inventory level have been budgeted, the level of production can be budgeted to meet those needs. As the production budget is dependent upon the sales budget, it is extremely important to accurately budget sales. If sales are underbudgeted, the firm may have a shortage of inventory and therefore lost sales. If, on the other hand, sales are overbudgeted, excess inventory may be produced which will result in high carrying costs for the inventory.

The production budget is developed in terms of units. In order to associate costs with the units, the firm must determine the underlying cost structure of its operating costs. The reader is referred back to Chapter 5 of this book for a discussion of the determination of cost behavior patterns.

As can be seen in Table 6.3, based upon sales and inventory needs, MR Corporation has budgeted production costs of $3,355,000 to meet those needs. It is at this point that the impact of inflation can perhaps best be seen in the budgeting process.

Suppose that MR Corporation's sales for 19X0 only reach the inflation adjusted sales budget of $4,800,000. What impact does that have on the corporation? Schedule 6.4 shows that by maintaining its budgeted production level of $3,355,000, it would be left with $715,000 in ending inventory or an excess inventory of approximately $200,000. In percentage terms, it would have 38% *excess* inventory on hand at the end of the period.

This serves to illustrate two problems that can arise if an enterprise uses nominal sales dollars instead of real sales dollars to project its future sales. First, it can result in a materially different sales budget (either overbudgeted or underbudgeted). This mistaken sales budget then impacts virtually all other facets of the business—production levels, inventory levels, operating costs, and cash flows.

SCHEDULE 6.4
Budgeted Ending Inventories

Beginning Inventories*	$ 480,000
Budgeted Production—see Table 6.3	3,355,000
Less: Budgeted Cost of Goods Sold—see Schedule 6.3	(3,120,000)
Budgeted Ending Inventories	$ 715,000

*From Figure 1, Chapter 2.

Budgeting of Other Operating Costs

The other operating costs are dependent upon the level of activity to be maintained by the enterprise and the underlying cost structure. Once again, the reader is referred to Chapter 5 for a discussion of the determination of cost behavior patterns during inflationary periods. The budget of the other operating costs is then a function of the level of activity to be maintained and the underlying cost structure of the firm.

Additional Problems—Allocation of Joint-Product Costs

An additional problem arises in the budgeting process if joint products are produced in the manufacturing process. This is common in many industries such as petroleum refining and cotton ginning. With joint products, more than one product results from the initial inputs.

The problem that arises is that prior to the point where the products split off and become individually salable or processable, all costs incurred in the manufacturing process benefit all resultant products. Therefore, a method must be used to allocate the common costs to the several resultant products.

The two common methods of allocating joint costs are based on (1) the relative physical quantities at the split-off point, and (2) the relative sales value of the products at the same point. If the joint products are measured in similar quantities—i.e., gallons, pounds, etc.—the use of the relative physical quantities approach is preferable since this approach will not be affected by inflation. The relative quantities of output would remain constant regardless of the changes in the manufacturing costs.

However, if the outputs are measured on a dissimilar basis, the relative sales value approach must be used. In this case, inflation will impact the allocation of the jointly incurred costs since inflation will affect the sales price of the products. If this approach must be used to allocate joint costs, the importance of an accurate sales projection is increased even more. The projection of sales of the joint products will impact the costs assigned to each product. This, in turn, will affect the profit margin of the joint products. By changing the profit margins of the joint products, the desired product mix may be changed. A change in the product mix can affect the projected sales figures since more of one product may be sold relative to the other product(s).

Since the method of allocating joint costs is arbitrarily selected in most instances, the costs associated with the products must also be arbitrary in nature. This also implies that the profit margins for each product must be somewhat arbitrary. Therefore, for purposes of projecting sales and determining desired product mixes, management would be best advised to disregard the *allocated* joint costs in making its decisions.

Summary

This chapter has shown that the sales budget is the key figure in the process of budgeting the operations of the enterprise. The sales budget affects the budgeted production level, operating costs, and cash flows of the enterprise.

If the enterprise budgets sales without reflecting the impact of inflation upon its sales, it runs the risk of materially misstating its sales budget. Since the sales budget permeates the operational budgeting process, this misstatement can result in a material misstatement of its other costs —and even to under- or over-producing its inventory. By adjusting past sales so that sales increases are stated in terms of real dollars, the enterprise will have a more accurate basis upon which to project its subsequent sales. By using this approach, the enterprise lessens the risk of operating at an inappropriate activity level in relation to its *real* sales level.

CHAPTER 7

A Practical Approach
to Variance Analysis
during Inflationary Periods

🔲🔲🔲🔲🔲🔲🔲🔲🔲🔲🔲

Budgeting the operations is the primary accounting tool used by management in planning the operations for the future. As such, budgeting is both a planning and a control tool. The budget is a quantative depiction of the plans of management, but it is also a benchmark to which actual performance can be compared. Chapters 5 and 6 examined the effect of inflation on the budgeting process. When the actual performance level differs from the budgeted performance level, variances will result. The process of investigating the causes of the variances is commonly referred to as *variance analysis*. This process is used by management as a control tool. The purpose of variance analysis is to signal to management when the operating process is not functioning according to the plan of operation. The variances act as a guide to management, showing which aspects of the operating process need attention.

When variances are determined to be significant, management investigates the operations so that the cause of the variance can be identified.

Once this has been done, management can institute corrective procedures so that future operations will be in accordance with the budgeted amounts. Since the budget is the benchmark by which actual performance is measured, the resultant variances will be impacted by inflation if management has not incorporated inflation into the budgeting process. The chapter will begin with a discussion of the computation of key variances. Then this chapter will illustrate how inflation can impact variance analysis.

Computation of Efficiency and Price Variances

Two commonly used types of variances are efficiency variances and price variances. Efficiency variances provide management with a measure of productivity. If the production process results in a smaller quantity of output for the given quantity of input, an unfavorable efficiency variance would result. On the other hand, the price variances indicate whether the per-unit costs are in line with expectations. If the cost of the output exceeds the expected level, an unfavorable price variance would result. For an in-depth discussion of variance analysis, the interested reader is referred to *Cost Accounting: A Managerial Emphasis*, by Horngren.[1]

Schedule 7.1 illustrates how an efficiency variance is computed. If it is deemed to be material, then management should investigate the cause of the variance. It should be noted that an efficiency variance can be computed for all aspects of the production process. Management should select the variances so as to most adequately be informed of the results of operations of the enterprise.

Schedule 7.2 illustrates the computation of a price variance. Once again, if the price variance is significant, it will need to be investigated. After the cause of the variance is determined, corrective action can be initiated.

As can be seen from Schedules 7.1 and 7.2, the efficiency variance reports whether the quantity of inputs used in the production process is appropriate, given the resultant quantity of outputs. The price variance measures whether the actual cost incurred is justified, given the quantity of inputs that were needed during the period. The next section will demonstrate how variance analysis can yield misleading results if inflation is not incorporated into the budgeting process.

---

[1] Horngren, Charles T. *Cost Accounting: A Managerial Emphasis* 4th ed. (Englewood Cliffs, NJ: Prentice-Hall, Inc., 1978).

SCHEDULE 7.1
Computation of Efficiency Variance

Assume the following information:

Standard Variable Overhead Cost per hour of Direct Labor	$3.00
Quantity of Units Produced	1,000
Standard Direct Labor Hours per unit Produced	5
Actual Direct Labor Hours Incurred	5,100

Expected Overhead Cost Based Upon Output	Expected Overhead Cost Based Upon Input
Standard Cost per Hour × Standard Hours ($3.00 per hour) × (1000 units × 5 hours per unit)	Standard Cost per Hour × Actual Hour ($3.00 per hour) × (5,100 hours)
$15,000	$15,300

Efficiency Variance:

Based upon Output	$15,000
Based upon Input	15,300
Efficiency Variance	$ 300 Unfavorable

The $300 unfavorable variance results because it required 100 hours more than expected to produce 1000 units of output.

SCHEDULE 7.2
Computation of Price Variance

Assume the following information:

Standard Variable Overhead Cost per Direct Labor Hour	$6.00
Actual Direct Labor Hours Incurred	50,500
Actual Overhead Costs Incurred	$313,100

Actual Overhead Costs	Expected Overhead Costs Based Upon Inputs
	Standard Cost per hour × Actual Hours ($6.00 per hour) × 50,500 hours
$313,100	$303,000

Price Variance:

Expected Cost based upon Input	$ 303,000
Actual Cost	313,100
Price Variance	$ 10,100 Unfavorable

The $10,100 unfavorable price variance results because the enterprise incurred overhead costs at a rate of $6.20 per direct labor hour ($313,100/50,500 hours) rather than the expected cost of $6.00 per direct labor hour.

Analyzing Efficiency Variances during Inflationary Periods

If inflation is not incorporated into the budgeting process, the most significant variance could result in the quantity of inventories maintained. Schedule 7.3 uses the data from Chapters 5 and 6 to develop the efficiency variance due to the quantity of inventory carried when inflation is not reflected in the budgeting process.

As can be seen from Schedule 7.3, MR Corporation is left with $260,000 in excess inventory. This represents an excess of 46% above the planned quantity of ending inventory. A closer examination of the figures reveals that the excess inventory is not the result of overproducing by the production department. Actual production costs exceeded expected production costs by only $45,000. The primary reason for excess inventory is that cost of goods sold was $195,000 less than expected because sales only approximated the inflation adjusted budgeted amount of $4,800,000

(Schedule 6.3) rather than the unadjusted sales budgeted amount of $5,100,000 (Exhibit 6.2). The resultant excess inventory was not from poor control in the production department, but rather from an overestimation of sales. This overestimation occurred because management did not incorporate inflation into its sales budget.

SCHEDULE 7.3
Excess Inventory—Budget Prepared without Incorporating Inflation

Budgeted Production Costs (Exhibit 6.3)	$3,355,000
Budgeted Ending Inventories (Exhibit 6.3)	520,000
Budgeted Cost of Goods Sold (Exhibit 6.3)	3,315,000

Assume that the following actual figures result:

Actual Production Costs	$3,400,000
Actual Ending Inventories	780,000
Actual Cost of Goods Sold	3,100,000

Budgeted Ending Inventories	Actual Ending Inventories
$520,000	$780,000

Excess Inventories:

Budgeted	$ 520,000
Actual	780,000
Excess	$ 260,000 Unfavorable

Schedule 7.4 shows the computation of excess inventory which would have resulted had the budgeted sales amount incorporated an inflation component. The excess inventory in Schedule 7.4 results from the combination of two factors. First, production levels exceeded the expected amount, and second, sales were less than expected. However, by having incorporated inflation into the initial sales budget, MR Corporation has only $60,000 of excess inventory rather than the $260,000 of excess inventory which would have resulted had the budget been prepared without incorporating inflation.

One point to notice is that variance analysis can lead to increased efficiency in the budgeting process. Assume that MR Corporation had prepared its budget without reflecting inflation. A thorough investigation of the cause of the excess inventories should bring to light the fact that the initial budget was unrealistic. If management is aware of this possibility, the variance analysis procedure can be used as both a control tool and an analysis of the budgeting process.

SCHEDULE 7.4
Excess Inventory—Inflation Incorporated into Budget

Budgeted Ending Inventories (Exhibit 6.3)	$520,000
Budgeted Cost of Goods Sold (Schedule 6.3)	3,120,000
Budgeted Production Level	3,160,000

Actual Results (assumed):

Actual Cost of Goods Sold	$3,100,000
Actual Production Costs	3,200,000
Actual Ending Inventories	580,000

Budgeted Ending Inventories	Actual Ending Inventories
$520,000	$580,000

Excess Inventories:

Budgeted	$ 520,000
Actual	580,000
Excess	$ 60,000

Analyzing Price Variances during Inflationary Periods

During inflationary periods, the underlying cost structure of the enterprise can change because of the inflationary pressures that are brought upon the operations of the enterprise. Chapter 5 discussed a preferable method of incorporating inflation into the analysis of cost behavior patterns. This section will examine price variances during inflationary periods. MR Corporation's budget of overhead costs is derived from Exhibit 5.4 when inflation is not incorporated into the cost behavior pattern. Exhibit 5.5 provides the data for budgeting overhead costs when inflation is incorporated into the cost behavior pattern.

Schedule 7.5 shows the computation of the overhead costs when inflation has not been incorporated into the cost behavior pattern. Schedule 7.6 shows the computation of the overhead price variance when inflation has been incorporated into the cost behavior pattern.

By ignoring inflation in the budgeting process, MR Corporation would appear to have an unfavorable price variance of $23,203 in overhead costs. This is a material variance which would warrant the attention of management. However, when inflation has been considered in the budgeting process, the same price variance is only $2,173. This may very well be an immaterial price variance which requires no special attention from management.

As a result of having neglected inflation in the budgeting process, MR Corporation will spend valuable time investigating a variance which is really immaterial. What the variance that MR Corporation is investigating really reflects is increased costs due to inflation—not increased costs due to poor operating procedures.

By ignoring inflation initially, MR Corporation wastes time and money in investigating its overhead costs. But just as in the case of excess inventories, if the corporation is aware of the possible effects of inflation, its investigation of the overhead variance could lead to the discovery of its incorrectly budgeted amounts. This discovery will allow the enterprise to incorporate inflation into subsequent budgets and prevent it from repeating its error of investigating immaterial variances.

SCHEDULE 7.5
Price Variance—Inflation Not Incorporated into Budget

Actual Machine Hours (X_2)	10,000
Actual Direct Labor Hours (X_3)	60,000
Actual Idle Time Hours (X_5)	5,000
Actual Overhead Costs	$110,000
Budgeted Overhead Costs*	86,797

*From Exhibit 5.4

Budgeted Overhead Costs = $103.097 + 1.440 \times (10) - .614 \times (50) = \$86,797$

Actual Costs	Budgeted Costs Based upon Actual Inputs
$110,000	$86,797

Price Variance:	
Actual	$ 110,000
Budgeted	86,797
Price Variance	$ 23,203 Unfavorable

SCHEDULE 7.6
Price Variance—Inflation Incorporated into Budget

Actual Machine Hours (X_2)	10,000
Actual Direct Labor Hours (X_3)	60,000
Actual Idle Time Hours (X_5)	5,000
Time Period (X_1)	14
Actual Overhead Costs	$110,000
Budgeted Overhead Costs*	107,827

*From Exhibit 5.5

Budgeted Overhead Costs: $52.527 + .155 \times (14) + 1.467 \times (10) + 60 \times (.641) = 107,827$

Actual Costs	Budgeted Costs Based upon Actual Inputs
$110,000	$107,827

Price Variance:

Actual	$ 110,000	
Budgeted	107,827	
Price Variance	$ 2,173	Unfavorable

Summary

This chapter has further illustrated how failure to incorporate inflation into the operating budgeting process can cause confusing results. Reported variances, since the computations of variances rely on the budgeted amounts, can be meaningful only if the underlying budgeted figures are accurate depictions of the anticipated results.

If the impact of inflation has been reflected in the initial development of the budget, then traditional variance analysis can be employed since the reported variances will be reflective of problem areas in the operations of the enterprise. However, if inflation has been ignored, then the reported variances may be largely attributable to the inflationary factor. When that is the case, management should be wary of potential inflationary effects as it investigates the material variances. In this way, management may be able to detect the effects of inflation through its investigation of variances. Then the effects of inflation can be incorporated into future budgeted amounts, thereby avoiding repetition of past erroneous variance reporting.

CHAPTER 8

Accounting for Inflation in Capital Budgeting Processes*

□□□□□□□□□□□□□

Capital budgeting involves the evaluation of capital investment proposals in terms of amounts, timing, and uncertainty of cash inflows and cash outflows and the selection between project alternatives based upon certain investment criteria. An often overlooked aspect of capital budgeting relates to the impact of inflation on capital budgeting techniques, particularly that of incorporating price level changes into net present value models. The purpose of this chapter is to examine how inflationary trends should be incorporated with capital budgeting processes.

On the Effect of Inflation on Capital Budgeting Processes

In a taxless world, inflation would impact cash flows and applicable discount rates in a comparable manner; therefore, inflationary effects on present value computations would be irrelevant. In the traditional model,

---

*This chapter is adapted from D.D. Raiborn and Thomas A. Ratcliffe, "Are You Accounting for Inflation in Your Capital Budgeting Process," *Management Accounting* (September 1979): 19–22.

$$NPV = -Co + \sum_{t=1}^{x} \frac{\overline{C}_t}{(1 + K)^t},$$

inflation implicity is contained in the overall discount rate (K) and remains constant throughout the life of a given project. But this implicit assumption of an unchanging price level is erroneous in that price level changes do occur over the life of a project.

Given this unrealistic assumption concerning an unchanging price level, the necessary estimation of future cash flows typically is analyzed in terms of existing prices. The acceptance criterion, the rate of return demanded by investors, is based on current capital costs which embody a premium for anticipated inflation. Seemingly, if this acceptance criterion encompasses an element of anticipated inflation, the estimated cash flows of the project also should be analyzed in anticipation of inflation so that the acceptance criterion and the estimated cash flows may be stated on an equivalent basis.

An increase in the general price level typically would increase further revenues, wages, and material costs of a project. The effect of anticipated inflation on the cash inflows and outflows of a particular project may not always be in the same direction; therefore, any assumptions used in present value analysis should be stated carefully. Various price level change assumptions should be analyzed to test the sensitivity of project acceptance to different changes in the general price level. Probability analysis also can be incorporated into the model by assuming various changes in the general price level and estimating the probability of their occurrence.

The traditional capital budgeting process involves the following steps:

1. Determine the initial net capital investment and the useful life of a project.
2. Determine incremental cash flows involving—
    a. estimation of future revenues, and
    b. estimation of future expenses by estimating:
        (1) incremental materials and labor,
        (2) incremental depreciation, and
        (3) incremental taxes.
3. Discount net cash flows at required rate of return. The impact inflation has on each of these steps is summarized in Exhibit 8.1.

EXHIBIT 8.1
The Effects of Inflation on Capital Budgeting Procedures

CAPITAL BUDGETING PROCEDURES	EFFECT OF INFLATION
1. Determination of initial net capital investment and life of project	NO EFFECT (The asset is purchased currently.)
2. Estimation of incremental future revenues	EFFECTED (Future revenues increase or decrease with general price level effects on sale of goods and services.)
3. Estimation of incremental future expense	EFFECTED (Future expenses increase or decrease with general price level effects on materials and labor.)
4. Determination of incremental depreciation	NO EFFECT (The depreciation charge is fixed at the time of asset acquisition.)
5. Determination of incremental taxes	EFFECTED (Incremental taxes are affected by the increase or decrease in sales and expenses and the tax consequences of depreciation charges based on historical cost.)
6. Determination of incremental cash flows	EFFECTED (Depreciation is based on historical cost; therefore, depreciation is constant as revenues and expenses increase or decrease with the price level.)
7. Discount cash flows to present value	EFFECTED (The discounting term should be multiplicative not additive in nature.)

Incorporating the Impact of Inflation into the Capital Budgeting Process

Capital budgeting in periods of increasing price levels involves the following modifications to the traditional process:

1. *Cash flow estimates.*
   Cash flows are affected by anticipated inflation in several ways:
   a. Cash inflows arising from the sale of products or services are affected by future prices.
   b. Cash outflows affect future wages and material costs.
   c. Depreciation charges *are not* affected since once an asset is acquired, future charges against income are known with certainty.
2. *The discount rate.*
   The cost of capital to an enterprise involves three components: the pure interest rate (i), an inflation adjustment (n), and a premium associated with the degree of risk (p). The relationship of these three factors typically is expressed in the denominator of the present value equation as $(1 + k)^t$. The traditional relationship can be defined further as $(1 + n + p + i)^t$, where n is the inflation adjustment factor, p is the risk premium, and i is the pure interest rate.

The additive relationship of the discount rate components ignores the fact that discount rates are stated as of the end of each period, but the discounting process occurs on a continuing basis; therefore, cost of capital will be understated and the real net present value overstated if the additive denominator is used and the compounding effect is ignored. The relationship may be stated better in the multiplicative form as $(1 + n)^t (1 + i + p)^t$. Only if the product of the inflation rate (r) and the real discount rate $(i + p)$ is sufficiently small can this relationship be depicted as additive: $(1 + i + p + n)^t$. Exhibit 8.2 illustrates the conversion of the traditional present value model to a model that incorporates changes in the general price level. From this illustration, it should be evident why net cash flows cannot be adjusted as a single amount for changes in the general price level, but the revenues and expenses (exclusive of depreciation) should be adjusted. To allow for inflation, the first part of the numerator is multiplied by the inflation adjustment factor. The second part of the numerator, the tax savings from depreciation, *is not* multiplied by the inflation index. The expansion of the denominator to allow for inflation also is illustrated.

EXHIBIT 8.2

Conversion of the Traditional Net Present Value Model

The conversion below illustrates how the net present value model is adjusted to incorporate general price level changes.

TRADITIONAL

MODEL: $NPV = -Co + \sum_{t=1}^{X} \dfrac{\overline{C}_t}{(1+K)^t}$

<u>CHANGES TO THE MODEL</u>

1.

The numerator, $\overline{C}_t$,

may be expanded to: $\overline{C}_t = [(I_t - O_t)(1 - T)] + D_t T$

$\overline{C}_t$ = estimated net cash flows for period t

I_t = estimated net cash inflows for period t

O_t = estimated net cash outflows for period t

T = corporate tax rate

D = fixed non-cash charges (i.e. depreciation)

2.

To allow for inflation the numerator may be changed to:

$\sum_{n=1}^{m} n[(I_t - O_t)(1 - T)] + D_t T$

n = inflation adjustment (GPL Index)

3.

The denominator may be expanded to: $(1 + i + n + p)^t$

i = pure interest rate

n = inflation adjustment

p = premium associated with risk

EXHIBIT 8.2 (continued)

4.

To incorporate the compounding affect, the expanded arithmetic demoninator should be changed to the multiplicative form which incorporates the compounding affects.

$$(1 + n)^t (1 + i + p)^t$$

5.

Substituting the conversion of the numerator and denominator, the revised NPV model is:

$$NPV = -Co + \sum_{t=1}^{X} \sum_{n=1}^{m} \frac{n[(I_t - O_t)(1 - T)] + D_t T}{(1 + n)^t (1 + i + p)^t}$$

How Inflation Impacts Capital Budgeting Decisions: A Case Example

The following case example should serve to illustrate potential problem areas in analyzing capital investment projects in the absence of introducing the impact of inflation into the decision processes. Assume MR Corporation is reviewing a project that involves a net cash outflow of $100,000 for a new machine that is estimated to have a useful life of four years. MR Corporation depreciates equipment on a straight-line basis. The corporate controller estimates the *real* cost of capital of the corporation adjusted for inflation to be 12%. The cost rate was computed by using an historical, pure interest rate of 4% plus an average premium demanded by the investors of 8%. The controller also has determined through consultation with economic advisors that the general price level index should rise by 10% per year for the next four years. MR Corporation anticipates the following revenues and expenses:

	Year 1	2	3	4
Revenues:	$ 60,000	$ 75,000	$ 75,000	$ 45,000
Expenses:				
Labor	$ 10,000	$ 10,000	$ 10,000	$ 8,000
Materials	$ 8,000	$ 12,000	$ 12,000	$ 8,000

After-tax cash flows, assuming no adjustment for price level changes, are computed in Exhibit 8.3. And Exhibit 8.4 illustrates the real cash flows of the machine purchase, assuming an increase in the general price level in each of the next four years of 10%. The project which at first appeared acceptable, now appears to be unacceptable.

EXHIBIT 8.3
Net Present Value Computation

PROJECT A
Assumption 1: No change in general price level.

	YEAR 1	YEAR 2	YEAR 3	YEAR 4
Revenues:	$60,000	$75,000	$75,000	$45,000
Expenses:				
Labor	10,000	10,000	10,000	8,000
Materials	8,000	12,000	12,000	8,000
Depreciation	25,000	25,000	25,000	25,000
Total Expenses	(43,000)	(47,000)	(47,000)	(41,000)
Before tax Profit	17,000	28,000	28,000	4,000
Taxes (50%)	(8,500)	(14,000)	(14,000)	(2,000)
After tax Profit	8,500	14,000	14,000	2,000
Add back:				
Depreciation	25,000	25,000	25,000	25,000
After tax cash				
flows	$33,500	$39,000	$39,000	$27,000

CONVERSION TO PRESENT VALUE OF CASH FLOWS

After tax cash flows	Discount factor (12%)	Present value of cash flows
$33,500	.89286	$ 29,910.81
$39,000	.79719	31,090.41
$39,000	.71178	27,759.42
$27,000	.63552	17,159.04
		$105,919.68
	Less cost of project:	(100,000.00)
	NET PRESENT VALUE:	$ 5,919.68

EXHIBIT 8.4
Net Present Value Computation

PROJECT A
Assumption 2: General price level increase of 10% each of the next four years.

	YEAR 1	YEAR 2	YEAR 3	YEAR 4
GPL Index	1.10	1.21	1.331	1.464
Revenues:	$66,000[(A)]	$90,750	$99,825	$65,880
Expenses:				
Labor	11,000	12,100	13,310	11,712
Materials	8,800	14,520	15,972	11,712
Depreciation	25,000	25,000	25,000	25,000
Total Expenses	(44,800)	(51,620)	(54,282)	(48,424)
Before tax Profit	21,200	39,130	45,543	17,456
Taxes	(10,600)	(19,565)	(22,771)	(8,728)
After tax Profit	10,600	19,565	22,772	8,728
Add back:				
Depreciation	25,000	25,000	25,000	25,000
Nominal after tax cash flows	$35,600	$44,565	$47,772	$33,728

[(A)]Revenue and cash expenses were converted to purchasing power equivalents of each year, i.e., Year 1 revenues of $60,000 $\times$ 1.1 = $66,000.

Without incorporating inflation adjustments into the capital budgeting model, the net present value computation is overstated. The net present value in Exhibit 8.3 is $5,919.68. Cash flows are computed for four years and then discounted by 12%, the pure interest rate plus the risk premium. The 12% discount factor contains no provision for inflation.

Exhibit 8.4 reflects the multiplication of revenues, materials, and labor estimates by the general price level index. An annual 10% inflation rate compounds to yield the following indices:

Year 1—1.0 * 1.1 = 1.1
Year 2—1.1 * 1.1 = 1.21
Year 3—1.21 * 1.1 = 1.331
Year 4—1.331 * 1.1 = 1.464

These indices are used first to inflate revenues and appropriate expenses to approximate cash flows expected each year and then used to deflate the resulting nominal cash flows. Nominal cash flows are converted to real cash flows (constant dollars) by dividing the nominal cash flows by the index applicable to each year. The real cash flows are then discounted by the 12% factor to yield a net present value of $1,554.50.

CONVERSION OF NOMINAL CASH FLOWS TO REAL CASH FLOWS

Nominal after tax cash flows	General Price Level Index	Real after tax cash flows
$35,600	1.10	35600/1.10 = $32363.64
44,565	1.21	44565/1.21 = 36830.58
47,772	1.331	47772/1.331 = 35891.81
33,728	1.464	33728/1.464 = 23038.25

CONVERSION TO PRESENT VALUE OF REAL CASH FLOWS

Real after tax cash flows	Discount factor (12%)	Present value of cash flows
$32363.64	.89286	$ 28,896.20
36830.58	.79719	29,360.97
35891.81	.71178	25,547.07
23038.25	.63552	14,641.26
		$ 98,445.50
	Less cost of project:	(100,000.00)
	NET PRESENT VALUE:	$−1,554.50

Summary of Capital Budgeting with Price Level Adjustments

Incorporating general price level adjustments into present value models utilized in capital budgeting decisions will not always result in information that would reverse the acceptance/rejection decision, but the adjustment always will yield a different net present value result. The adjustments should be considered to improve decision-making analysis. The following factors should be considered in the capital budgeting process when price level adjustments are used:

1. Even though sales dollars, profits, and cash flows may increase with a rise in the general price level, the *real* rate of return will decrease with inflation.
2. During a period of inflation, the real cost of an asset is not reflected totally through depreciation charges; therefore, taxable income will be overstated.

3. The *real* income tax rate increases with the rate of inflation and the age of the asset (step 2 in Exhibit 8.2 illustrates this phenomenon).
4. The effect of inflation usually is more significant for individual projects than for portfolios, depending on the size of the general price level adjustment, the pattern of cash flows between given projects, and the diversity of the portfolio.
5. General price level changes can affect the evaluation of mutually exclusive projects.

To prevent the erroneous acceptance of capital investment projects and provide optimum resource allocation, the technique proposed in this chapter should be incorporated into the capital budgeting process during times of changing prices.

CHAPTER 9

Accounting for Inflation in the Oil and Gas Industry*

□□□□□□□□□□□□

In 1978, the Securities and Exchange Commission (SEC) announced that oil and gas producing companies would soon be required to implement an accounting and reporting system radically different from the traditional historical cost models utilized in the industry. The new form of accounting, entitled Reserve Recognition Accounting (RRA), would require supplemental disclosures on a value-type basis; these disclosures currently do not supplant the basic financial statements for oil and gas producers. Companies affected by the SEC rules recently issued the first set of financial statements involving the RRA disclosures, and it would be no overstatement to conclude that formalization of these disclosures has been extremely difficult in practice. The purpose of this chapter is to provide an overview of the operational aspects of developing the RRA disclosures. While this chapter will be especially interesting to those associated with the oil and gas industry, it should also prove beneficial to all readers attempting to understand and implement inflation-adjusted disclosures.

---

*Special gratitude should be offered to Professor Robert J. Koester at Texas Tech University for his contribution to insuring the technical accuracy of this chapter.

Developments Leading to RRA

While the controversy over the appropriate accounting method to be used in the oil and gas industry is not new, recent accounting and socio-economic developments have focused increasing attention on this particular industry. The rationale for this oil and gas industry focus could be a result of one or more factors, including the embryonic stage accounting in the oil and gas industry is (was) in, and the economic and social significance of products from this industry.

Regardless of the reasons for this attention, the "appropriate method" debate traces at least as far back as the full costing versus successful effort debates of the 1960s and 1970s. Congressional intervention in 1975 through the Energy Policy and Conservation Act proved to be a significant stimulus to furthering these controversial debates. This legislation required the SEC to develop a single method of accounting and reporting for oil and gas producing companies so that a national energy base might be developed. The SEC was allowed to rely on the Financial Accounting Standards Board (FASB) as a source for developing this method of accounting. The SEC initially followed this choice and, in December 1977, after careful study and evaluation of various accounting alternatives, the FASB promulgated Statement of Financial Accounting Standards (SFAS) No. 19 entitled "Financial Accounting and Reporting for Oil and Gas Producing Companies." SFAS No. 19 would have required oil and gas producers to report under a form of successful efforts accounting.

The FASB conclusions in SFAS No. 19 were discounted significantly when the SEC issued Accounting Series Release (ASR) No. 253 in August 1978 and concluded that neither the full costing nor the successful efforts form of accounting was acceptable for reporting on oil and gas producing activities. Instead, the SEC announced plans to study and begin implementation of RRA. This method would reflect as a surrogate for current value the net present value of estimated future oil and gas production determined at current costs and current prices. Instead of a net income number, RRA would result in a current earnings number that is the net future benefits of discovered reserves in excess of the net present and future costs related to those reserves. In October 1979, the SEC issued ASR No. 269, which provides the first set of final rules under RRA and requires supplemental disclosure on an RRA basis for all oil and gas producing companies that are SEC registrants. The FASB has indicated its plans to issue an exposure draft which, if adopted into a formal statement, would require the same or similar disclosures by all oil and gas producing companies, whether or not these companies are SEC registrants.

Recognizing that such a formidable project would take at least three years to fully develop, the SEC, in the interim development of RRA, is allowing oil and gas producing companies to report under either the full costing or the successful efforts method of accounting. The SEC issued ASR Nos. 257 (successful efforts) and 258 (full costing) to provide operational guidance to SEC registrants in implementing these methods of accounting.

RRA Is Not Historical Cost Accounting

Several substantive changes in financial reporting have been instituted as a result of SEC actions concerning RRA. Some of the basic themes of RRA that are in conflict with the traditional historical cost approaches to accounting in the oil and gas industry are discussed below.

Determining the Critical Event

Perhaps the single most important issue in controversies surrounding RRA is that the SEC has shifted the critical event in measuring progress in the earnings process from the point of sale to the point of discovery of oil and gas reserves. The end result of this change in thought is that oil and gas producers should report an economic benefit (earnings) when new reserves are discovered while substantially no earnings should be recognized when those reserves are produced and sold. Pros and cons of this position could be argued in terms of the realization concept utilized in the traditional historical cost model. Per this realization notion, historical cost reserves typically are recognized when an exchange has taken place between buyer and seller (so that an objective measure of revenues exists) and the earnings process is virtually complete (so that substantially all risks and rights of ownership of the property transfer to the buyer). Given the ready marketability of oil and gas reserves, the SEC obviously believes that the earnings process is virtually complete when the reserves are discovered, and since an ascertainable market price for the reserves generally exists, there appears to be no need to await a buy/sell transaction to develop objective measures of earnings. Therefore, the SEC promotes the idea that the critical event in the earnings process for oil and gas producers occurs at the point of discovery of reserves.

The Current Value Issue

It is a commonly held view that implementation of RRA will result in a current value of oil and gas reserves. This conclusion is substantially erroneous.

The first problem with such a view is the difficulty of defining what constitutes proved reserves—those reserves that are economically feasible to develop and produce given the current economy and technology. Because of the nature of the oil and gas industry, many reserves become "proved" not because they are discovered but because of economic and political events that transpire and make previously discovered unproved reserves suddenly economically feasible to develop and produce. An example would be a marginal field which, under previous pricing regulations, was not feasible to develop, but during a current period of price deregulation, becomes efficient to develop and produce.

Another problem with the RRA model is that *future* oil and gas production is included in the discounting process at *current prices* and *current costs* and, as such, it would seem to be difficult to conclude that RRA represents even a good surrogate for the current value of future net revenues. Because current prices and current costs are used and then discounted to present value at an arbitrary 10% discount rate, in most cases these computations will result in a substantial understatement of the current value of oil and gas reserves.

Financial Statement Presentation

It should be noted that, currently, the RRA disclosures are supplementary in nature and that the SEC has announced no firm plans to substitute these disclosures for the primary financial statements. However, this fact does not diminish the computational difficulties inherent in formulating the disclosures.

The first statement in the RRA disclosures is a summary of *economic* results of operations, not revenues minus expenses as in the traditional historical cost financial statements. Based on the present value of oil and gas reserves, economic benefits of oil and gas exploration activities must be determined and then economic detriments are deducted from this amount. The resultant net number should be indicative of the economic results of oil and gas acquisitions and exploration.

The second RRA statement summarizes the changes in present value of oil and gas reserves. This is not a statement of financial position and addresses no assets other than crude oil and natural gas reserves. However, it should be noted that the SEC has utilized this valuation method in establishing the capitalization limit in the historical cost statement of financial position for property and equipment of full costing companies.

On the Content of RRA Statements

RRA is illustrated through statement development from the following facts. On January 1, 19X9, MR Corporation initiated oil and gas exploration activities. A 40% tax rate is assumed throughout this example for simplicity. Transactions for the first two years are presented here.

In 19X9—acquired leases to three properties and explored as follows:

Lease	Bonus	Geological and Geophysical Costs	Drilling Costs
A	$ 4,000	$20,000	$100,000 (all intangible)
B	$ 8,000	-0-	-0-
C	$10,000	$50,000	$150,000 (2/3 intangible)

Proved reserves were discovered on Lease C and it was estimated that total production over a four-year life would be:

> 19Y0—22,000 barrels
> 19Y1—17,000 barrels
> 19Y2—14,000 barrels
> 19Y3—12,000 barrels

Current market price for crude is $42 per barrel and lifting costs are estimated to be $5 per barrel. It is estimated that development costs of $85,000 will be incurred in 19Y0. Also, plant removal and site restoration costs are estimated to be $42,000, and these costs will be incurred in 19Y3.

In 19Y0—Lease B is surrendered and a delay rental of $6,000 is paid for Lease A. In addition, $100,000 (all tangible) is to be paid to develop Lease C. During 19Y0, 25,000 barrels of crude are produced and sold for $46 per barrel. Lifting costs now are $6 per barrel. Estimates of future crude production from Lease C are as follows:

> 19Y1—20,000 barrels
> 19Y2—18,000 barrels
> 19Y3—15,000 barrels

Exhibits 9.1 and 9.2 and related schedules illustrate how these facts should be transformed into RRA statements.

Developing the Results Statement

The statement of results of operations as illustrated in Exhibit 9.1 depicts the economic results of oil and gas exploration activities. Although the title of the statement refers to oil and gas producing activities, it should be noted that this statement primarily addresses activities through the exploration stage and makes no evaluation of current development or production activities. The same can be concluded of the "bottom line" of this statement which is, in effect, economic benefits less economic detriments of oil and gas exploration activities.

EXHIBIT 9.1
Summary of Oil and Gas Producing Activities
on the Basis of RRA (Thousands of Dollars)

	19X9	19Y0
Additions and Revisions to Estimated Proved Oil and Gas Reserves:		
Additions to Estimated Proved Reserves—Gross (Schedule 9.1)	$ 2,216	$ -0-
Revisions to Estimates of Reserves Proved in Prior Years		
Changes in Prices (Schedule 9.4)	-0-	159
Other (Schedule 9.4)	-0-	450
Accretion of Discount (Schedule 9.4)	-0-	185
Subtotal (Schedule 9.5)	$ 2,216	$ 794
Evaluated Acquisition, Exploration, Development, and Production Costs:		
Costs Incurred	(330)	(14)
Present Value of Estimated Future Development and Production Costs (Schedule 9.1)	(370)	-0-
Subtotal	$ (700)	$ (14)
Additions and Revisions to Proved Reserves over Evaluated Costs	$ 1,516	$ 780
Provision for Income Taxes (Schedules 9.2 and 9.6)	(588)	(314)
Results of Oil and Gas Producing Activities on the Basis of RRA	$ 928	$ 466

The first line on the statement addresses additions that actually are newly defined proved reserves. These proved reserves may be new discoveries or may be the result of economic and/or political events on previously discovered marginal reserves that currently meet the definition of proved reserves. As previously noted, this amount is calculated by applying current prices and current costs to estimated future production and then discounting these values to present value using a 10% discount rate. See Schedules 9.1 and 9.5 for illustrations of these computations.

Since the estimation of future production is at best an inexact art, it will be necessary to make numerous revisions to previously reported information. The SEC has identified three categories of changes. The "changes in prices" line applies to future production only. That is, if prices have increased from the previous year, the present value model must be revised to reflect anticipated future production at currently existent prices. This calculation in practice may represent future revenues net of future production costs or it also may be shown gross of production costs. See Schedule 9.4 for computational guidance.

The "accretion of discount" line refers to the resultant holding gain because the present value model has moved one more year closer to production. Rather than require a detailed computation changing the discount factor for future production of each year, the SEC allows an approximation taking 10% of the beginning value of the reserves. See Schedule 9.4 for a computational approach.

The subtitle "other revisions" includes essentially three levels of computation: (1) changes in the estimation of reserve quantities, (2) changes in the rate of production that will affect the current value model, and (3) the interaction of all other revisions (this would be similar to a joint price-efficiency variance in a standard cost system). Because of the very inexact nature of reserve estimation, this "other revisions" category (even though a plug number) will usually be very large in relationship to the other numbers on the statement. (See Schedule 9.4.)

Evaluated costs are those costs which are associated only with the additions to proved reserves identified in the top portion of the statement. The costs incurred include current exploration costs, both dry holes and discovery wells, geological and geophysical costs, delay rentals, test well contributions, and acquisition costs where doubt as to quality of acquisition has been removed. Future development and production costs are those related only to additions to proved reserves reported in the top portion of the statement. As with future revenues, these costs must be reported at current costs and are discounted to present value using the arbitrary 10% discount factor. (See Schedules 9.1 and 9.5.)

SCHEDULE 9.1
Future Cash Flows for 19X9 (Thousands of Dollars)

	19Y0	19Y1	19Y2	19Y3	Total	Present Value
Sales	$ 924	$ 714	$ 588	$ 504	$ 2,730	$ 2,216 (a)
Production Costs	(110)	(85)	(70)	(60)	(325)	(264)(b)
Development Costs	(85)	-0-	-0-	-0-	(85)	(77)(c)
Plant Removal	-0-	-0-	-0-	(42)	(42)	(29)(d)
Estimated Future Net Revenues	$ 729	$ 629	$ 518	$ 402	$2,278	$ 1,816(e)

(a) $924 * .90909 = $ 840
$714 * .82645 = $ 590
$588 * .75132 = $ 442
$504 * .68301 = $ 344

Present Value of
Sales   = $2,216

(b) $110 * .90909 = $100
$ 85 * .82645 = $ 70
$ 70 * .75132 = $ 53
$ 60 * .68301 = $ 41
Present Value of
Production Costs = $264

(c) $85 * .90909 = $77 (Present
Value of Development Costs)

(d) $42 * .68301 = $29 (Present
Value of Plant Removal and
Site Restoration Costs)

(e) Present Value of Estimated
Future Development and
Production Costs =
$264 + $77 + $29 = $370

SCHEDULE 9.2
Tax Computation for 19X9

Present Value of Reserves—Ending (Schedule 9.1)	$1846
Tax Basis—Ending (see Schedule 9.3)	(142)
Future Taxable Income	1704
Tax Rate	40%
Income Tax	682
Less Present Value of Investment Tax Credit	9
Net Tax for Future Operations	673
Less Previously Accrued Tax	-0-
Provision for Future Taxes	673
Current Tax (see Schedule 9.3)	(85)
Provision for Taxes	$ 588

SCHEDULE 9.3
Tax Liability Computations

19X9

End-of-Year Tax Basis Computation:

Lease Bonus ($4,000 + $8,000 + $10,000)	$ 22,000
Geological and Geophysical Costs ($20,000 + $50,000)	70,000
Tangible Drilling Costs (1/3 * $150,000)	50,000
Ending Basis	$ 142,000

Tax Computation:

Revenue	$ -0-
Intangible Drilling Costs	(200,000)
Taxable Income	$ (200,000)
Income Tax (40%)	$ 80,000
Investment Tax Credit	5,000
Net Tax	$ 85,000

19Y0

End-of-Year Tax Basis Computation:

Beginning Basis	$ 142,000
Development Costs	100,000
Abandonment of B	(8,000)
Amortization of C*	(67,250)
Ending Basis	$ 166,750

$$\frac{*\$100,000 + \$60,000 + \$50,000}{78,000 \text{ barrels}} * 25,000 \text{ barrels} = \$67,250$$

Tax Computation:

Revenue		$1,150,000
Lifting Costs	$150,000	
Delay Rental	6,000	
Abandonment of B	8,000	
Amortization of C	67,250	231,250
Taxable Income		$ 918,750
Income Tax (40%)		$ 367,500
Investment Tax Credit		(10,000)
Net Tax		$ 357,500

203

SCHEDULE 9.4

**Calculation of 19Y0 Revision of Estimates of Reserves Proved
in Prior Years Due to Changing Prices,
Accretion of Discount, and Other Changes**

Step 1—Determine Net Sales Prices

19Y0 Net Sales Price ($46 - $6)	=	$40
19X9 Net Sales Price ($42 - $ 5)	=	$37
Increase in net sales price		$ 3

Step 2—Net Sales Price Change Times Estimated Production

19Y0 = 22,000 barrels * $3	=	$ 66,000
19Y1 = 17,000 barrels * $3	=	$ 51,000
19Y2 = 14,000 barrels * $3	=	$ 42,000
19Y3 = 12,000 barrels * $3	=	$ 36,000
Total		$195,000

Step 3—Determine Present Value of Cash Flows Using Revised Net
    Sales Price (Thousands of Dollars)

19Y0 = $ 66,000 * .90909 = $60
19Y1 = $ 51,000 * .82645 = $42
19Y2 = $ 42,000 * .75132 = $32
19Y3 = $ 36,000 * .68301 = $25
        $195,000 $159

Step 4—Determine Accretion of Discount Amount

10% of Beginning Value of Reserves = 10% * $1846 = $185

Step 5—Determine "Other Revisions" Line

This amount is a plug figure—$794 - $185 - $159 = $450

SCHEDULE 9.5
Future Cash Flows for 19Y0 (Thousands of Dollars)

	19Y1	19Y2	19Y3	Total	Present Value
Sales	$920	$828	$690	$2,438	$2,038 (a)
Production Costs	(120)	(108)	(90)	(318)	(266)(b)
Development Costs	-0-	-0-	-0-	-0-	-0-
Plant Removal	-0-	-0-	(42)	(42)	(32)(c)
Estimated Future Net Revenues	$800	$720	$558	$2,078	$1,740 (d)

(a) $920 * .90909 = $ 836
    $828 * .82645 = $ 684
    $690 * .75132 = $ 518

Present Value
  of Sales $2038

(b) $120 * .90909 = $109
    $108 * .82645 = $ 89
    $ 90 * .75132 = $ 68

Present Value of
Production
Costs $266

(c) $42 * .75132 = $32 (Present
     Value of Plant Removal
     and Site Restoration Costs)

(d) Present Value of
    Beginning Reserves   = $1740
    Net Cash Flow   900*
    Present Value at End
     of Year of Beginning
     Reserves $2640**

* Revenues ($1,150) - Pro-
  duction Costs ($150) -
  Development Costs
  ($100)   = $900

** Total Revisions = 19Y0 Present
   Value of Reserves Minus 19X9
   Present Value of Reserves =
   $2,640 - $1,846 (see Schedule 9.1)
   = $794

SCHEDULE 9.6
Tax Computation for 19Y0

Present Value of Reserves—Ending	
(see Schedule 9.5)	$1740
Tax Basis—Ending (see Schedule 9.3)	(167)
Future Taxable Income	1573
Tax Rate	40%
Income Tax	629
Less Previously Accrued Tax (see Schedule 9.2)	(673)
Provision for Future Taxes	(44)
Current Tax (see Schedule 9.3)	358
Provision for Taxes	$ 314

The two subtotals in the statement refer first to total economic benefits of oil and gas acquisition and exploration activities and second to total economic detriments to the same activities. The line "additions over evaluated costs" refers to the net effect of these two economic factors.

The provision for taxes is computed by adding to the increase or decrease in deferred tax computed on an RRA basis the tax liability of the current period. It should be noted that this amount will not be the same as the provision for income taxes on the historical cost income statement. Deferred taxes typically will decrease during years when production is greater than new discoveries. Schedules 9.2, 9.3, and 9.6 should be examined carefully so that an understanding of these tax complexities may be attained.

The Changes Statement

The second statement is illustrated in Exhibit 9.2, and basically is a summary of the changes in the current value model. The statement title and bottom three lines properly address the purpose of the statement. Notice in the bottom three lines that the approach is to calculate the net increase or decrease in estimated future net revenue and compare this amount with the present value number reported the previous year.

The primary number in the increases section will be the "additions and revisions" as reported during the current year in the results statement. These are reported at gross amounts and still refer to future quantities at current prices discounted at 10%.

If reserves are purchased in place, they are reported at their RRA computed value. This typically will result in a lower value being assigned to the reserves than the amount of the purchase price, and the excess should be deferred and charged to revisions or impairments on future changes statements.

The "reduction in future development costs" line refers to those current expenditures that eliminate the need to deduct future development costs from the present value model. That is, these costs no longer represent a future cash outflow in determining the previously defined present value.

EXHIBIT 9.2
Changes in Present Value of Estimated Future Net Revenue from Proved Oil and Gas Reserves

	19X9	19Y0
Increases:		
Additions and Revisions (Exhibit 9.1)	$2,216	$ 794
Less: Related Estimates of Future Development and Production Costs	(370)	-0-
Net Additions	$1,846	$ 794
Expenditures that Reduced Estimated Future Development Costs (Tangible—Lease C)	-0-	100
Subtotal	$1,846	$ 894
Decreases:		
Sales of Oil and Gas, Net of Production Costs	-0-	1,000
Net Increase (Decrease)	$1,846	($106)
Beginning of Year	-0-	1,846
End of Year	$1,846	$1,740

The primary decrease in the present value model will be sales of oil and gas produced which are reported at actual prices net of actual production costs. The difference between these actual amounts and the related present value amounts will be reflected in the revision section of the results statement. Sales of reserves in place are reported at actual sales price.

Summary of Implications of RRA Disclosures

There are several distinct implications all accountants should be aware of in the development of RRA. Even though the model is not a precise current value model, it certainly is a step toward implementing current value accounting. The RRA emphasis is on future cash flows, and those cash flows, though defined in present terms as far as costs and prices go, are discounted to reflect some form of present value.

The SEC requirements already have resulted in incorporating the RRA technique into the financial statements. Full-costing companies must limit their capitalization of oil and gas properties and wells to a value essentially equivalent to the RRA amount. This result implies that the SEC is not reluctant to implement these techniques into the primary financial statements of oil and gas producers.

If RRA concepts are to be required in the primary financial statements, a distinct change in their nature and purpose will be evident. That is, the income statement will no longer be centered on the difference between revenues and expenses but, rather, would report economic changes as a result of operations. Balance sheet amounts would no longer be computed on the basis of historical costs but would be concerned with explicit attempts at valuation.

The purpose of this chapter has been to provide some technical guidance in attempts to understand and implement RRA disclosures. The positions advanced in this chapter should not be used as a substitute for a careful analysis of the authoritative literature by those attempting to implement the technical requirements of RRA.

CHAPTER **10**

Accounting for Inflation in the Real Estate, Banking, Insurance, Regulated and Manufacturing Industries

🔲🔲🔲🔲🔲🔲🔲🔲🔲🔲🔲🔲

In addition to the problems of accounting for the exploration and extraction of natural resources on a current cost and constant dollar basis, other industries face unique problems in implementing the reporting requirements of Statement of Financial Accounting Standards (SFAS) No. 33, "Financial Reporting and Changing Prices." Among the industries that have special reporting problems with regard to SFAS No. 33 are the real estate industry, the banking and insurance industries, regulated businesses, and the manufacturing industry. This chapter will discuss the special problems faced in these industries and present illustrative disclosures for each.

Real Estate Industry

Paragraph 19 of SFAS No. 33 provided a special exemption from the current cost reporting requirements for income-producing properties of real estate enterprises. However, SFAS No. 41, "Financial Reporting and Changing Prices: Specialized Assets—Income-Producing Real Estate," requires that enterprises must make both current cost and constant dollar disclosures for these assets. Such enterprises are still required to make the historical cost/constant dollar disclosures required of other enterprises. In making the historical cost/constant dollar disclosures, real estate enterprises would follow the same computational procedures illustrated in Chapter 2.

In making the current cost disclosures, the enterprise may use *either* historical cost/constant dollar information or estimates of current cost for income-producing property. However, SFAS No. 41 does not provide specific guidelines for deriving the current cost information. Income-producing property is typically a very important asset to a real estate enterprise. While it may be possible to measure the current cost of income-producing properties and the related depreciation, frequently there are complicating factors that make it difficult, if not impossible, to directly compute the current cost of income-producing properties.

When an enterprise reports current cost information, a surrogate for the current cost amount may be computed. Typically, income-producing properties are leased under long-term contracts. As such, it is possible to derive a surrogate for current cost by computing the net present value of all future cash flows. This is illustrated in Schedule 10.1.

SCHEDULE 10.1
Net Present Value—Income-Producing Properties

Income-Producing Properties	Acquisition Date	Cash Inflows per Year*	Cash Outflows per Year**	Historical Cost***
A	1/1/X2	$30,000	$5,000	$100,000
B	1/1/X3	35,000	7,000	150,000
C	1/1/X5	50,000	12,000	200,000

Applicable Discount Rate:
19X6   9%
19X7   10%
19X8   12%

*Cash inflows occur at the beginning of the year—hence present value computations use annuity due amounts.
**Cash outflows occur at the end of the year—hence present value computations use rdinary annuity amounts.
***Accelerated depreciation is used in part to offset the effect of rising prices. Each property has an eight-year life and is rented for an eight-year period.

SCHEDULE 10.1 (continued)

<u>To determine the Average Current Cost for 19X6:</u>

Step 1. Compute the net present value of future cash flows as of beginning of 19X6:

Cash flows	×	Factor	=	Present Value of Cash Flows

Property A:
| Inflows* | $30,000 × 3.53130 = $105,939 |
| Outflows** | 5,000 × 3.23972 = (16,199) |

Net Present Value
Discounted at 9%
for 4 Years   <u>$ 89,740</u>

Property B:
| Inflows* | $35,000 × 4.23972 = $148,390 |
| Outflows** | 7,000 × 3.88965 = (27,228) |

Net Present Value
Discounted at 9%
for 5 Years   <u>$121,162</u>

Property C:
| Inflows* | $50,000 × 5.48592 = $274,296 |
| Outflows** | 12,000 × 5.03295 = (60,395) |

Net Present Value
Discounted at 9%
for 7 Years   <u>$213,901</u>

Step 2. Compute the net present value of future cash flows as of the beginning of 19X7:

	Cash flows	×	Factor	=	Present Value of Cash Flows
Property A:					
Inflows*	$30,000	×	2.73554	=	$ 82,066
Outflows**	5,000	×	2.48685	=	(12,434)
Net Present Value Discounted at 10% for 3 Years					$ 69,632
Property B:					
Inflows*	$35,000	×	3.48685	=	$122,040
Outflows**	7,000	×	3.16986	=	(22,189)

SCHEDULE 10.1 (continued)

Net Present Value
   Discounted at
   10% for 4 Years $ 99,851
                                                                   ──────────

Property C:
   Inflows* $50,000   ×   4.79079   = $239,540
   Outflows**   12,000   ×   4.35526   =   (52,263)
Net Present Value   ──────────
   Discounted at
   10% for 6 Years $187,277
                                                                   ══════════

       Step 3. Compute the average current cost for 19X6:

       (Current Cost—beginning of 19X6 + Current Cost—beginning of 19X7)/2 = Average Current Cost—19X6

       Property A ($89,740 + $69,632)/2 = $79,686
       Property B ($121,162 + $99,851)/2 = $110,507
       Property C ($213,901 + $187,277)/2 = $200,589

To determine the Average Current Cost for 19X7:

       Step 4. Compute the net present value of future cash flows as of the beginning of 19X8:

	Cash flows	×	Factor	=	Present Value of Cash Flows
Property A:					
Inflows*	$30,000	×	1.89286	=	$ 56,786
Outflows**	5,000	×	1.69005	=	(8,450)
Net Present Value					
Discounted at					
12% for 2 Years					$ 48,336
Property B:					
Inflows*	$35,000	×	2.69005	=	$ 94,152
Outflows**	7,000	×	2.40183	=	(16,813)
Net Present Value					
Discounted at					
12% for 3 Years					$ 77,339
Property C:					
Inflows*	$50,000	×	4.03735	=	$201,868
Outflows**	12,000	×	3.60478	=	(43,257)

SCHEDULE 10.1 (continued)

Net Present Value
  Discounted at
  12% for 5 Years   <u>$158,611</u>

  Step 5. Compute the average current cost for 19X7:

  (Current Cost—beginning of 19X7 + Current Cost—begining of 19X8)/2
  = Average Current Cost—19X7

  Property A   ($69,632 + $48,336)/2 = $58,984
  Property B   ($99,851 + $77,339)/2 = $88,595
  Property C   ($187,277 + $158,611)/2 = $172,944

<u>To compute Current Cost Depreciation for 19X7:</u>

  Step 6. Compute current cost depreciation for 19X7:

  Average Current—19X6 — Average Current Cost—19X7 = Current
  Cost Depreciation—19X7

  Property A $79,686 — $58,984 = $20,702
  Property B   110,507 — 88,595 = 21,912
  Property C   200,589 — 172,944 = <u>27,645</u>

  Total Current Cost Depreciation—   <u>$70,259</u>
  19X7

As Schedule 10.1 shows, the computation of the net present value of the future cash flows is impacted by both time (in that there is one less year to receive and pay cash as we progress from year 19X6 to 19X7, etc.) and the appropriate interest rate. Since the average current cost encompasses computations from the beginning of two years, it also is impacted by the changing interest rate. Therefore, it is critical that an appropriate interest rate be selected if the real estate enterprise opts for using the net present value of future cash flows as its measure of current cost. Another point to be made is that the net present value of future cash flows is the recoverable amount for assets held for use. As such, this is the *maximum* value that can be used as the current cost of such assets.

The general presumption is that depreciation methods, useful life estimates, and salvage values of assets should be the same for current cost purposes as are used for historical cost purposes. However, SFAS No. 33 provides an exception to this general presumption in that if the depreciation methods and estimates have been chosen partly to allow for changing prices, different depreciation methods may be used in computing current cost depreciation amounts. As Schedule 10.1 indicates, accelerated depreciation has been chosen to offset subsequent price changes. Therefore, it is appropriate to employ a different depreciation method for current cost purposes. Since the net present value of the future cash flows represents the value of the asset to the enterprise, the change in the net present value of the future cash flows from one period to the next must represent the decline in the value of the asset during that period. For that reason, depreciation has been calculated in step 6 of Schedule 10.1 as the change in the current cost of the asset (i.e., the decline in the value of each property or, alternatively stated, the value used up, in 19X7).

The historical cost/constant dollar computations would be identical to those illustrated for MR Corporation in Chapter 2. An illustration of the real estate disclosures can also be found in *Illustrations of Financial Reporting and Changing Prices.*[1] However, in computing the current cost income, if a real estate enterprise opts to use current cost amounts, the method depicted in Schedule 10.1 is appropriate. The *disclosure* of the current cost information would be identical to that shown in Chapter 3.

Banking and Insurance Industries

In many respects, the problems faced by banking and insurance enterprises are similar. With respect to current cost and constant dollar adjustments, most banks and insurance enterprises have relatively small amounts of inventory and depreciable assets.

In spite of arguments to the contrary, the Financial Accounting Standards Board (FASB) did not provide a special exemption to the banking and insurance industries from the reporting requirements of SFAS No. 33. As a matter of fact, by adding the second size criterion that public enterprises with total assets in excess of $1 billion are required to comply with SFAS No. 33, the FASB has specifically included many large banks and insurance companies who do not have enough inventory and property, plant, and equipment to meet the first size test. (See Chapter 2 for a complete discussion of who is required to comply with SFAS No. 33.)

There are, however, two general exceptions that apply to all enterprises which may reduce the reporting requirements for banks and insurance companies. The first is that if current cost amounts do not materially differ from historical cost/constant dollar amounts, only the

---

[1] Financial Accounting Standards Board. *Illustrations of Financial Reporting and Changing Prices* (Stamford, CN: Financial Accounting Standards Board, December 1979), pp. 91–102.

historical cost/constant dollar disclosures need be made. It is probable that most banks and insurance companies will benefit from this materiality test, and they will need to report only the historical cost/constant dollar amounts. The second materiality test is one that applies to all promulgated generally accepted accounting principles (GAAP). The provisions of SFAS No. 33 need not be applied to immaterial items. It is possible that many banks and insurance companies will not need to make either the historical cost/constant dollar or current cost income computation on the grounds of materiality.

There are other problems that are even more complex. For both banking and insurance enterprises, the purchasing power gain or loss is likely to be significant since these enterprises hold a large amount of monetary items. Since the purchasing power gain or loss measures the change in purchasing power of the monetary items held during the period, the classification of items as monetary and nonmonetary could significantly affect the amount of the reported purchasing power gain or loss. This effect is even more critical when the effect on income is considered. The effect of inflation on items classified as monetary is reported immediately through the purchasing power gain or loss. Therefore, this amount is excluded from income from continuing operations. On the other hand, the effect of inflation on nonmonetary assets is recognized over the productive life of the assets (through depreciation expense) and is included in income from continuing operations. Thus classification of items as monetary or nonmonetary affects both the timing of income recognition and the classification of the component of income. The definition (and hence classification) of monetary and nonmonetary items has been subject to considerable debate in the insurance industry. In particular, items such as loss reserves for claims, deferred policy acquisition costs, and unearned premiums have created difficulty in the past. The FASB defined monetary items as:

> *Monetary asset:* money or a claim to receive a sum of money, the amount of which is fixed or determinable without reference to future prices of specific goods or services.
> *Monetary liabilities:* an obligation to pay a sum of money, the amount of which is fixed or determinable without reference to future prices of specific goods or services.[2]

However, as the continuing controversy in the insurance industry indicates, the general definitions do not necessarily provide definitive guid-

---

[2] Financial Accounting Standards Board. "Financial Reporting and Changing Prices," *Statement of Financial Accounting Standards No. 33* (Stamford, CN: Financial Accounting Standards Board, September 1979), par. 47.

ance in the classification of all items. To supplement the general definitions of monetary items, the FASB provided a list of specific balance sheet items, indicating which are to be considered monetary and which should be treated as nonmonetary. That list is reproduced in the Appendix to Chapter 2 of this *Handbook*. For now, the definition and supplemental list provided by the FASB would appear to indicate that the monetary treatment is called for the controversial items. This is consistent with the FASB's task force recommendation on the treatment of assets and liabilities of banking and insurance enterprises.[3]

Another problem with the disclosure of the purchasing power gain or loss is the potential for financial statement users to misunderstand the significance of the statistic. A critical factor for banks is the impact of inflation upon interest income and interest expense. The purchasing power gain or loss does not provide a direct measure of the impact of inflation upon interest income and interest expense. As a consequence, additional disclosures may be helpful in assessing the effect of inflation upon financial institutions.

Whereas the prices of goods and services in the economy are directly related to the prices of other goods and services (i.e., for a manufacturing concern, as the price of its inputs rises, the price it charges for its outputs must also increase), the price of borrowing and lending funds (i.e., the interest rate charged) is more closely related to the *rate of change*—not the absolute amount of change—in the prices of goods and services. For example, when the rate of inflation declines, the interest rate is also likely to decline. The interest rate may return to its previous level (e.g., it may fall to say 8%); however, the prices of goods and services will remain at their current level (i.e., the *prices* of goods and services will not decline to previous levels). In addition, interest rates are subject to other pressures such as shifts in credit demands, monetary policy, and usury laws.

For these reasons, it is critical that the required constant dollar disclosures be supplemented with an analysis of the effect of inflation upon interest income and interest expense. One possible supplemental disclosure

---

[3] *Ibid.*, par. 171.

is illustrated in Exhibit 10.1. As this exhibit indicates, rather than showing a modest increase in net interest income from 19X4 to 19X8, net interest income decreased by $311 when adjusted for inflation.

EXHIBIT 10.1
Disclosure of Effect of Inflation
on Interest Income and Interest Expense
Constant Dollar Amounts in Average-for-the-Year 19X8

	19X8	19X7	19X6	19X5	19X4
Interest Income:					
Historical Cost/Nominal Dollars	$4,977	$4,445	$4,154	$3,882	$3,733
Historical Cost/Constant Dollars (Schedule 10.2)	4,977	4,785	4,761	4,706	4,939
Interest Expense:					
Historical Cost/Nominal Dollars	$3,139	$2,832	$2,551	$2,278	$2,109
Historical Cost/Constant Dollars (Schedule 10.2)	3,139	3,049	2,924	2,761	2,790
Net Interest Income (Expense):					
Historical Cost/Nominal Dollars	$1,838	$1,613	$1,603	$1,604	$1,624
Historical Cost/Constant Dollars (Schedule 10.2)	1,838	1,736	1,837	1,945	2,149
Increase (Decrease) in Net Interest Income:					
Historical Cost/Nominal Dollars	$ 255	$ 10	$ (1)	$ (20)	—
Historical Cost/Constant Dollars	102	(101)	(108)	(204)	—

SCHEDULE 10.2
Computation of Constant Dollar Interest—
Average 19X8 Constant Dollars

For Interest Income:

Step 1. Compute interest income in average-for-the-year 19X8 constant dollars:

Interest Income ** × (19X8 average CPI/base year CPI)* = Interest Income in Average 19X8 Constant Dollars

19X8	$4,977 × (195.4/195.4) =	$4,977
19X7	4,445 × (195.4/181.5) =	4,785
19X6	4,154 × (195.4/170.5) =	4,761
19X5	3,882 × (195.4/161.2) =	4,706
19X4	3,733 × (195.4/147.7) =	4,939

*From Schedule 2.1
**From Exhibit 10.1

Step 2. Compute interest expense in average-for-the-year 19X8 constant dollars:

Interest expense × (19X8 average CPI/base year CPI) = Interest Expense in Average 19X8 Constant Dollars

19X8	$3,139 × (195.4/195.4) =	$3,139
19X7	2,832 × (195.4/181.5) =	3,049
19X6	2,551 × (195.4/170.5) =	2,924
19X5	2,278 × (195.4/161.2) =	2,761
19X4	2,109 × (195.4/147.7) =	2,790

For Net Interest Income (expense):

Step 3. Compute net interest income (expense) in average-for-the-year 19X8 constant dollars:

Interest Income in 19X8 Constant Dollars — Interest Expense in 19X8 Constant Dollars = Net Interest Income (Expense) in 19X8 Constant Dollars

19X8	$4,977 − $3,139 =	$1,838
19X7	4,785 − 3,049 =	1,736
19X6	4,761 − 2,924 =	1,837
19X5	4,706 − 2,761 =	1,945
19X4	4,939 − 2,790 =	2,149

The effect of inflation upon banking and insurance enterprises is not as well comprehended by users of financial statements. Banks and insurance enterprises have two disclosure outlets to pursue, in conjunction with each other, to impress upon financial statement users how inflation has impacted the enterprise. First, since interest income and interest expense constitute a major portion of the operations, supplementary disclosures should reflect the impact of inflation upon these amounts. Second, as discussed in Chapter 4, a management discussion of the supplementary information is required by SFAS No. 33. Banks and insurance enterprises should fully exploit this opportunity to discuss the unique problems described above caused by inflation in these industries.

Regulated Businesses

Enterprises that are regulated have a unique problem in preparing financial statements in accordance with generally accepted accounting principles (GAAP). Due to the rate-making process, items of revenue and expense are often recognized for regulatory purposes in different time periods than they would be if they were recognized in accordance with GAAP. In recognition of this fact, Accounting Principles Board Opinion (APBO) No. 2—Addendum[4] specified certain circumstances under which different treatment of items was acceptable for regulated industries.

One of the significant operating constraints which distinguishes a regulated business from a nonregulated enterprise is that regulated businesses (particularly utilities) may not be permitted to recover more than historical cost/nominal dollar amounts in their selling prices. As such, it has been argued that inventory, property, plant, and equipment, and the related expenses of a regulated enterprise should not be stated in excess of the historical cost/nominal dollar amounts for purposes of computing either constant dollars or current cost income, since to do so would state the items in excess of their recoverable amounts.

The contrasting view is that regulated enterprises are subject to the same erosion of capital as are nonregulated enterprises. As a consequence, the presentation of constant dollar and current cost income amounts may lead to a better public understanding of the operations of regulated enterprises and may provide a more useful basis to use in assessing the ability of the regulated enterprises to maintain capital.

Since regulated enterprises are subject to the effects of inflation, the FASB concluded that constant dollar and current cost disclosures should be made by these enterprises. Therefore, in making these disclosures, such

---

[4]Accounting Principles Board. "Accounting Principles for Regulated Industries," *Addendum to Opinion No. 2* (New York: American Institute of Certified Public Accountants, 1962).

enterprises should measure assets at historical cost/constant dollar amounts and current cost amounts, and make appropriate adjustments for lower recoverable amounts. Failure to consider recoverable amounts— which may very well be historical cost/nominal dollar amounts due to the rate-making process—could give a misleading impression of the worth of the assets employed by the enterprise.

In measuring the expenses for constant dollar and current cost disclosures, there are considerations that point to two alternatives: (1) measure expenses at historical cost/constant dollars and current cost or recoverable amount, if lower, in all situations, or (2) measure expenses at historical cost/constant dollar and current cost or lower recoverable amount unless replacement of the asset would be undertaken under current economic conditions, in which case lower recoverable amounts would be ignored.

The difference between the two alternatives can best be seen through an example. Exhibits 10.2 (constant dollar) and 10.3 (current cost) provide illustrations of the two alternatives. As can be seen from Exhibit 10.2, the reduction to net recoverable amounts of $266,029 is excluded from income from operations and included as a component of the price-level effects under alternative 1. Under alternative 2, the reduction to net recoverable amounts is included in income from continuing operations through increased depreciation charges. Exhibit 10.3 shows that the same effect is true under the current cost approach.

The second alternative would appear to be preferable for several reasons. First, it provides a basis for the assessment of income from continuing operations assuming that the assets will be replaced. In addition, the amount that an enterprise has sacrificed by using the service potential of the assets is better measured by current costs than by recoverable amounts when the assets are to be replaced. An enterprise that is affected by rate regulation differs from other enterprises because it is likely to replace assets even though the current cost of the assets exceeds the recoverable amounts. Furthermore, the recoverable amounts will be lower than current cost only because of the effect of rate regulation. Replacement will therefore be a worthy investment because subsequent rates will be based upon the expenditures incurred to replace the assets. For these reasons, it would appear that alternative 2 is preferable for disclosing the effects of changing prices upon a regulated enterprise.

Since regulated enterprises have unique operating conditions, the management discussion can be very effective in telling their story to financial statement users. As such, the second alternative can have two potential benefits. First, it will allow management to explain dividend and reinvestment policies to investors and potential investors in light of the future costs it expects to incur in order to maintain its operating capacity. Second, increased future costs can be highlighted is subsequent rate requests which will be filed with the regulatory bodies. Exhibit 10.4 illustrates the constant dollar and current cost disclosures (using the statement format) that a regulated enterprise would make using the second alternative.

EXHIBIT 10.2
Historical Cost/Constant Dollar Disclosures for Regulated Enterprises Restated to Average-for-the-Year 19X9 Constant Dollars

	Historical Cost/ Nominal Dollars (Assumed)	Historical Cost/ Constant Dollars Alternative 1	Historical Cost/ Constant Dollars Alternative 2
Sales	$1,352,000	$1,352,000	$1,352,000
Operating Expenses (exclusive of depreciation)	$1,144,000	$1,144,000	$1,144,000
Depreciation (Schedule 10.3)	92,000	170,004	436,033
	$1,236,000	$1,314,004	$1,580,033
Income (Loss) from Continuing Operations	$ 116,000	$ 37,996	$ (228,033)
Reduction to net recoverable amount (Step 3, Schedule 10.3)		$ (266,029)	
Gain from decline in purchasing power of amount owed*		148,256	$ 148,256
		$ (117,773)	$ 148,256

*Computations of gain or loss from change in purchasing power are illustrated in Chapter 2.

SCHEDULE 10.3
Computation of Historical Cost/Constant Dollar Depreciation Expense

For Alternative 1:

Step 1. Determine recoverable amount (since rates allow for amounts to be recovered to be historical cost, recoverable amounts are based upon historical cost):

Historical Cost/Nominal Dollar $\times$ Average 19X9 CPI/ $=$ Recoverable
Net Property, Plant,   Year-End CPI   Amounts
    and Equipment

Beginning of 19X9 $2,918,000 \times (217.1/202.9) = \$3,122,217$
End of 19X9 $2,826,000^* \times (217.1/228.4) = 2,686,184$

*Assume that no additions were made in 19X9, therefore the only change is due to net depreciation of $92,000.

Step 2. Compute historical cost/constant dollar depreciation (see Chapter 2 for illustration of computational procedures):

Historical cost/constant dollar depreciation $170,004
(alternative 1)

For Alternative 2:

Step 3. Determine adjustment to depreciation expense for recoverable amounts*:

Recoverable Amounts (beginning of year)	Historical Cost/ — Constant Dollar — Depreciation	Recoverable Amounts (end of year)	Adjustment for = Net Recoverable Amounts
$3,122,217	— $170,004	— $2,686,184 =	$266,029

*If there were additions during the year, the amount of additions would be added in this equation in computing the adjustment for recoverable amounts.

Step 4. Adjust depreciation expense for recoverable amounts:

Depreciation Expense + Adjustment = Depreciation Expense (alternative 2)

$170,004   + $266,029 = $436,033

EXHIBIT 10.3
Current Cost Disclosures for Regulated Enterprises
Restated to Average-for-the-Year 19X9 Constant Dollars

	Historical Cost/ Nominal Dollars	Current Cost Alternative 1	Current Cost Alternative 2
Sales	$1,352,000	$1,352,000	$1,352,000
Operating Expense (exclusive of depreciation)	$1,144,000	$1,144,000	$1,144,000
Depreciation (Schedule 10.4)	92,000	245,766	413,063
	$1,236,000	$1,389,766	$1,557,063
Income (Loss) from Continuing Operations	$ 116,000	$ (37,766)	$ (205,063)
Increase in specific prices of property, plant and equipment (Schedule 10.5)		$ 673,376	$ 673,376
Reduction to net recoverable amount (Step 2, Schedule 10.4)		$ (167,297)	
Effect of inflation (Schedule 10.5)		(696,346)	(696,346)
Excess of increase in specific prices over increase in general price-level after reduction to net recoverable amount (Schedule 10.5)		(190,267)	(22,970)
Gain from decline in purchasing power of amounts owed (Exhibit 10.2)		148,256	148,256
Net Amount		$ (42,011)	$ 125,286

SCHEDULE 10.4
Computation of Current Cost Depreciation

For Alternative 1:

    Step 1. Compute current cost depreciation on lower recoverable amounts:

    Current Cost Depreciation $245,766

    (see Chapter 3 for illustration of computation of current cost depreciation)

For Alternative 2:

    Step 2. Compute specific price increase in excess of general price increase:

	Current Cost/ Nominal Dollars	Factor	Current Cost/ Average 19X9 Constant Dollars
Beginning of Year	$5,652,020	×(217.1/202.9)=	$6,047,578
Additions	-0-		-0-
Depreciation (Alternative 1)	(245,766)		(245,766)
End of year	(6,079,630)	×(217.1/228.4)=	(5,778,842)
Increase (Decrease)	$ 673,376		$ (22,970)

Increase on specific prices of property, plant, and equipment	$673,376
Effect of general prices	(696,346)
Excess of increase in general prices over increase in specific prices	$ (22,970)

For Alternative 2:

    Step 3. Compute adjustment for net recoverable amounts*:

Recoverable Amount (beginning of year)	— Current Cost Depreciation	Specific Price Increase excess of general price + level increase	Recoverable Amount — (end of yr)	Adjustment for net Recoverable = Amount
$3,122,217	— $245,766	— $22,970	— $2,686,184	= $167,297

*If there were additions during the year, the amount of additions would be added in these equations in computing the adjustment for recoverable amounts.

SCHEDULE 10.4 (continued)

Step 4. Adjust current cost depreciation for recoverable amounts:

Current Cost Depreciation (alternative 1)	+	Adjustment for Recoverable Amounts	=	Current Cost Depreciation (alternative 2)
$245,766	+	$167,297	=	$413,063

SCHEDULE 10.5
Computation of Increase in Specific Prices of Property, Plant, and Equipment

Alternative 1 (where amounts are reduced to lower recoverable amounts):

	Current Cost/ Nominal Dollars	Net Recoverable Amounts Current Cost/Average 19X9 Dollars
Beginning of year	$5,652,020	$3,122,217*
Additions	-0-	-0-
Depreciation	(245,766)	(245,766)
End of year	(6,079,630)	(2,686,184) *
Increase (Decrease)	$ 673,376	$ (190,267)

*From Step 1, Schedule 10.3.

Increase in specific prices of property, plant, and equipment	$ 673,376
Reduction to net recoverable amounts (step 3, Schedule 10.4)	(167,297)
Effect of general price level (step 2, Schedule 10.4)	(696,346)
Excess of increase in general price level over increase in specific prices	$ (190,267)

Alternative 2 (where amounts are not reduced to net recoverable amounts for items which will be replaced):

Increase in specific prices of property, plant, and equipment	$ 673,376
Effect of general price level	(696,346)
Excess of increase in general price level over increase in specific prices	$ (22,970)

EXHIBIT 10.4
Regulated MR Corporation
Statement of Income from Continuing Operations
Adjusted for Changing Prices
For the Year Ended December 31, 19X9
(Average-for-the-Year 19X9 Dollars)

	As Reported in Primary Statements	Adjusted for General Inflation	Adjusted for Changes in Specific Prices (Current Costs)
Sales	$1,352,000	$1,352,000	$1,352,000
Operating Expenses	$1,144,000	$1,144,000	$1,144,000
Depreciation	92,000	436,033	413,063
	$1,236,000	$1,580,033	$1,557,063
Income (Loss) from Continuing Operations	$ 116,000	$ (228,033)	$ (205,063)
Gain from decline in purchasing power of net amounts owed		$ 148,256	$ 148,256
Increase in specific prices of property, plant, and equipment held during the year*			$ 673,376
Effect of increase in general price level			(696,346)
Excess of increase in general price level over increase in specific prices			$ 22,970

*At the end of the year, current cost of property, plant and equipment, net of accumulated depreciation was $5,778,842.

Manufacturing Industry

Manufacturing enterprises have a greater problem in implementing the disclosure requirements of SFAS No. 33 than do retailing enterprises. Manufacturing concerns produce products. Of necessity, the manufacturing facilities must be in working order to produce the products. Therefore, a portion of the cost of the facilities must be allocated to the cost of the finished products. For a manufacturing enterprise, then, the inflation-adjusted depreciation affects both the operating expenses and the cost of goods sold.

Retailing enterprises that use LIFO for valuing their inventories have been provided with a simplifying assumption in computing constant dollar and current cost of goods sold. SFAS No. 33 states that:

> (w)here inventories and cost of sales are accounted for under the LIFO method in the primary financial statements the only adjustment normally required in computing income from continuing operations would be to eliminate the effect of changing prices on any prior period LIFO layer liquidations.[5]

However, manufacturing enterprises may not be able to use this simplified approach because of the potential impact depreciation can have on the inventories and cost of goods sold.

Exhibit 10.5 provides a comparison of the current cost of goods sold that would be reported by a manufacturing enterprise when LIFO costs are not adjusted for increased depreciation charges, and the cost of goods sold when LIFO costs are adjusted for increased depreciation charges. As Exhibit 10.5 indicates, there will be significant increase to current cost of goods sold when current cost depreciation on manufacturing facilities materially exceeds historical cost depreciation. This is true because the major portion of the total manufacturing costs is included in the cost of goods sold with a relatively small portion of those costs being deferred as an additional LIFO layer. As a consequence, the majority of the increased depreciation charge will also be charged to current cost of goods sold. Since constant dollar adjustments will also cause a material increase in depreciation charges, a similar adjustment will be needed for computing cost of goods sold on a constant dollar basis.

---

[5] Financial Accounting Standards Board. "Financial Reporting and Changing Prices," *Statement of Financial Accounting Standards No. 33* (Stamford, CN: Financial Accounting Standards Board, September 1979), par. 212.

EXHIBIT 10.5
Cost of Goods Sold—Current Cost Basis

	As Reported in Primary Financial Statements LIFO-no adjustment	LIFO adjusted
Beginning Inventories	$75,767	$75,767
Cost of Goods Manufactured (Schedule 10.5)	563,483	569,675
Cost of Goods Available for Sale	$639,250	$645,442
Less Ending Inventories (Schedule 10.6)	80,763	80,820
Cost of Goods Sold	$558,487	$564,622

SCHEDULE 10.6
Adjustments for Increased Depreciation

For LIFO Adjustment:

Step 1. Determine additional depreciation charges on a current cost basis (see chapter 3):

$6,192—assumed increased depreciation on current cost basis

Step 2. Adjust manufacturing costs to reflect additional depreciation:

Cost of Goods Manufactured (unadjusted)	+	Additional Depreciation	=	Cost of Goods Manufactured (unadjusted)

$563,483 + $6,192 = $569,675

Step 3. Determine new LIFO layer:

Ending Inventories − Beginning Inventories = New LIFO Layer (unadjusted)

$80,763 − $75,767 = $4,996

Step 4. Determine portion of manufacturing costs retained in ending inventory:

SCHEDULE 10.6 (continued)

Increase in Inventories during Year/Total Manufacturing Costs = Percent of Costs Retained in Ending Inventories

$4,996/$563,483 = .9%

Step 5. Adjusted new LIFO layer for additional depreciation:

New LIFO Layer + (Additional Depreciation × Percent in Ending Inventories) = New LIFO Layer—Adjusted

$4,996 + ($6,192 × .9%) = $5,053

Step 6. Determine adjusted current cost of goods sold:

Beginning Inventories + Adjusted Manufacturing Costs − Adjusted Ending Inventories = Adjusted Current Cost of Goods Sold

$75,767 + $569,675 − $80,820 = $564,622

If a basis other than LIFO is used to value the inventories, cost of goods sold will need to be adjusted by both manufacturing and retailing enterprises. This adjustment process is illustrated in Chapter 2 for the constant dollar disclosures and in Chapter 3 for the current cost disclosures. Again, however, manufacturing enterprises will find this to be a more difficult task than will retailing enterprises. Manufacturing enterprises will need to adjust the manufacturing costs and inventory amounts (as shown in Schedule 10.6) for the computations when FIFO is used, while retailing enterprises need only adjust inventory amounts when average-for-the-year constant dollars are used.

Management Discussion

As Chapter 4 indicated, the management discussion of the supplementary information gives management a viable outlet to tell its story about the impact of inflation upon the operations of the enterprise. Among the factors management should highlight are the effective tax rate based upon the constant dollar and current cost information and the potential erosion of capital.

Management teams of enterprises in certain industries have an additional difficulty in that the effects of inflation upon their enterprises are unique because of the industry in which they operate. As a consequence, the management discussion of the supplementary data can serve a dual purpose. It can allow management to discuss the impact of inflation upon the operations of the enterprise and in addition provide management with the opportunity to explain the special constraints faced by the enterprise as it tries to combat the effects of inflation (e.g., the restriction to recovery of cost for regulated enterprises).

Summary

This chapter has discussed the problems of complying with the disclosure requirements of SFAS No. 33 for enterprises in four types of industries: real estate, banking and insurance, regulated, and manufacturing. Enterprises in these industries have additional problems in disclosing the effects of inflation, problems which do not confront a retailing enterprise. Disclosure of additional information beyond the minimally required supplementary disclosures may significantly aid the financial statement users in evaluating the performance of the enterprise. This chapter has discussed the methods that can be used to develop the additional information and the manner of disclosure applicable to the additional information.

CHAPTER 11

How to Use Ratio Analysis for Short-Term Decisions

□□□□□□□□□□□□

In analyzing the short-term creditworthiness of an enterprise, short-term creditors and management of the enterprise are concerned with the short-term liquidity of the enterprise. Furthermore, the ability to continue to generate cash in the future is equally important since the enterprise must maintain its short-term liquidity.

Ratio analysis is often used as a tool in evaluating the performance of the enterprise. Two types of ratios that are used in evaluating the short-term operating performance of the enterprise are (1) liquidity ratios and (2) efficiency ratios. This chapter will illustrate the use of ratio analysis for short-term decisions and discuss the impact that inflation can have upon the liquidity and efficiency ratios. A summary of the ratios is provided in the Appendix to Chapter 12.

Liquidity Ratios

The general objective of liquidity ratios is to indicate the firm's ability to meet its short-term financial obligations. As such, these ratios focus upon the relative amount of the enterprise's liquid assets in comparison to its short-term obligations. Two commonly used measures of short-term liquidity are the current ratio and the acid-test ratio.

The *current ratio,* computed by dividing current assets by current liabilities, has long been employed as a barometer of the liquidity of an enterprise. Since current assets represent the pool from which liquidity is generated, their ratio to current liabilities represents a measure of the enterprise's ability to meet its short-term obligations as they come due.

Another measure of liquidity which has developed in recent years is the *acid-test ratio.* It is computed by dividing quick assets (cash, short-term receivables and marketable securities) by current liabilities. Since inventories must be sold and then the receivables must be collected before cash is available, it is often argued that the current ratio is not a stringent enough measure of the enterprise's short-term liquidity. The acid-test ratio overcomes this problem by using only the cash and near-cash items in the computation.

Schedule 11.1 presents the liquidity ratios for MR Corporation for three years. By computing the ratios for three years, a creditor can see

SCHEDULE 11.1
Liquidity Ratios of MR Corporation

Current Ratio (Current Assets ÷ Current Liabilities):
  (from Figure 2.1)

	19X7	19X8	19X9
Current Assets	$1,995,000	$2,061,000	$2,537,000
Current Liabilities	$ 242,891	$ 215,793	$ 227,532
Working Capital	$1,752,109	$1,845,207	$2,309,468
Current Ratio	8.21	9.55	11.15

Acid-Test (Quick Assets ÷ Current Liabilities):

	19X7	19X8	19X9
Quick Assets	$1,595,000	$1,641,000	$2,057,000
Current Liabilities	$ 242,891	$ 215,793	$ 227,532
Net Quick Assets	$1,352,109	1,425,207	$1,829,468
Acid-Test Ratio	6.57	7.60	9.04
Purchasing Power Loss (see Schedule 2.7 for an illustration of this computation)	$ (3,892)	$ (19,060)	$ (68,437)

not only what the corporation's liquidity position is presently, but also, the trend in its liquidity. In analyzing the short-term liquidity position of an enterprise, it is important to use the trend of the liquidity position. By employing trend analysis, it can be seen whether the enterprise is improving its position or becoming progressively less liquid. An analysis of MR Corporation's short-term position will be presented following the discussion of the efficiency ratios.

Efficiency Ratios

Efficiency ratios provide information on how well the enterprise is using its assets. For evaluating the short-term position of the enterprise, it is important to evaluate the efficiency with which the enterprise employs its short-term assets.

The two primary operating current assets (exclusive of cash) are the receivables and the inventory. The liquidity ratios measure whether the enterprise has the ability to meet its short-term obligations. However, it is significant to note that the receivables represent a material amount of the current assets of MR Corporation. Liabilities typically cannot be retired directly by the receivables, but rather the liabilities are retired with the cash collected from the receivables. It is important, then, to determine how rapidly the receivables will be collected, thereby generating cash. The average collection period for receivables provides the financial statement reader with a measure of the approximate time that elapses between the sale of merchandise and the collection of cash. The average collection period for receivables is computed by dividing the days in a year by the receivable turnover (credit sales divided by average receivables).

The inventory turnover ratio provides a measure of the utilization of the inventory. A higher inventory turnover would indicate that the enterprise sells its inventory relatively quickly. As a consequence, receivables are generated more rapidly. A higher inventory turnover would reduce the operating cycle and allow the enterprise to carry a smaller portion of liquid assets than would be needed with a lower inventory turnover. The inventory turnover ratio is computed by dividing the cost of goods sold by the average inventory for the year.

Schedule 11.2 presents the short-term efficiency ratios for MR Corporation for the three years 19X7, 19X8, and 19X9. As is the case for the liquidity ratios, it is important to evaluate the efficiency ratios in the context of their recent trend. Also, it is important to note that the inventory turnover ratio has been computed using historical cost/nominal dollar amounts, historical cost/constant dollar amounts, and current cost/constant dollar amounts. This will aid the financial statement reader in evaluating MR Corporation's ability to meet its future as well as its present obligations.

SCHEDULE 11.2
Efficiency Ratios for MR Corporation

Collection Period for Receivables (Days in Year ÷ Receivables Turnover):
(from Figures 2.1 and 2.2)

	19X7	19X8	19X9
Sales	$2,400,000	$3,200,000	$4,000,000
÷ Average Receivables	$1,021,875	$1,213,500	$1,386,750
Receivable Turnover	2.34 times	2.64 times	2.88 times
Collection Period	155 days	138 days	127 days

Inventory Turnover (Cost of Goods Sold ÷ Average Inventories):
(from Figures 2.1, 2.2, 2.3, 2.4, 3.3, and 3.4)

	19X7	19X8	19X9
Historical Cost/Nominal Dollar			
Cost of Goods Sold	$1,560,000	$2,080,000	$2,600,000
	$ 350,000	$ 410,000	$ 450,000
Inventory Turnover	4.46 times	5.07 times	5.78 times
Historical Cost/Constant Dollar (end-of-year 19X9)			
(constant dollars)			
Cost of Goods Sold	$1,603,928	$2,472,758	$2,790,192
Inventories	$ 442,639	$ 482,726	$ 477,926
Inventory Turnover	3.62 times	5.12 times	5.84 times
Current Cost/Constant Dollar			
Cost of Goods Sold	$1,998,579	$2,471,851	$2,795,066
Inventories	$ 451,637	$ 488,869	$ 482,832
Inventory Turnover	4.43 times	5.06 times	5.79 times

Analysis of MR Corporation's Short-Term Position

As Schedule 11.1 indicates, MR Corporation has maintained a very liquid position from 19X7 through 19X9. This is indicated by the very high current ratio and acid-test ratio maintained throughout the time period. Further, the corporation has an upward trend in each ratio.

Maintaining adequate liquidity is important; however, there is a danger in maintaining too much liquidity. MR Corporation has had an increase in its acid-test ratio from 6.57 in 19X7 to 9.04 in 19X9. In a time of significant price increases, it may be inadvisable to hold a significant amount of liquid (and hence, to a large degree, monetary) items. This is reflected in the dramatic increase in the purchasing power loss suffered by the corporation. It suffered a purchasing power loss of $68,437 in 19X9. This loss represents approximately 10% of its net monetary items.

To further evaluate MR Corporation's short-term position, the efficiency ratios should be studied. The inventory turnover ratio has shown a steady increase from 19X7 to 19X9 (see Schedule 11.2) regardless of whether it is computed on a historical cost/nominal dollar, historical cost/constant dollar, or current cost/constant dollar basis. It has increased to nearly six times per year in 19X9. This indicates that the corporation sells and replaces its inventory, on the average, every two months. As a consequence, the inventory turnover ratios are very similar under all three bases. By having a high turnover, MR Corporation is not faced with significant price increases on each acquisition. On the other hand, if it had a lower inventory turnover, it would make inventory purchases on a less frequent basis and be susceptible to more significant price increases between acquisitions.

The collection period for receivables must be evaluated in conjunction with the inventory turnover. As Schedule 11.2 indicates, the trend of the collection period is positive in that the collection period is declining. However, although it is declining, it still took an average of 127 days to collect its receivables in 19X9. The long collection period itself leads directly to the high liquidity ratios since a large amount of receivables remain on hand waiting to be collected. This effect increases as MR Corporation increases its sales from year to year. Furthermore, receivables are monetary items. As a consequence, the long collection period indirectly leads to an increase in the purchasing power loss each year. Perhaps most importantly, receivables, in themselves, are nonproductive assets. They can be converted into cash—a potentially productive asset—but in the form of receivables, they are nonproductive.

Since MR Corporation has an inventory turnover level of six times per year, it sells its inventory every 60 days (approximately). That fact, along with the collection period for receivables, means that it is making sales more rapidly than it collects the cash from the sales. The persistence of this pattern, then, can only lead to further increases in and holding of receivables. This would further compound the problem which already exists; that MR Corporation is holding a large amount of nonproductive assets.

After an analysis has been made of both the inventory turnover and the collection period for receivables, the operating cycle can be evaluated. (The operating cycle is the time it takes an enterprise to begin with cash, acquire inventory, sell the inventory, plus the time required to collect the receivables.) In 19X7, the operating cycle for MR Corporation was approximately 237 days. This was reduced to 210 days in 19X8 and 190 days in 19X9. Over the three-year period, the corporation has successfully reduced its operating cycle by 47 days (or 20%). However, its operating cycle in 19X9 of 190 days still is in excess of half the year. This long operating cycle forces it to maintain a large amount of cash on hand to meet two needs: first, it needs cash to pay its current obligations as they come due, and second, it needs cash to finance its other daily activities. As a consequence, MR Corporation is forced to maintain a *cash* balance which is approximately double the amount of its current liabilities.

Recommendations for Improving Short-Term Operations

At present, MR Corporation is holding far too much in monetary assets—both in cash and in receivables. This is caused primarily by the long time period needed to collect its receivables, although it has improved its collection period in the past three years.

MR Corporation needs to undertake aggressive action to drastically reduce its collection period. It would be desirable to reduce the collection period to approximately 45 days. If this were done, its operating cycle would be significantly reduced. By reducing the operating cycle, it could operate with less cash on hand. As a consequence, a significant portion of the cash currently needed to operate the enterprise would be nonessential to the daily operations. As such, that cash could be invested, thereby converting a non-income generating asset into one that does produce revenue.

Summary

This chapter has reviewed the short-term evaluation of an enterprise in inflationary time periods. When inflation persists, it is even more important than usual to maintain a proper liquidity position. If the enterprise is overly liquid, it will suffer severe purchasing power losses from the erosion of the purchasing power on the monetary items held. If, on the other hand, the enterprise does not maintain enough liquid assets, it runs the risk of being caught in a credit pinch. As was discussed in Chapter 10, interest rates tend to move in conjunction with inflation rates. As a consequence, if an enterprise must borrow because it is short of liquid assets, a substantial interest rate is likely to be incurred during high-inflation periods.

As can also be seen from this chapter, maintaining a proper operating cycle is critical to maintaining a proper liquidity position. Since, in inflationary periods, it is more difficult to collect receivables on a timely basis, the enterprise must carefully monitor its collection period so that its operating cycle will not increase significantly.

The following chapter will discuss the problems of evaluating the long-term potential of an enterprise in inflationary periods. It will discuss the potential implications that the short-term position—as discussed here—may have on the long-term position of the enterprise. It will also discuss potential solvency indicants as well as the potential for future economic growth by the enterprise.

CHAPTER 12

How to Use Ratio Analysis for Long-Term Decisions

□□□□□□□□□□□□

For long-term creditors, stockholders, and potential long-term investors, the long-term creditworthiness of the enterprise is of greater importance in evaluating investment alternatives than is its short-term liquidity. This is not to say that long-term investors will ignore the liquidity position of the enterprise, but rather, the analysis of its short-term position will provide a supplement for the analysis of its long-term position.

Ratio analysis also can be used to aid the investor in evaluating the long-term capabilities of the enterprise. Two categories of ratios that are used in evaluating the long-term operating potential are (1) long-term solvency ratios, and (2) profitability and return ratios. This chapter will discuss the use of ratios in analyzing the long-term operating potential of an enterprise that is operating in an inflationary environment. A summary of the ratios is provided in the Appendix to this chapter.

Long-term Solvency Ratios

The primary objective of long-term solvency ratios is to provide the investors with an indicant of the ability of the enterprise to meet both the principal and interest payments on its outstanding long-term obligations. This differs from the objective of the liquidity ratios discussed in the previous chapter in that the long-term solvency ratios stress the long-term financial and operating capabilities of the enterprise.

The first long-term solvency ratio normally analyzed is the debt to equity ratio. This is computed by dividing total liabilities by total stockholders equity. As such, the numerator incorporates both short-term and long-term debt. This measure of solvency is based upon the notion that the larger the portion of capital provided by creditors, the greater is the risk sustained by the creditors. Conversely, that same high proportion of debt financing leads to a greater return for the stockholders (i.e., trading on equity or using financial leverage). However, the debt to equity ratio does not distinguish between the different degrees of risk taken by the creditors. For example, some of the long-term creditors may have secured borrowings. As such, their risk is not as great as the risk of the unsecured creditor. Despite this shortcoming, it is still widely used as a general indicator of the risk being taken by the creditors.

In addition to providing an indicator of the risk assumed by the creditors, the debt to equity ratio also provides a measure of the financial risk to the common stockholders. Financial risk is typically measured in terms of volatility in earnings to the common stockholders. As the degree of debt increases, the common stockholder is more susceptible to earnings fluctuations, since the interest charges must be paid before income can accrue to the common stockholder. In general, the greater the amount of debt an enterprise incurs, the greater will be its earnings volatility and hence its financial risk. As a consequence, the debt to equity ratio provides an indicant of risk incurred by both the stockholders and the creditors.

As a supplement to the debt to equity ratio, the ratio of long-term debt to equity is often evaluated. This ratio provides a more direct measure of the long-term financing provided by creditors and stockholders. This ratio provides essentially the same information as does the debt to equity ratio except that it excludes the short-term creditors from the computation. This is done since short-term creditors provide operating assets (such as acquisition of inventories) whereas long-term creditors provide financial capital for expansion purposes (such as borrowing to build a new factory).

Another measure of the risk to the long-term creditors is provided by the times interest earned figure. The times interest earned is computed by dividing income before interest and taxes by the fixed interest charges. This number measures the margin of safety of the fixed payments to be made to creditors. The ratio indicates the ability of the enterprise to meet its fixed charges out of its current earnings. The higher the ratio, the larger the margin of safety provided to the creditors.

Profitability and Return Ratios

Profitability and return ratios provide the financial statement user with a basis for evaluating the operational performance of the enterprise. By comparing revenues with invested capital, these ratios provide an indicant of the efficiency of the enterprise in using the capital that has been invested by creditors astockholders.

The first return ratios computed for MR Corporation are net sales to stockholders' equity (net sales divided by average total stockholders' equity) and net sales to total assets (net sales divided by average total assets). These ratios provide the financial statement user with a measure of the gross amount that the enterprise is generating for every dollar invested. Net sales to stockholders' equity makes that comparison only for the investment provided by stockholders, whereas the net sales to total assets ratio provides the information based upon all invested capital.

The return on assets (computed by dividing net income by average total assets) and return on equity (computed by dividing net income by average stockholders' equity) ratios provide a means for evaluating the net return on invested capital after all operating expenses have been deducted. As is the case with the net sales to stockholders' equity and net sales to total assets, the return on equity ratio provides an indicant of the return per dollar invested by the stockholders, while the return on assets ratio provides an indicant of the return per total dollar invested. These ratios differ in purpose from the long-term solvency ratios in that they provide a measure of operating efficiency rather than financial efficiency.

Another measure of operating efficiency is the return on sales—computed by dividing net income by net sales. Return on sales indicates how many operating costs are being incurred in order to generate revenues. Return on sales provides a link between the net sales to total assets or stockholders' equity ratio and the return on assets or equity ratio. Also, the trend of the return on sales ratio is very important. A declining trend may indicate that the productive assets are becoming old and less efficient and may need replacement soon.

Perhaps the most widely used single figure in evaluating the performance of the enterprise is its earnings per share (EPS). The EPS provides a measure of the income available to the common stockholder for each share of stock held. Corporate management often defines its policy goals in terms of the effect upon EPS of certain actions. It provides a general guideline as to the amount of income available to the common stockholder and also a basis for future expectations about the enterprise.

A natural extension of the evaluation of EPS is the price-earnings (PE) ratio. This is computed by dividing the market price per share by the EPS. This ratio provides a measure of how much the investor is paying to receive the EPS. Stock prices are based upon expectation of future earning performance of the enterprise. Therefore, enterprises which have prospects of high earnings growth would have higher PE ratios than would enterprises with prospects of lower earnings growth. The PE ratio is an indicator of the future earnings prospects of the enterprise as anticipated by the stock market.

Another important ratio from the stockholders' perspective is the dividend payout ratio—dividends divided by net income. This ratio measures the percentage of net income being returned to the stockholders. The ratio provides an indicator of the dividend policy of the enterprise. It also reflects the expectations of management regarding the uncertainty associated with future earnings.

Analysis of MR Corporation's Long-term Position

As an examination of Schedule 12.1 shows, MR Corporation has been reducing its relative borrowings over the past three years. This is true on all three measurement bases—historical cost/nominal dollars, historical cost/constant dollars, and current cost/constant dollars. As a consequence, the stockholders are being asked to provide a greater portion of the invested capital.

This trend is further substantiated by examining the trend of the times interest earned figure. Again, on all three measurement bases, the figure has increased dramatically. Using the current cost/constant dollar base—which provides for replacement of operating facilities in its computation of net income—the times interest earned is in excess of ten times. Or, income could decline by a factor of ten and MR Corporation would still be able to cover its fixed charges out of current earnings.

The figures on Schedule 12.1 would appear to indicate that MR Corporation is not using enough financial leverage. It appears that the stockholders are accepting a greater portion of the burden for providing additional invested capital. As a consequence, creditors—who are already in a less risky position than the stockholders—are being asked to take even less risk while the stockholders are being asked to accept more financial risk.

Theoretically, if the stockholders are accepting more financial risk, they can expect a greater operating return. As Schedule 12.2 shows, the gross return (net sales to stockholders' equity and total assets) has increased dramatically in the last three years. This is true for all three measurement bases. Is this trend still evident when net return is computed?

SCHEDULE 12.1
Long-Term Solvency Ratios

Debt to Equity Ratio (Total Liabilities ÷ Total Stockholders' Equity):
(from Figures 2.1, 2.3, and 3.3)

	19X7	19X8	19X9
Historical Cost/Nominal Dollars			
Total Liabilities	$1,487,970	$1,330,570	$1,401,410
Total Stockholders' Equity	$1,312,030	$1,569,430	$1,898,590
Debt to Equity	1.13	.85	.74
Historical Cost/Constant Dollars (end-of-year 19X9 constant dollars)			
Total Liabilities	$1,826,181	$1,497,823	$1,401,410
Total Stockholders' Equity	$1,806,323	$2,031,655	$2,237,220
Debt to Equity	1.01	.74	.63
Current Cost/Constant Dollars			
Total Liabilities	$1,826,181	$1,497,823	$1,401,410
Total Stockholders' Equity	$1,907,290	$2,174,880	$2,299,605
Debt to Equity	.96	.69	.61

Long-Term Debt to Equity Ratio:

	19X7	19X8	19X9
Historical Cost/Nominal Dollars			
Long-Term Liabilities	$1,214,456	$1,089,963	$1,137,657
Stockholders' Equity	$1,312,030	$1,569,430	$1,898,590
Long-Term Debt to Equity	.93	.69	.60
Historical Cost/Constant Dollars			
Long-Term Liabilities	$1,490,498	$1,214,589	$1,137,657
Total Stockholders' Equity	$1,806,323	$2,031,655	$2,237,228
Long-Term Debt to Equity	.83	.60	.51
Current Cost/Constant Dollars			
Long-Term Liabilities	$1,490,488	$1,214,589	$1,137,657
Total Stockholders' Equity	$1,907,290	$2,174,880	$2,299,605
Long-Term Debt to Equity	.78	.56	.49

Times Interest Earned (Income before Interest ÷ Fixed Interest Charges):
(from Figures 2.1, 2.2, 2.3, 2.4, 3.3, and 3.4)

SCHEDULE 12.1 (continued)

	19X7	19X8	19X9
Historical Cost/Nominal Dollars			
Interest Expense	$ 85,012	$ 75,527	$ 79,636
Earnings before Interest and Taxes (EBIT)	$ 572,012	$ 735,527	$ 923,636
Times Interest Earned	6.73	9.74	11.60
Historical Cost/Constant Dollars			
Interest Expense	$ 106,979	$ 88,282	$ 83,781
EBIT	$ 678,387	$ 798,262	$ 888,021
Times Interest Earned	6.34	9.04	10.60
Current Cost/Constant Dollars			
Interest Expense	$ 106,979	$ 88,282	$ 83,781
EBIT	$ 662,415	$ 790,534	$ 880,794
Times Interest Earned	6.19	8.95	10.51

SCHEDULE 12.2
Profitability and Return Ratios

(Information from Figures 2.1, 2.2, 2.3, 2.4, 3.3, and 3.4)

Net Sales to Stockholders' Equity and Net Sales to Total Assets:

	19X7	19X8	19X9
Historical Cost/Nominal Dollars			
Net sales	$2,400,000	$3,200,000	$4,000,000
Average Total Stockholders' Equity	$1,217,065	$1,440,730	$1,734,010
Average Total Assets	$2,550,000	$2,850,000	$3,100,000
Net Sales to Stockholders' Equity	1.97	2.22	2.30
Net Sales to Total Assets	.94	1.12	1.29
Historical Cost/Constant Dollars (end-of-year 19X9 constant dollars)			
Net Sales	$2,945,513	$3,740,566	$4,208,400
Average Total Stockholders' Equity	$1,698,670	$1,918,989	$2,134,442
Average Total Assets	$3,392,783	$3,580,991	$3,548,058

SCHEDULE 12.2 (continued)

Net Sales to Stockholders' Equity	1.73	1.94	1.97
Net Sales to Total Assets	.87	1.04	1.19

Current Cost/Constant Dollars

Net Sales	$2,945,513	$3,740,566	$4,208,400
Average Total Stockholders' Equity	$1,772,466	$2,041,085	$2,237,243
Average Total Assets	$3,475,631	$3,703,087	$3,686,859
Net Sales to Stockholders' Equity	1.66	1.83	1.88
Net Sales to Total Assets	.85	1.01	1.14

Return on Assets (Net Income ÷ Total Assets):

	19X7	19X8	19X9
Historical Cost/Nominal Dollars			
Net Income	$ 316,550	$ 429,000	$ 548,600
Average Total Assets	$2,550,000	$2,850,000	$3,100,000
Return on Assets	12.4%	15.1%	17.7%
Historical Cost/Constant Dollars			
Net Income	$ 334,159	$ 418,502	$ 425,013
Average Total Assets	$3,392,783	$3,580,991	$3,548,058
Return on Assets	9.8%	11.7%	12.0%
Current Cost/Constant Dollars			
Net Income	$ 388,501	$ 460,760	$ 344,165
Average Total Assets	$3,475,631	$3,703,087	$3,686,859
Return on Assets	11.2%	12.4%	9.3%

Return on Equity (Net Income ÷ Stockholders' Equity):

	19X7	19X8	19X9
Historical Cost/Nominal Dollars			
Net Income	$ 316,550	$ 429,000	$ 548,600
Average Stockholders' Equity	$1,217,065	$1,440,730	$1,734,010
Return on Equity	26.0%	29.8%	31.6%
Historical Cost/Constant Dollars			
Net Income	$ 334,159	$ 418,502	$ 425,013
Average Stockholders' Equity	$1,698,670	$1,918,989	$2,134,442
Return on Equity	19.7%	21.8%	19.9%

SCHEDULE 12.2 (continued)

Current Cost/Constant Dollars

Net Income	$ 388,501	$ 460,760	$ 344,165
Average Stockholders' Equity	$1,772,466	$2,041,085	$2,237,243
Return on Equity	21.9%	22.6%	15.4%

Return on Sales (Net Income ÷ Net Sales):

	19X7	19X8	19X9
Historical Cost/Nominal Dollars			
Net Income	$ 316,550	$ 429,000	$ 548,600
Net Sales	$2,400,000	$3,200,000	$4,000,000
Return on Sales	13.2%	13.4%	13.7%
Historical Cost/Constant Dollars			
Net Income	$ 334,159	$ 418,502	$ 425,013
Net Sales	$2,945,513	$3,740,566	$4,208,400
Return on Sales	11.3%	11.2%	10.1%
Current Cost/Constant Dollars			
Net Income	$ 388,501	$ 460,760	$ 344,165
Net Sales	$2,945,513	$3,740,566	$4,208,400
Return on Sales	13.2%	12.3%	8.2%

Earnings per Share:

	19X7	19X8	19X9
Historical Cost/Nominal Dollars	$11.31	$15.32	$19.59
Historical Cost/Constant Dollars	11.93	14.95	15.18
Current Cost/Constant Dollars	13.88	16.46	12.29

Price-Earnings Ratio (Market Price ÷ Earnings Per Share):

	19X7	19X8	19X9
Historical Cost/Nominal Dollars	2.7 times	2.0 times	1.8 times
Historical Cost/Constant Dollars	3.2 times	2.3 times	2.3 times
Current Cost/Constant Dollars	2.7 times	2.1 times	2.8 times

Dividend Payout Ratio (Dividends ÷ Net Income):

	19X7	19X8	19X9
Historical Cost/Nominal Dollars	40.0%	40.0%	40.0%
Historical Cost/Constant Dollars	46.5%	46.2%	51.6%
Current Cost/Constant Dollars	40.0%	41.9%	63.8%

To answer this question, one must examine the trend of return on assets and return on equity. On an historical cost/nominal dollar basis, the

increase in both return ratios is quite impressive. When the ratios are computed on an historical cost/constant dollar basis, the increase is modest, at best. When the return ratios are computed on a current cost/constant dollar basis, it becomes apparent that there has been a *real decline* in the return provided to the common stockholder. This is further substantiated by examining the return on sales ratio. On either an historical cost/nominal dollar or historical cost/constant dollar basis, the return on sales has been relatively constant over the past three years. On a current cost/constant dollar basis, there is a declining trend in the return on sales.

It would appear that MR Corporation is not reinvesting in productive assets. As a consequence, the unsophisticated investor could be misled by the historical cost/nominal dollar figures. The ratios computed on that basis indicate that MR Corporation has a smooth growth trend. The EPS figures substantiate this trend on an historical cost/nominal dollar basis. It also appears that there is a significant growth in EPS when computed on an historical cost/constant dollar basis. However, once again, on a current cost/constant dollar basis, there is a decline in EPS.

In light of the earnings trend, what is MR Corporation's dividend policy? As can be seen from the dividend payout ratio, it would seem that it intends to pay 40% of its earnings in dividends. In real terms, however, it paid nearly two-thirds (63.8%) of its real earnings in dividends in 19X9.

The general sophistication of the stock market can perhaps best be seen be examining the PE ratio. As has been shown, MR Corporation is having a real decline in its earning power. The PE ratio on a historical cost/nominal dollar basis has steadily declined. Since the PE ratio reflects the expectations of the market of the future earning potential of the corporation, it seems that the market does not have favorable expectations of its future earnings.

In summary, then, it appears that MR Corporation has had a real decline in earning power. This has happened primarily because it has not borrowed funds to use for plant expansion. Further, the dividends paid have not allowed it to retain enough earnings to reinvest in productive assets.

Analysis of Going Concern Potential— Bankruptcy

In light of the short-term and long-term trends of MR Corporation's operations, the question of its continued existence should be addressed. If it continues its current operating trends, its long-run potential is gloomy at best.

As was seen in Chapter 11, MR Corporation is maintaining too much liquidity. This results in a loss of purchasing power when significant inflation persists. In addition to the short-term position maintained, it is not taking advantage of its borrowing potential. As a consequence, it is allowing its facilities to become outdated and inefficient. Its low PE ratio will make it difficult for it to generate additional equity capital. It will then be forced to obtain additional borrowings. By having delayed those actions, it will pay higher prices for its equipment. This will mean that additional borrowings will be necessary at higher interest rates.

In essence, by relying on historical cost/nominal dollar information, MR Corporation has ignored the effect that inflation has had on its operations. As one can see, when the impact of inflation is incorporated into the analysis of its operations, it is apparent that there has been a significant negative trend in its operations.

Summary

Chapters 11 and 12 have shown how inflation impacts the operations of an enterprise. If the effect of inflation is not incorporated into the short-term and long-term analysis, misleading inferences may be drawn. This can lead to poor investment decisions by investors and creditors. Even more critical is the danger that it can lead to poor operating decisions by the management of the enterprise. The poor operating decisions can then jeopardize the future operating potential of the enterprise. These two chapters have highlighted this potential negative result and have shown how the impact of inflation can be incorporated into ratio analysis.

APPENDIX

Summary of Ratios Used

Liquidity Ratios:

Current Ratio
$$\frac{\text{Current Assets}}{\text{Current Liabilities}}$$

Acid Test Ratio
$$\frac{\text{Quick Assets}}{\text{Current Liabilities}}$$

Efficiency Ratios:

Collection Period for Receivables
$$\frac{365 \text{ days}}{\text{Sales/Average Receivables}}$$

Inventory Turnover
$$\frac{\text{Cost of Goods Sold}}{\text{Average Inventory}}$$

Long-term Solvency Ratios:

Debt to Equity
$$\frac{\text{Total Liabilities}}{\text{Total Stockholders' Equity}}$$

Long-term Debt to Equity
$$\frac{\text{Long-term Liabilities}}{\text{Total Stockholders' Equity}}$$

Times Interest Earned
$$\frac{\text{Income before interest and taxes}}{\text{Fixed Interest Charges}}$$

Profitability and Return Ratios:

Net Sales to Stockholders' Equity
$$\frac{\text{Net Sales}}{\text{Average Stockholders' Equity}}$$

Net Sales to Total Assets
$$\frac{\text{Net Sales}}{\text{Average Total Assets}}$$

Return on Assets
$$\frac{\text{Net Income}}{\text{Average Total Assets}}$$

Return on Equity
$$\frac{\text{Net Income}}{\text{Average Stockholders' Equity}}$$

Return on Sales
$$\frac{\text{Net Income}}{\text{Net Sales}}$$

Earnings per Share

$$\frac{\text{Income Available to Common Stockholders}}{\text{Average Shares Outstanding}}$$

Price-Earnings

$$\frac{\text{Market Price}}{\text{Earnings per Share}}$$

Dividend Payout

$$\frac{\text{Dividends}}{\text{Net Income}}$$

CHAPTER 13

The Practical Implementation of Inflation Accounting

□□□□□□□□□□□

Accounting numbers being adjusted to incorporate the effects of changes in purchasing power of the dollar and/or changes in the prices of specific goods and services no longer need to be discussed in hypothetical terms. For the first time in the history of promulgated accounting principles, inflation accounting numbers are required to be disclosed in published financial statements. And management accountants, financial analysts, and other users of accounting information are beginning to utilize inflation adjusted data in decision-making processes. The purpose of this chapter is to summarize how inflation accounting numbers are having an impact on financial accounting and reporting and on economic decisions being made on the basis of accounting information.

Financial Accounting and Reporting

Chapters 2 through 4 of this book are devoted to providing some practical guidance to those attempting to implement the disclosure requirements of Statement of Financial Accounting Standards (SFAS) No. 33. These chapters also should be beneficial to those attempting to gain an understanding of the nature, source, and usefulness of the required inflation accounting disclosures.

For the first time in the development of financial reporting standards in the private sector, the Financial Accounting Standards Board (FASB) is requiring that certain large, publicly traded enterprises disclose accounting information on both a constant dollar (general purchasing power) and a current cost (specific purchasing power) basis. While the development of these disclosures involves complex measurement issues, the authoritative literature to date provides little guidance in addressing and solving these issues. And this general nature of the authoritative literature is not necessarily a negative characteristic; this approach does provide latitude for the exercise of professional judgment and introduces a chance for flexibility in developing constant dollar and current cost disclosures during the initial years of disclosure. But practitioners attempting to develop these required disclosures currently need some guidance that, hopefully, can be found in this book.

It will be noticed that the financial reporting chapters in this book comprehend much more than the required minimum disclosures under the FASB reporting requirements. This broad approach should prove beneficial to those attempting to formulate comprehensive inflation-adjusted disclosures and to adapting to subsequent disclosure requirements related to inflation. For example, the FASB explicitly notes in SFAS No. 33 that the conclusions in that document will be reviewed comprehensively within five years from its issuance (September 1979). It seems safe to conclude that many of the disclosures required in SFAS No. 33 are tenuous and will be changed as experimentation with these disclosures unfolds. By focusing not only on current minimum disclosure requirements but also on comprehensive restatements of historical cost numbers, the reader of this book should be able to adapt the implementation skills currently utilized to reflect the requirements of subsequent authoritative literature issuances.

The general rules discussed in Chapters 2 through 4 should be adaptable in understanding disclosure requirements for specialized industries as discussed in Chapters 9 and 10. Already the Securities and Exchange Commission (SEC) had adopted complex and comprehensive disclosure requirements for the oil and gas industry that necessitate the development of surrogates for the current value of proved oil and gas reserves for SEC registrants. And it seems likely that the FASB will follow with similar required disclosures for (perhaps an expanded group of) oil and gas producers. Also, the development of disclosure guidelines in other specialized industries, e.g., real estate, banking, insurance, and retailing, is part of the planned agenda of the FASB. The extensive efforts of the FASB and the SEC in this area indicate that only the initial stages of inflation accounting disclosures currently are being witnessed; it is safe to conclude that the development of inflation accounting and reporting is to be a long-run pragmatic reality.

The Reality of Inflation Now Is Being
Reflected in Corporate Financial Reports

The impact of inflation on reported accounting numbers has been somewhat mystical in the past. But now published financial reports are being issued that include the required constant dollar and current cost disclosures. And the results of these initial computations are significant. The inflation-adjusted numbers reported by most corporations reflect profits that are much smaller than reported under historical costing. At the same time, inflation has driven up the value of corporate assets so that most companies are "worth" much more than historical cost numbers indicate.

With the inflation-adjusted numbers indicating a decline in corporate profitability, the percentage of profits being negated by taxes is much larger. And corporate management is highlighting this fact in a number of annual reports in what seemingly is a drive to reduce applicable taxes.

Examples of the significant differences in disclosed numbers under the three valuation bases (historical costs, constant collars, and current costs) are not difficult to find. Ford Motor Company disclosed 1979 profits reducing from $1.17 billion under conventional historical cost accounting to $330 million under constant dollar accounting and $213 million on a current cost basis. Ford paid $467 million in dividends.

American Telephone & Telegraph (A T & T), which paid 62 percent of its profits in dividends under historical costing, paid 162 percent of current cost profits in dividends. A T & T labeled these results misleading in its annual report. And Georgia Pacific, a timber producer, reflected profits that declined more than 50 percent when adjusted for inflation, but the value of corporate assets increased by about 50 percent.

Some have asserted that many companies are in the process of a very slow liquidation. And, with profits declining in light of increasing asset amounts, corporate profitability does look much less impressive. This is especially true in regard to taxation in that most companies are paying a high rate of income taxes. For example, Ford figures that its income tax provision was 38 percent of reported historical cost profits, but 127 percent of profits calculated on a current cost basis. While the profit structure of many corporations seems weakened by the disclosure of inflation-adjusted numbers, the impressive increase in asset valuation may make several companies likely takeover prospects.

The SFAS No. 33 disclosures are required of about 1200 of the largest companies, but these numbers are still experimental in nature and analysts are cautioning that it would be risky to use them in making company comparisons. This caveat is especially emphasized when making comparisons of companies in different industries.

Managerial Use of Inflation-Adjusted Numbers

Chapters 5 through 8 of this book represent an attempt to provide some insights as to how inflation-adjusted accounting numbers may be used in managerial decision-making processes. And it seems safe to conclude that much of the information being developed for external reporting purposes will at least be considered in managerial analysis.

The chapters selected for inclusion in this managerial section are not all-inclusive. But, they appear to be good points of departure in attempting to understand the impact of inflation on managerial decision-making. And all of this inflationary impact will not be reflected in the SFAS No. 33 disclosures. For example, in Chapter 8 an analysis of capital budgeting in an inflationary environment is presented that utilizes numbers that are foreign to the external reporting process.

Chapters 11 and 12 should provide some insight as to the significance of inflation-adjusted numbers. The ratio analysis conclusions derived from analyzing numbers developed from different valuation bases obviously could vary. And the problems inherent in this analytical process will not be limited to sophisticated investor groups but will be widespread throughout the investing community.

Summary

While U.S. generally accepted accounting principles are not as inflation oriented as, for example, accounting in Great Britain, where current cost information may be used as the basic financial report, the inflation-adjusted data now is required to be disclosed and should prove useful. The development of these "new accounting numbers" will not be an easy task, especially during the initial years of requiring disclosure. But users of financial information should have better information from which to assess the impact of inflation on the reporting entity. And company management will be forced to examine the same numbers. If this book has aided in the implementation and/or understanding of inflation accounting, it will have served its purpose.

Index

WESTMAR COLLEGE LIBRARY